A Garland Series

RENAISSANCE DRAMA

A COLLECTION OF
CRITICAL EDITIONS

edited by
STEPHEN ORGEL
The Johns Hopkins University

A Critical Edition of
THE POLITICIAN
by James Shirley

ROBERT J. FEHRENBACH

GARLAND PUBLISHING, INC.
NEW YORK & LONDON • 1980

All volumes in this series are printed on
acid-free, 250-year-life paper.

Library of Congress Cataloging in Publication Data

Shirley, James, 1596–1666.
  A critical edition of The politician by James Shirley.

  (Renaissance drama)
  Bibliography: p.
  I. Fehrenbach, Robert J., 1936–   II. Title.
III. Series.
PR3144.P6   1980   822'.4   79-54337
ISBN 0-8240-4455-X

CONTENTS

ACKNOWLEDGMENTS

Happily, I have the opportunity to acknowledge those who assisted me in preparing this edition, first as a dissertation some years ago, and more recently in its revised form as presented here. I am grateful for the many courtesies shown me by the staffs of the libraries in which I did my research: the Bibliothèque Nationale in Paris, the British Museum, the Victoria and Albert Museum, the Library of Congress, and especially the Folger Shakespeare Library. I am indebted as well to the library staffs at the Widener, at Duke University, and at the University of Texas for providing information without which I could not have completed this study.

For their special assistance, I wish to recognize and thank Howard M. Nixon, Deputy Keeper of the Department of Printed Books at the British Museum, T. M. MacRobert, Deputy Keeper of the Library at the Victoria and Albert Museum, and June Moll, Librarian of the Humanities Research Center Library at the University of Texas. For giving me access to his dissertation on The Politician, I thank Professor Edward Huberman of Rutgers, and for her aid with the Latin texts, I

I am grateful to Dr. Margaret Aston. The frontpiece, a photograph of the title page of the 1655 quarto of The Politician in the Humanities Research Center Library at the University of Texas, appears with that library's kind permission, and the introductory section on the printing of the play was first published in Studies in Bibliography.

To Professor Donald K. Anderson, Jr. of the University of Missouri I wish to express a special appreciation for the suggestions and many hours of patient consultation he gave me during the preparation of this edition in its earlier form as a doctoral thesis. Considerably revised in its introduction and notes, the edition which appears here has been spared numerous errors as a result of the careful reading given the revised version in all its stages by my wife, Dee. Her keen eye and valuable criticism have saved me much embarrassment. And to Gloria Hall, who with good humor met the unusual difficulties that this publication format--to say nothing of my manuscript--presented her as she prepared the typescript, I am greatly in debt. Finally, I owe a special thanks to my colleague, Professor J. B. Savage, who seems always to have good ideas.

Williamsburg, Virginia   R. J. F.
August, 1979

INTRODUCTION

I. BIBLIOGRAPHICAL AND TEXTUAL

Date

No play with the title, The Politician, appears in the office-book of Sir Henry Herbert, the Master of Revels during the period that Shirley was writing.[1] On May 26, 1641, however, Herbert's records show that he licensed "The Politique Father, by James Shirley."[2] Several of Shirley's plays appeared in print with titles different from those assigned them in licensing,[3] and the first person to suggest that The Politique Father licensed in 1641 might be The Politician

---

[1]Joseph Quincy Adams (ed.), The Dramatic Records of Sir Henry Herbert (New Haven: Yale University Press, 1917). These records are compiled from information found in Edmond Malone's variorum edition of Shakespeare (London: C. Baldwin, 1821) and in George Chalmers' An Apology for the Believers in the Shakespeare-Papers (London: Thomas Egerton, 1797). Both Malone and Chalmers had access to the manuscript of Herbert's office-book, now lost, which Malone, in An Historical Account of the Rise and Progress of the English Stage (London: Henry Baldwin, 1790), pp. 225-226, says "does not furnish us with a regular account of the plays at court every year," a fact which may account for the missing Politician. It is also possible that Malone and Chalmers did not cite every entry in Herbert's office-book.

[2]Adams, p. 39.

[3]The Beauties was licensed in 1633 and published as The Bird in the Cage in 1638; Rosania of 1641 was printed as The Doubtful Heir in 1652; The Faithful Servant (licensed, 1629) became The Grateful Servant (printed, 1630); The Duke licensed, 1631), became The Humorous Courtier (printed, 1640).

v

published in 1655 was Alexander Dyce in the 1833 edition of Shirley's works.[4] Although this conjecture has been supported by many, almost from the outset it was challenged, and the prevailing scholarly opinion today is that the two titles do not refer to the same play.[5]

Fragmentary evidence indicates that The Politician was written while Shirley was in Ireland (from late 1636 to about spring 1640[6]) and first performed there. It was probably presented at the Salisbury Court Theatre in London before the closing of the theatres in 1642, as was certainly another of Shirley's plays having close associations with The Politician: The Gentleman of Venice. The latter was

---

[4]Alexander Dyce in the introduction to The Dramatic Works and Poems of James Shirley, [edited] by William Gifford [with an introduction] by Alexander Dyce (London: John Murray, 1833), I, xxxviii.

[5]The Politique Father is thought to be the original title of the play that was printed in 1652 as The Brothers. The Play licensed as The Brothers in 1626 is believed to be lost. The most comprehensive expressions of the opponents and the supporters of this view are found in the works of Robert Forsythe and Arthur H. Nason. Forsythe in The Relations of Shirley's Plays to the Elizabethan Drama (New York: Columbia University Press, 1914), pp. 173-77, insists that The Politician is the play licensed as The Politique Father in 1641. But Forsythe's position is virtually destroyed by Nason in James Shirley: Dramatist (New York: Arthur H. Nason, 1915), pp. 47-68, who takes the position summarized above. For an early but somewhat eccentric expression of what has now become the prevailing opinion regarding the licensing and printing of these plays, see F. G. Fleay, "Annals of the Careers of James and Henry Shirley," Anglia, 8 (1885), 410-411. The most recent comment on this issue is by Gerald Eades Bentley in The Jacobean and Caroline Stage (Oxford: Clarendon Press, 1956), V, 1138.

[6]Allan H. Stevenson, "Shirley's Years in Ireland," Review of English Studies, 20 (1944), 22 and 27.

doubtless composed while Shirley was in Ireland, for it was licensed on October 30, 1639,[7] three years after Shirley went to Ireland and six months before he returned to England. It is very probable that The Gentleman of Venice was produced in Dublin, and it was in fact performed at the Salisbury Court Theatre sometime between November, 1639, and the interdiction of the stage. Because of these and the other relationships with The Gentleman of Venice discussed below, and because of other evidence that The Politician was performed on the Irish stage and at Salisbury Court by 1640,[8] it is reasonable to conjecture that The Politician was licensed and first performed in 1639-40, having been written sometime after the spring of 1638. For it was on April 23, 1638, that Shirley's The Royal Master was licensed by Herbert,[9] and from the dedication and commendatory verses in the 1638 first edition of the play and from information on its title-page,[10] The Royal Master can be identified as the first play Shirley wrote in Ireland.

---

[7]Adams, p. 38.

[8]For a full discussion of the stage history of The Politician see pp. lii-lxiv.

[9]Adams, p. 37.

[10]James Shirley, The Royal Master: As it was Acted in the New Theater in Dublin (London: T. Cotes and John Crooke, 1638). See the dedication to the Earl of Kildare, sigs. A2^r-A2^v and the commendatory verses, sigs. A3^r-B2^r.

The Play and the Catalogues

Among the list of "severall playes" entered in the Stationers' Register on September 9, 1653, by Humphrey Moseley is found: "The Polititian by James Shirley."[11] Two years later there appeared for sale a play, the title-page of which reads: "THE POLITITIAN, A TRAGEDY, Presented at Salisbury Court BY HER MAJESTIES SERVANTS; WRITTEN By JAMES SHIRLEY. LONDON, Printed for Humphrey Moseley and are to be sold at his Shop at the Princes Armes in St. Pauls Church-yard. 1655."[12] The play was issued in two formats, octavo and quarto, as was The Gentleman of Venice, also printed by Humphrey Moseley in 1655[13] after he had entered the latter play in the Stationers' Register on July 9, 1653,[14] exactly two months before the entry of The Politician is dated. Although both plays are printed in two formats, both formats of each play were printed from a single type-setting, a bibliographical curiosity discussed below.

---

[11]G. E. Briscoe Eyre (ed.), A Transcript of the Registers of the Worshipful Company of Stationers: 1640-1708 A.D. (London: [n.p.] 1913), I, 429.

[12]As found on the title-page of the quarto in the John H. Wrenn Collection in the University of Texas Library, Austin.

[13]THE GENTLEMAN OF VENICE A Tragi-Comedie Presented at the Private house in Salisbury Court by her Majesties Servants. Written by JAMES SHIRLEY. LONDON, Printed for Humphrey Moseley and are to be sold at his shop at the Princes Armes in St. Pauls Church-yard. 1655. (As found on the title-page of a quarto in the Folger Shakespeare Library, Washington, D.C.)

[14]Eyre, I, 423.

In a separate list of advertised publications printed
in two issues, the first of which emerged about the end of
1655[15] and the last of which came out about the middle of
January, 1656, Humphrey Moseley publicized those books for
sale at his shop.[16] Under "Playes lately Printed" are
found "The Gentleman of Venice, a Tragi-Comedy by James
Shirley" and "The Polititian, a Tragedy by James Shirley."[17]
The first list of printed dramas appended to a play is
found with The Careless Shepherdes by T[homas]. G[off].
published by Richard Rogers and William Ley in 1656. The
catalogue is "of all such Plays that ever were Printed."[18]
The Politician is not found in this list of about 500 titles,
and although a play entitled "Gentleman of Verona" exists,
the title The Gentleman of Venice does not. W. W. Greg believes that "Gentleman of Verona" might be a mistake of The
Gentleman of Venice, but, of course, it is also possible
that "Gentleman of Verona" is an erroneous duplication of
Two Gentlemen of Verona, a possibility Greg apparently
thinks more likely.[19]

---

[15]All dates are new style except where noted.

[16]W. W. Greg, A Bibliography of the English Printed
Drama to the Restoration (London: The Bibliographical Society, 1957), III, 1178.

[17]Greg, III, 1179.

[18]T[homas]. G[offe]., The Careless Sheperdes (London:
Richard Rogers and William Ley, 1656), sigs. [A2^r]-[A4^r].

[19]Greg, III, 1321.

Another play published in 1656, The Old Law, has a list of over 620 plays appended to it. The advertisement reads: "[A]n exact and perfect catalogue of all the Playes, with the Authors Names, and what Comedies, Tragedies, Histories, Pastoralls, Masks, Interludes, more exactly Printed then ever before."[20] This list, printed by Edward Archer, was the first catalogue in which an attempt was made to classify the dramas according to type. Among the plays listed to sell are: "Politician C[omedy]. Iames Shirley"[21] and "Gentleman of Venice H[istory]. Iames Shirley."[22]

From an examination of the play titles found on these lists, Greg argues that Rogers and Ley's catalogue appeared near the end of 1655 or in the first weeks of 1656 and that Archer's list appeared in the summer of 1656.[23] If The Politician (along with The Gentleman of Venice) was published in time to be included in a late 1655, early 1656 advertisement issued by the printer of the play, but too late to appear in another printer's catalogue issued about the same time, yet was to appear in still another bookseller's catalogue issued in the summer of 1656, it seems likely that The Politician was printed in the last months of 1655.

---

[20] Phil. Massinger, Thomas Middleton, William Rowley, The Excellent Comedy called The Old Law (London: Edward Archer, 1656), sigs. (a[1ʳ])-(b[4ʳ]).

[21] Massinger, et al., sig. b2ᵛ.

[22] Massinger, et al., sig. a3ᵛ.

[23] Greg, III, 1319.

Subsequent seventeenth-century catalogues carry citations of The Politician, and it appears as if no cataloguer
paid a great deal of attention to the title-page of the 1655
edition. No seventeenth-century bibliographer seems to have
read the play save Gerard Langbaine, and he only after he
had listed the play in his first two catalogues. Aside
from Langbaine, all the bibliographers appear to have relied
entirely upon Archer's list and never to have seen Moseley's
advertisement. Furthermore, there is no indication that
any cataloguer in the seventeenth century saw an octavo
copy.

In 1658, William London, advertising the "Most Vendible Books in England" cites: "The Politician. 4°".[24] In
both of Francis Kirkman's catalogues (1661 and 1671), The
Politician is listed erroneously as a comedy[25] as it is in
Langbaine's list of plays "ever yet Printed and Published,
till this present year 1680."[26] William Winstanley in 1687
follows Kirkman and Archer and lists The Politician as a

---

[24] [William London,] A Catalogue of the Most Vendible
Books in England (London: [William London,] 1658), sig.
F[f 1]v.

[25] [Francis Kirkman,] A True, perfect, and exact Catalogue ([London: Francis Kirkman, 1661,]) p. 12; A True,
perfect, and exact Catalogue ([London: Francis Kirkman,
1671,]) p. 11.

[26] [Gerard Langbaine and Nicholas Cox,] An exact Catalogue of all Comedies, tragicomedies, . . . That were ever
yet Printed and Published, till this present year 1680 (Oxford: Nicholas Cox, 1680), p. 11.

comedy.[27] Langbaine, in 1688, follows his predecessors and again lists it as a comedy and only indicates the quarto format.[28] But in 1691 Langbaine clearly shows that he has looked at a copy of the first edition and that he has read it. In An Account of the English Dramatick Poets, he writes:

> Politician, a Tragedy presented at Salisbury Court, by Her Majesty's Servants; and printed 4°. Lond. 1655. This Play is dedicated to Walter Moyle, Esquire. A Story resembling this, I have read in the first Book of the Countess of Montgomery's Urania, concerning the King of Romania, the Prince Antissius, and his Mother-in-Law.[29]

Gildon's 1699 revision of Langbaine's 1691 publication repeats this essential information.[30]

Only one of the eighteenth-century bibliographers and literary historians gives any indication that he examined the play before listing it in his work. Giles Jacob, in 1719, follows Langbaine and Gildon in his citation,[31] and W. R. Chetwood in 1756 adds nothing, listing only the name of the play, the fact that it is a tragedy, and the date of

---

[27] William Winstanley, The Lives of the Most Famous English Poets (London: H. Clark, 1687), pp. 138-139.

[28] Gerard Langbaine, Momus Triumphans: or the plagaries of the English Stage (London: Nicholas Cox, 1688), p. 22.

[29] Gerard Langbaine, An Account of the English Dramatick Poets (Oxford: George West and Henry Clements, 1691), p. 481.

[30] Gerard Langbaine, The Lives and Characters of the English Dramatic Poets; also an exact Account of all the Plays that were ever yet Printed in the English Tongue (London: Nich[olas] Cox and William Turner, 1699), p. 133.

[31] G[iles]. J[acob]., The Poetical Register or the Lives and Characters of the English Dramatic poets with an account of their Writings (London: E. Curll, 1719), p. 240.

its publication.[32] But D. E. Baker in The Companion to the
Playhouse, 1764, adds to the information previously given
that the action of the play takes place in Norway.[33] The
anonymous Playhouse pocket-companion of 1779 erroneously
lists the play as a tragicomedy,[34] and Egerton's Remembrancer of 1788 offers no new information.[35]

In the nineteenth century, some bibliographers contri-
bute additional information about the 1655 edition of The
Politician, while others are satisfied to repeat old knowledge gleaned from previous lists. All of the works published in the early part of the 1800's connected with the
name of James Barker offer nothing new,[36] and in the 1812
edition of Biographia Dramatica (a continuation of D. E.
Baker's eighteenth-century work) the only addition is the
critical comment that The Politician "is not one of

---

[32][William Rufus Chetwood,] Theatrical Records (London:
R. and J. Dossley, 1756), p. 38.

[33][D. E. Baker,] The Companion to the Playhouse (London: T. Becket, P. A. Dehondt, C. Henderson, and T. Davies,
1764), I, sig. R[2]^r.

[34]The Playhouse pocket-companion (London: Richardson
and Urquhart, 1779), p. 110.

[35][John and Thomas Egerton (comps.),] Egerton's Theatrical Rembrancer (London: T. and J. Egerton, 1788), p. 54.

[36]W. C. Oulton (ed.), Barker's Continuation of Egerton's Theatrical Remembrancer (London: Barker & Son, 1801),
p. 274; W. C. Oulton (ed.), Barker's Complete List of Plays
(London: Barker & Son, [1804], p. 274; and [W. C. Oulton
(ed.),] The Drama Recorded; or, Barker's List of Plays (London: J. Barker, 1814), p. 142.

Shirley's best productions."[37] Halliwell's Dictionary of

Old English Plays (1860) is nothing but a verbatim repetition

of the 1812 Biographia Dramatica regarding The Politician.[38]

It is W. C. Hazlitt who, in 1876, adds to the bibliographical

information of the play, for Hazlitt is the first to note,

in print,[39] that the play was published in octavo and

quarto formats and the first to give a collation of both

issues. From his citations it appears as if the quarto

that Hazlitt saw was a volume that contained only The Poli-

tician, but that the octavo issue of the play was bound with

The Gentleman of Venice.[40] After Hazlitt, nothing of any

bibliographical significance was written about The Politi-

cian until Edward Huberman's essay in The Library in 1937[41]

and until Greg's description of the play in A Bibliography

of the English Printed Drama to the Restoration.[42]

---

[37]D. E. Baker, Isaac Reed, and Stephen Jones, Biographia Dramatica (London: Longman, Hurst, Rees, Orme,
and Brown, 1812), III, 169.

[38]J. O. Halliwell, A Dictionary of Old English Plays
(London: John Russell Smith, 1860), p. 197.

[39]Edward Huberman, "Bibliographical Note on James Shirley's The Polititian," The Library, 18 (1937), states on
p. 108: "It seems that the first catalogue of any sort to
indicate that there were both quarto and octavo copies is in
manuscript, apparently in early nineteenth-century hand, in
the British Museum. . . . B. M. Additional MS. 29712, fol.
284."

[40]W. C. Hazlitt, Collections and Notes, 1867-1876
(London: Reeves and Turner, 1876), p. 386.

[41]Pp. 104-108, see note 39 above.

[42]Greg, passim, especially III, 861.

The Printing

    The printing of a play in two formats in one edition
was an extremely rare practice in the seventeenth century.[43]
Nonetheless, it is clear that The Politician and its companion piece, The Gentleman of Venice, were so issued.
Huberman correctly notes about the octavo and quarto sizes
of The Politician: "Except for their size and signatures,
. . . these two are exactly alike."[44] This fact poses a
problem for bibliographers, for it is unsatisfactory to say
that two copies of a play that contain different signatures
and collations, to say nothing of the different sizes, are
of one edition. It is equally unsatisfactory, however, to
say that two copies of the same play which are obviously
printed from a single type-setting (and in the seventeenth-
century this meant that they were printed at the same time)
represent two different editions. It is wise to accept
Greg's solution and call these copies "simultaneous issues"
of one edition.[45] But the apparent signature errors require

---

    [43]W. W. Greg, "The Printing of Mayne's Plays," Oxford
Bibliographical Society: Proceedings and Papers, 1 (1927),
255-262.

    [44]Huberman, p. 104. On pp. 104-105 Huberman gives as
additional evidence (apart from a study on the typography
with the naked eye) that the two sizes were printed from
the same type: "I have repeatedly applied McKerrow's
ruler test and found it to show every time that the pages
in the two sizes were printed from the same type, and without alteration in spacing." (See Ronald B. McKerrow, An
Introduction to Bibliography for Literary Students [Oxford:
Clarendon Press, 1928], p. 183.)

    [45]Greg, Bibliography, IV, xxxv.

an explanation and have led scholars to attempt to determine,
on the basis of the signature misprints in the copies of The
Politician, the priority of the printing of its two formats,
gaining thereby knowledge about printing house practices
during the 1650's.

Huberman's study of the misprints led him to conclude
that the octavo and quarto sheets of this bibliographical
rarity were printed in no consistent order.[46] Sometimes, he
argues, the octavo sheets were printed first and the appropriate quarto sheets followed in the press; at other times
the process was reversed. In his description of The Poli-
cian in A Bibliography of the English Printed Drama to the
Restoration, Greg agrees with Huberman's analysis of the
printing procedure.[47] A closer examination of several key
copies of the 1655 edition which contain previously over-
looked odd variants--in addition to the apparent signature
errors--reveals that a consistent order of printing was in
fact used and that additional copies of a pre-Restoration
drama must be added to the list of fakes made up by the in-
famous bibliophile, Thomas J. Wise.

The close printing relationship of The Gentleman of
Venice and The Politician is relevant to a discussion of
the priority of the two sizes of The Politician, for if
the publications were intimately related in the press, they
probably would have been printed by the same procedure, and

---

[46]Huberman, p. 107.

[47]Greg, II, 861.

the second to have come from the press would surely have been machined by the same process as the first.

Both plays were published in quarto sizes to match many of Shirley's plays previously printed in quarto, and in octavo formats to fit with Shirley's recently published octavo volume, Six New Playes (1653), also issued by Humphrey Moseley. This is the only logical explanation that accounts for this unusual and complicated printing procedure.[48] Greg, who discusses the octavo issues of the two plays as a "collection," believes it quite probable that only the quarto issues of the two plays were sold separately and that the octavo copies were always sold bound together as a supplement to Six New Playes.[49]

In addition, the two 1655 publications contain typographical similarities which indicate their proximity in the press. "James Shirley" on the title-page of both sizes of both plays is from the same typesetting. The imprint is exactly the same in all copies save for two small but significant variations to be discussed later. The head-

---

[48]One of the octavo copies of the play in the Victoria and Albert Museum is bound with The Gentleman of Venice and Six New Playes (V8a). P. Nissen in his monograph, James Shirley: Ein Beitrag zur englischen Litteraturgeschichte (Hamburg: Lütcke and Wülff, 1901), p. 24n, states that he found the two plays bound with Six New Playes in the Hamburger Stadtbibliothek. These, however, like those in the Victoria and Albert Museum, appear to have been added to the larger volume at a date later than 1655.

[49]III, 1124-1125. The British Museum and the Victoria and Albert Museum each house one such octavo "collection" of The Gentleman of Venice and The Politician.

line, "The Epistle Dedicatory," is the same in both publications as is the signature "JAMES SHIRLEY" on the same page.[50] Also, the rules and the type of the word FINIS are the same in both plays.[51] All of these identical typographical features have been verified by measurement. Several identical head ornaments are found in both publications, and only these two plays of Shirley's carry the head-line, albeit of different typography, "The names and small Characters of the Persons"[52] and contain brief descriptions of each character in the dramatis personae.[53] In the rest of the plays printed by Humphrey Moseley in 1655,[54] none of these similarities exists except for an occasional similar ornament. All this evidence indicates that The Gentleman of Venice and The Politician were very close in the press, one probably being printed immediately after the other.

Two variations exist in the otherwise identical imprints of both plays. A gap, the width of one piece of type, appears between the H and the u in Humphrey in the quarto issues of The Gentleman of Venice and in both sizes

---

[50]Sig. A2^v in both plays.

[51]P. 78 (sig. L2^v) in The Gentleman of Venice and p. 74 (sig. L2^v) in The Politician.

[52]The Gentleman of Venice reads: "The names with some small Characters of the Persons." (sig. A3^r)

[53]Sigs. A3^r-A3^v in each play.

[54]Philip Massinger, Three New Playes, Lodowick Carlell, The Passionate Lovers, and R[obert]. B[aron]., Mirza.

of The Politician. Greg believes that this gap occurred
when the compositor made the change from the octavo forme to
the quarto forme in the course of printing The Gentleman of
Venice and that this space was carried over into the printing
of the title page of The Politician.[55] Furthermore, the e
in be is properly placed in the imprint in The Gentleman of
Venice but is raised significantly in the imprint in The
Politician. These two typographical variations indicate that
The Gentleman of Venice was printed first and that the imprint, which was set up correctly, experienced some minor,
unnoticed variations as it stood in type or was transferred
from one galley to another. For The Politician to have been
printed first, we would have to believe that the compositor
corrected one error in the imprint (in be) and ignored
another even more obvious mistake (in Humphrey).

Because of the various limitations connected with early
printing it is highly unlikely that an entire work, unless
it were an extremely short piece, stood in type at any one
time. It is much more reasonable to assume that a forme or
two was placed in type and after the desired number of
sheets were printed, the type was distributed and reused for
other formes. Similarly, when one work was printed in both
octavo and quarto formats from a single typesetting, it is
unlikely that one size was printed entirely before the other
size went to the press. It is more likely that a printer

---

[55]Greg, II, 857.

first imposed the type-pages in one forme and printed the sheets of the appropriate format; then he reimposed the type-pages in the other forme, made the necessary signature changes, and machined the sheets of the other size. The question of the printing priority of the two sizes of each of these two plays is, then, a question of which sheets were printed first, not which entire format. Greg warns that it is unwise to assert that a printing priority of octavo sheets to quarto sheets, or quarto to octavo, was consistently followed.[56] But if all of the evidence suggests one process, only extreme caution would prohibit one from making a reasonable conjecture about the printing priority of the sheets.

No octavo copy of The Gentleman of Venice contains any signature misprint.[57] In three quartos examined by Huberman, in all of the quartos examined by and brought to the attention of Greg, and in the one quarto of The Gentleman of Venice I examined, B1-B3 are misprinted C1-C3 and quires A and E are fully signed.[58] Greg notes that in the quarto, A2 and K2 are left unsigned while the signature K2 appears on K4.[59] All of these misprints in the quarto (except the

---

[56]In a letter to Huberman printed in Huberman's article, p. 107.

[57]Greg, II, 857.

[58]Huberman, p. 106 and Greg, II, 857. The copy I examined is in the Folger Shakespeare Library.

[59]Greg, II, 857.

misplacement of K2 on K4 and the omission of A2 which indicate nothing but carelessness) can be explained by the re-
tention of all or part of the octavo signatures when the
compositor reimposed the play for the quarto issue. A4
does not appear in quarto, but it is normal for octavo. E4
appears where C4 appears in octavo (p. 33 of both sizes);
the E is correct for quarto, but the 4 is correct for octavo. Finally, those sheets (B1-B3) that are misprinted
C1-C3 in the quarto issue are right for octavo. From the
first-mentioned variation in the imprint (the gap between
the H and the u in Humphrey) and from the misprinted signatures, it is reasonable to believe, as does Greg,[60] that
the octavo sheets were printed before the quarto sheets in
The Gentleman of Venice.

In all quarto copies of The Politician, only one misprint of a signature is found: A4, which already has been
noted, as unusual for the quarto but normal for octavo, appears in the quarto issue. Unlike The Gentleman of Venice,
however, there are apparent signature misprints in two of
the octavo copies; the remainder of the smaller-sized
copies carry correct signatures. In an octavo issue in the
British Museum (hereafter referred to as A8) C2 is misprinted as E2, and in another octavo in the University of
Texas Library (hereafter referred to as T8) C3 is misprinted

---

[60]Greg, II, 857.

as E3, C5-C6 as F1-F2, D2-D3 as G2-G3, and D6 as H2.[61] All

of these misprints are correct signatures for quarto. From

an examination of the unusual A4 signature in all the quar-

tos and the several misprints in two of the octavos, both

Greg[62] and Huberman[63] conclude that some sheets were printed

first in octavo and then reimposed in quarto and that

others went first to the press in quarto and were reimposed

in octavo.

In my examination of A8 and T8, however, I discovered:

(1) those leaves with the supposed signature misprints, con-

tain typographical variants identical with those found in

the regular quarto sheets;[64] (2) an occasional leaf in T8

and A8 which is unsigned in both octavo and quarto and

which corresponds in pagination (e.g. [K3] in quarto and

[E7] in octavo are both page 67) contains the typographical

characteristics of the quarto leaf instead of those of the

---

[61]Greg, II, 861 and Huberman, p. 107, agree with
these findings. In addition, Huberman says that he has
been informed by the University of Texas Library that
another octavo incorrectly reads Ll for Fl (p. 105). The
present staff of the Library at Austin is unable to find
such an octavo; still such a "misprint" would only support the findings of this present study.

[62]Greg, II, 861.

[63]Huberman, p. 107.

[64]For example, on p. 29 (sig. E2 in quarto and BM8,
sig. C2 in the other octavos), a comma is properly placed
after the word danger in the first line in all the quartos
and A8; in the other octavo copies it is raised to the
top of the r. On the same page the numeral 29 is un-
clearly printed in all the quartos and A8; it is dis-
tinctly printed in all the other octavo copies.

octavo leaf; (3) in those leaves with signature misprints
(as well as those unsigned leaves that share typographical
variants with the corresponding quarto leaves) the chain-
lines are horizontal, normal in quarto, while the chain-
lines of the rest of the leaves are vertical, an octavo
characteristic; and (4) the watermark in each of the suspected leaves, where it can be determined, is in the quarto
position. In short, octavo copies BM8 and T8 are filled
with inserts, cutdown leaves from quarto copies, and like
the other octavos, do not contain misprints. The only
authentic misprint in both sizes of The Politician is the
A4 in the quarto copies.

Further evidence that T8 and A8 are modern made-up
copies and do not represent "confusion of sheets in bind-
ing some of the individual volumes" which Huberman offers
as another possible explanation[65] is that A8 is in the
Ashley Library in the British Musuem and T8 is in the
Wrenn collection of the University of Texas Library, the
two private libraries with which Thomas J. Wise, the
famous fraudulent bibliophile, had this closest

---

[65]Huberman, p. 107.

association.[66] D. F. Foxon, who discovered Wise's deceptive handiwork with pre-Restoration plays, cites all of the
plays in Wise's Library (the Ashley Library) that appear to
be made up. The Politician, not found in that list, clearly
should be added.[67]

The evidence and conclusions about the printing of The
Politician, then, are these: it was printed in both octavo
and quarto issues, probably as soon as The Gentleman of
Venice, also printed in simultaneous issues, cleared the
press. As the octavo sheets of the latter probably were
printed before the quarto sheets, there is no reason to believe that the process would have been changed for The Politician. Moreover, the one authentic signature misprint in

---

[66]It is possible that Wise, aware of the authentic misprints in The Gentleman of Venice, decided to make up copies of The Politician thinking that the model of the former
would give credibility and even a touch of authenticity to
the made-up texts of the latter. One wonders at the extent
of Wise's deception when he reads the bibliographical comment on The Politician in the Wrenn Catalogue (A Catalogue
of the Library of the Late John Henry Wrenn, compiled by
Harold B. Wrenn and edited by Thomas J. Wise [Austin: University of Texas, 1920], IV, 145) in which Wise notes the
signature "misprints" in the octavo T8 and explains them by
saying that the play was "first set up in quarto" and then
reimposed in octavo.

[67]Thomas J. Wise and the Pre-Restoration Drama: A
Study in Theft and Sophistication (London: The Bibliographical Society, 1959), pp. 37-41. It appears as if the
quarto leaves used to complete the imperfect quartos were
taken from the now imperfect quarto presently in the Aitken collection at the University of Texas Library. The
quarto inserts in A8 and T8 account for all but two of
the missing leaves in the Aitken quarto. Wise, of course,
provided Aitken with copies of pre-Restoration plays as he
did Wrenn.

The Politician indicates the octavo-to-quarto procedure.
Apparently the compositor benefitted from the signature errors in The Gentleman of Venice and made only one in the
printing of The Politician.

The Earlier Editions

The 1655 edition of The Politician was the only available copy of the play until the nineteenth century. The
play, then, was among those "which are to be found only in
the British Museum and in some scarce private libraries[68]
as expressed by Charles Lamb in Specimens of English Dramatic Poets, 1808. Lamb reprints Haraldus' death-bed scene
with his mother, Marpisa, without any significant critical
comment.[69] In Biographia Dramatica, 1812, the editors express their desire that a "corrected edition of all this
author's [Shirley's] pieces" be published. At the end of
this plea is noted: "At the time of passing this sheet
through the press, we are informed, that Mr. Murray, bookseller, in Fleet street, has such an edition in the
press."[70] Twenty years later, in his Account of the English
Stage, 1832, John Genest deplores the fact that William
Gifford and his publisher John Murray often promised but

---

[68]Charles Lamb, Specimens of English Dramatic Poets,
Who Lived About the Time of Shakespeare (London: Longman,
Hurst, Rees, and Orme, 1808), p. v.

[69]Lamb, pp. 470-472.

[70]D. E. Baker, et al., p. 668.

never produced a collection of Shirley's dramatic and poetic works. Noting that Gifford died in 1826, Genest chides the unnamed editorial successor (Alexander Dyce) for the delay in producing the long promised works.[71] One year later in 1833, with great praise,[72] the six-volume collection was issued. The first five volumes are the editorial work of Gifford, and the last volume and the brief biographical and critical commentary found in Volume I are the products of Alexander Dyce. The Politician, found in Volume V, then, is the responsibility of Gifford.

The play is edited from a quarto, its spelling modernized; the characters' names are made uniform; some stage directions and scene designations are added and a few textual emendations made, not all of them noted by the editor. The lines are not numbered. "The names and small Characters of the Persons" are deleted from the text and placed in a footnote; there is one interpretive comment (p. 130n) and one gloss (p. 139n).

In 1934, as part of the requirement for a degree of Doctor of Philosophy at Duke University, Edward Huberman edited The Politician.[73] The text is a photostatic copy of

---

[71]John Genest, Some Account of the English Stage from the Restoration in 1660 to 1830 (Bath: H. E. Carrington, 1832), IX, 542-543.

[72]Quarterly Review, 49 (1833), 27.

[73]Edward Huberman, "James Shirley's 'The Polititian'" (unpublished Doctoral thesis, Duke University, Durham, North Carolina, 1934).

one of Wise's made-up copies (T8) with textual notes, most
of which refer to misprints and Gifford's emendations and
modernizations. Huberman is the first to develop Langbaine's
hint that the source of The Politician is The Countess of
Montgomery's Urania, and he further argues for part of Sidney's Arcadia as a source. His critical commentary, generally judicious and sound as it is on the characters, the
plot construction and verse, is directed too often towards
noting Shirley's use elsewhere of theatrical conventions and
language found in The Politician. And insisting that
Gotharus is a tragic figure, he argues that the play should
be considered a tragedy, not a tragicomedy. His explanatory
glosses provide primarily cross-references to plays by Shirley and by his contemporaries and predecessors; less attention is given to explaining the seventeenth-century language and attitudes found in The Politician. Huberman's
observations about the date of the play's composition and
about its early performances repeat previous scholars'
unsupported conjectures. His findings in regard to the
bibliographical problems of The Politician have already
been discussed.

This Edition

The present modern-spelling text is based on a collation
of thirteen copies (six octavo, seven quarto) of the 1655
first edition of The Politician, the scene printed by Charles
Lamb in Specimens of English Dramatic Poets, 1808, and the

edition by William Gifford found in his and Alexander Dyce's
1833 edition of Shirley's complete works. Occasional reference is made to Edward Huberman's 1934 dissertation, but not
to his text since he did not provide a newly edited text of
the play.

The quarto in the John H. Wrenn collection in the Library at the University of Texas is the copy-text of the
present edition, each page of which contains appropriate
textual and explanatory notes. Variants that are acciden-
tals (except where corrections have been made[74]) are not
cited in the notes; substantive variants, along with emendations by previous editors that have been accepted in the
present text, are always noted. Characters' names have
been regularized and all contracted forms of names have been
written in full. All additions to stage directions and
speech prefixes have been placed in brackets; when such an
emendation is from a previous editor, that fact is noted in
the textual notes. Dashes are used only to indicate (1) an
interruption in a speech, and (2) a speaker's shifting his
speech to another character. The use of periods, semicolons,
exclamation marks and question marks is based on an interpretation of the text, but restraint has been practiced.

The orthography and the punctuation of the text have
been modernized silently though certain seventeenth-century

---

[74]In the textual notes, these corrections are identified only as occurring in a quarto copy or an octavo copy.
In section C of Appendix I, can be found the particular
copy (or copies) in which these variants appear.

spellings have been retained. For example, all contractions (save where noted), such as wo'not and y'ave have not been changed. The policy of the seventeenth-century compositor on elisions has been followed: thus, both resolved and re-solv'd appear in the text. Certain words, now out of general use, have been retained because of their flavor, and their contribution, at times, to metrical balance. These works include chirurgeon and soldade; they are appropriately glossed.

The act designation as found in the quarto has been followed; a scene division has been included whenever the stage is cleared of all characters; and the lines have been numbered, starting anew with each scene. The lines have been regularized in accordance with dramatic blank verse tradition.[75]

The textual notes are found above the solid line at the bottom of the page, the explanatory notes below. Stage directions are indicated by the line number on which they are found (e.g., S.D. 236) or by the addition of a numeral indicating the position of the stage direction in relation to a line of verse (e.g., S.D. 236.1 refers to the first line of the stage direction following line 236). An earlier editor is identified by his last name. Meanings of words taken from the Oxford English Dictionary were in use during Shirley's time.

Finally, the abbreviations used in the notes are:

---

[75]In section D of Appendix I a list is provided of all unusually irregular lines in the copy-text.

Gifford	William Gifford (ed.) The Dramatic Works and Poems of James Shirley, with additional notes by Alexander Dyce. 6 vols. London: John Murray, 1833.
Huberman	Edward Huberman. "James Shirley's 'The Polititian.'" Unpublished Doctoral thesis, Duke University, Durham, North Carolina, 1934.
Lamb	Charles Lamb (ed.). Specimens of English Dramatic Poets. London: Longman, Hurst, Rees, and Orme, 1808.
O	The Polititian. London: Humphrey Moseley, 1655 (octavo size).
OED	Oxford English Dictionary.
Q	The Polititian. London: Humphrey Moseley, 1655 (quarto size).
S.D.	stage direction.
S.P.	speech prefix.

II. HISTORICAL

Source

Coming as he does at the end of a prolific period of English drama, Shirley is often and justifiably described as an imitative dramatist. Robert Forsythe, however, over emphasizes that derivative quality. One all but receives the impression from Forsythe's study that Shirley did little else except rewrite old plots, characters, and situations.[76] To counter such an approach to Shirley, however, does not require suggesting that Shirley was entirely original at a time in dramatic history when the use of old plots and successful stage conventions was accepted practice. But to identify the characters and incidents in The Politician which have similarities with others in earlier dramas, the interested reader is directed to Forsythe. The discussion presented here is of the relationship of The Politician to the work which provides the source for the main plot and central characters of the play. Other selected literary similarities are left for brief mention in the explanatory notes and the critical section of this introduction.

The major candidates for the source of the plot of The Politician are tales found in two romances: The Countess of Montgomery's Urania (1621) by Lady Mary Wroth and The Countess of Pembroke's Arcadia (1590) by Sir Philip Sidney. Not coincidentally the titles of these two works are similar; the relationship of these romances and the importance of that relationship upon the source-study of The Politician are discussed below. But first, each of the works is examined separately.

---

[76]The Relations of Shirley's Plays to the Elizabethan Drama (New York: Columbia University Press, 1914).

As previously mentioned, Gerard Langbaine first suggested a source for The Politician in 1691. He wrote: "A Story resembling this, I have read in the first Book of the Countess of Montgomery's Urania, concerning the King of Romania, the Prince Antissius, and his Mother-in-Law."[77] Nothing was added to this observation and no one developed the lead that Langbaine gave until Edward Huberman examined the Urania as the source of The Politician in 1934.[78] The Urania is the product of one of the first woman literati in English history. Lady Mary Wroth, the niece of Sir Philip Sidney and Mary Sidney, the Countess of Pembroke, and the daughter of Robert Sidney, was heir to a love of literature and the arts. Naturally, it would seem, she became a patroness of a variety of literary figures including George Chapman and Ben Jonson who dedicated The Alchemist to her in 1610.[79] In 1621 Lady Mary, who had married Sir Robert Wroth in 1604, brought out a large folio volume consisting of four books and running to over six hundred pages of prose romances and related lyrics.[80] The work is similar

---

[77]An Account of the English Dramatick Poets, p. 481.

[78]Huberman, "James Shirley's 'The Polititian,'" pp. 2-15.

[79]Sir Leslie Stephen and Sir Sidney Lee (eds.), The Dictionary of National Biography (Oxford: University Press, 1917), XXI, 1076-1077.

[80]Lady Mary Wroath [Wroth], The Countesse of Mountgomeries Urania (London: John Marriott and John Grismand 1621). All further references to the work appear in the text.

in style and method but far inferior in poetry and art to Sidney's Arcadia. It has become generally accepted that the Urania was, in part, a satirical attack upon various persons in Jacobean court society. Because of the many protests about the "scandalous allusions," some of the protests having been made to James himself, Lady Mary withdrew the book from the market protesting her innocence while reputedly fanning the fires of gossip by hinting at the identity of her fictitious characters to some of her close friends.[81]

The story to which Langbaine referred in Book I of the Urania is woven in a tangle of tales of lovers, pirates, heroes, beauties, villains and pastoral folk. The first twenty-six pages of Book I contain several stories of love and sorrow, all of which are unified by the goddess-shepherdess, Urania. At one point she and her new found lover, Parselius, are captured by a pirate, Sandringal, who in turn becomes engaged in a battle with still another group of pirates and is defeated. The victor is Leandrus, the betrothed of Antissia, daughter of the King of Romania. As it turns out, Sandringal, some time earlier when he was in the service of the king, was to have transported Antissia, along with a magnificent dowry, to Leandrus. But Sandringal absconded with the dowry, turned pirate and lost

---

[81]Because of the book's withdrawal, the volume has become extremely rare. For more detailed discussion of this literary tempest see: B. G. MacCarthy, Women Writers: Their Contribution to the English Novel 1621-1744. 3rd Impression (Dublin: Cork University Press, 1946), pp. 62-63, and John J. O'Conner, "James Hay and 'The Countess of Montgomerie's Urania,'" N&Q, 200 (1955), 150-152.

Antissia in the process. One of Sandringal's prisoners, Allimarlus, briefly mentions the sad tale of Antissia and Sandringal's treason, and then he embarks on another tale of "greater affliction" (p. 27).

Antissius, Prince of Romania and brother to Antissia, married virtuous and lovely Lucenia, and the son born of this union was likewise named Antissius. But the king, after his "vertuous" queen died, married the "young, politique and wicked" widow of a "Noble man in the Countrie." The king, "passionately doting on her," banished his son from Romania on the advice of his wife, who hated the prince (p. 27). Allimarlus says that the old and sad king could trust few in the court, the new queen "hauing taken care that her Minions and fauorites should most attend his person" (p. 28). Here the story directly related to The Politician stops as Allimarlus relates various tales connected with his search for Antissia. At one point, however, he refers to an attempt by two men, now slain in battle, to violate a beautiful young woman. They schemed "yet to be certaine, with a good fashion dissembling their inward intent, (as well they could, for they were Courtiers)" (p. 31). Of course, she is Antissia and Allimarlus rescues her (p. 32).

Leandrus then tells of his adventures after which the whole group sails for Italy, but because of fire on ship they are diverted to an unknown and charmed land where they experience strange adventures and finally are separated. Parselius is taken by Allimarlus away from this weird land

in a boat guided by an old man, Seleucius, who, as luck will
have it, is the brother of the King of Romania. The boatman
tells the story already related by Allimarlus concerning
Antissius' marriage to Lucenia and the birth of their son.
He then refers to the king's second wife as that "malitious
creature . . . [guilty of] treason, adultery, witchcraft, and
murder" (p. 42). She plotted the prince's death and the few
honest courtiers left warned the king of his wicked queen
(p. 42). Finally he believed them, but then she flattered
him excessively and generally kept in his good graces.
"[W]hat but for policy, she cared little for" (p. 43). She
was able to have those who had spoken unkindly, but truth-
fully, of her, banished or executed. Antissius, accused of
"popularity and aspiring to the Crowne" was banished with
his family to a castle twenty miles away, then finally given
permission to leave and live with his uncle, Seleucius (p.
43).

The people, disliking the queen, looked to Antissius,
which angered her considerably. She then made it appear as
if Antissius were plotting to overthrow his father, and the
ruler asked advice of the courtiers (now, of course, all her
minions) who counseled him to call Antissius to court but in
a manner not to arouse his suspicion (p. 44). This the king
did and Seleucius now adds that had he been there when the
messenger came he would have advised against Antissius'
going. But Antissius went "doubting no treason." The prince
was met by a Captain, Lisandrinus, loyal to Antissius but

sent by the queen with his soldiers to escort the son to his
father's court. This act of the queen puzzled Antissius who
nonetheless innocently accepted the escort, and they all
rode toward the city together. On the outskirts of Constantinople, the court being situated there, the travelers were
attacked and only the Captain and ten of his men survived.
The prince's body was returned to Seleucius (p. 45), and
while Seleucius reflected on young Antissius as the heir
both to woe and to Romania, Lucenia wept over the body of
the slain prince "kissing the pale lips of her dearest love"
(p. 46). She then proceeded to her chamber to commit sui-
cice. Seleucius, the Captain and the servants of Antissius
all vowed revenge (p. 47), and the old uncle took the or-
phaned prince, Young Antissius, and came to where they are
now (p. 48).

Leandrus comes upon this group and they all row on together until they see a ship, which they hail and in which
they set sail for Greece only to land in Morea. The loyal
Captain appears, but the narrator leaves this group to tell
other tales, none of which relates to The Politician.
Finally, the narrative returns to Seleucius, Antissius the
younger, and the Captain, the last of whom continues the
story of the King of Romania and his wicked queen.

The queen had successfully achieved making her son heir
to the throne and getting herself named regent in the event
the king should die while her son was in his minority. To
hasten matters, she called a servant, one of her "favourites,"

to her private chambers to plot the king's murder. She
flattered him and dissembled with him, pledging singular
love for him and promising to marry him when her husband was
dead. Of course, he promptly promised to kill the king (p.
58). The murderous plot was successful and the queen
feigned grief nicely. At a banquet she poisoned many who
suspected her, but she took care to spare her "minion" to
whom she explained that a quick marriage would be indecorous
(p. 59). But the the traitorous servant soon found that she
had other reasons for postponing the marriage, for he caught
her vainly trying to seduce the Ambassador of Morea (p. 60).
Enraged, he vowed to tell all. A trial was held; he con-
fessed his guilt and both she and the minion were put to
death in the midst of turmoil generated by the revelations
of such a corrupt court. The people, taking advantage of
this instability in the government, revolted and are at present, according to the Captain, holding Constantinople under
siege and are calling for the young Antissius. The Captain
has been sent by the "General," apparently the leader of the
rebellion (p. 61).

Antissius and his great-uncle accept the call and set
sail for Romania. They arrive, with many of the characters
already discussed in their company, and are greeted with
"unspeakable joy," the General "yeelding all into his
[Antissius'] hands, and taking his authority from him."
The usurper (the queen's son) calls for a private battle of

three men from each side to determine who should rule (p.
61). The challenge is accepted, Antissius' side wins the
day, and he is proclaimed King with great joy (pp. 62-63).
The rest of the romance does not relate to The Politician.

There are many similarities between this tale and Shirley's play, including characters, incidents, and at least one
minor verbal similarity.[82] The King of Romania is gullible,
essentially weak, easily led; the King of Norway in Shirley's play is likewise malleable and credulous. But although the actions of the Romanian can, in part, be explained by a passion for his wife akin to lust, he is not
the lecherous figure that Shirley makes his Norwegian king
in the first part of his play. The queen in both plots is
a widow of a good Lord, a wicked step-mother who dislikes
her step-son and plots his death (albeit unsuccessfully in
the play) for the advancement of her own issue, and uses a
favorite at court. Though Shirley's queen is an adulteress,
she in no way attains the licentious heights of the apparently pathologically sex-driven queen of Romania. Furthermore, Marpisa in The Politician, though responsible for at
least two deaths, does not murder and slaughter her enemies
wholesale in the grotesque manner of the queen in Lady
Mary's romance. In short, Shirley's queen is a more

---

[82]In the Urania, p. 27, the King of Romania is described as "passionately doting" on his second wife and in
the brief description of the King of Norway in "The Names
and Small Characters of the Persons" of The Politician is
found: " . . . passionately doting upon Queen Marpisa."

believeable character although she shares many of the same
characteristics with the queen in the Urania.

Shirley's Turgesius combines the qualities of both
Prince Antissius and Antissius the Younger. Prince Antissius is often referred to as "vertuous" and he certainly is
trusting, loyal, and dutiful, both as a subject and as a son.
He is innocent to the point of naive; therefore, in spite of
his apparent military prowess, he loses his life in a battle
created by intrigue and deception. His son, as well as he,
is extremely popular and deeply loved by the people. All
of these characteristics are found in Turgesius, and though he
does not lose his life as a result of naiveté, until the
critical moment has passed, there is some doubt whether he
will survive the deceit of others.

The prototype for Olaus is Seleucius. Both are uncles
to the princes (Olaus is great-uncle to Turgesius, Seleucius
is uncle to one Antissius and great-uncle to the other),
both are loyal and good men and both find their respective
nephews dangerously naive. Olaus, of course, is an irascible, blunt soldier, and if Shirley needed a model for this
type other than those already found on the Jacobean and
Caroline stage, he might have turned to the loyal captain,
Lisandrinus. Thus Olaus could be a combination of loving
uncle (Seleucius) and brave and loyal warrior (Lisandrinus).

But perhaps Lisandrinus, the loyal captain who survives the ambush designed for his death as well as the

prince's, became Aquinus in Shirley's play. For both are
used by the intriguers to give false assurance to the prince,
and both are marked for death. The appearance and offers of
both Lisandrinus and Aquinus, though completely loyal, give
the respective princes cause to ponder; but in each case the
prince trustingly accepts the soldier's proffered aid.
Huberman suggests that Aquinus might in part be modeled after Allimarlus, the first teller of the tale.[83] But aside
from the man's devotion and loyalty to the royal house, there
is little else to suggest that he is the prototype for
Aquinus.

About the only things the sons of the two wicked queens
have in common are (1) their mothers are determined that the
young men shall become king (though the Queen of Romania is
more concerned that she should be regent than that her son
should be king), and (2) they both die in the course of the
story. The peculiar personality of Haraldus, Marpisa's
child, is nowhere to be found in the almost faceless son of
the Romanian mother.

Albina in The Politician bears some resemblance to Lucenia in the Urania. They are both singularly virtuous and
attractive, their husbands were given them by the king, they
are loyal and loving wives, and they are both excessively
grief-stricken at the deaths of their husbands. Albina is

---

[83]Huberman, "James Shirley's 'The Polititian,'" pp.
14-15.

a more prominent character than Lucenia, and certainly she
is treated by her husband, Gotharus, in a manner that in no
way resembles the relationship of Antissius and Lucenia.
Near the end of the play, we are led to believe that Albina
will become the wife of Turgesius thereby making still
another, though very minor, connection between the two
stories.

The major figure of Gotharus, Shirley's titular character, has few roots in the Urania. Of course, the unnamed
servant, minion, lover, and betrayer of the Romanian queen
in Lady Mary's work resembles Gotharus, but that servant is
but a shadow of Shirley's politician. Gotharus is a full-
blooded figure; the minion in the Urania is a thin character,
best indicated by his namelessness. The suggestion, perhaps, of Gotharus is in the Urania, but the politician of
the play is mainly Shirley's creation.

Still other similarities exist in the two works. The
unsavory court in Romania, full of flatterers and minions
calls to mind the palace in Norway, which, though not as
thoroughly rotten, has its share of parasites. Witchcraft
is associated with the Queen of Romania as it is with Marpisa, and they both, apparently, favor poison as the instru-
ment of murder. Like Marpisa's favorite, the minion of the
Romanian queen causes her downfall, and neither woman is as
entirely honest with him as she purports to be. The banish-
ment of the prince to Seleucius' house in the Urania is
similar to Turgesius' being sent away to war with Olaus.

Antissius is called to court under the guise of friendship, but the purpose is to do him harm; likewise Turgesius' invited return to his father's city is a trick to have him murdered. And as Antissius' body is brought to Seleucius' castle, so Turgesius' "body" is returned to Olaus' palace. Finally, the rebels, who leave something to be desired as a social force according to Lady Mary in the Urania ("the people [are] apt to take any occasion to stirre new afflictions" [p. 61]), nonetheless are honest and well-meaning folk and recognize and follow good authority when they see it. Shirley, in his play, certainly leaves no doubt that he feels the rebels are a dangerous mob despite their loyalty to the good prince and their condemnation of the evil Gotharus. They too cease their rebellion when the proper authority presents itself.

Huberman in his 1934 thesis on The Politician was the first to suggest part of the Arcadia of Sir Philip Sidney as a source for Shirley's play.[84] The story cited by Huberman is in the fifteenth chapter of the Second Book of the 1590 edition of Sidney's work.[85] In brief, the tale is as follows: The King of Iberia, by his first wife, is blessed

---

[84]Huberman, "James Shirley's 'The Polititian,'" p. 16. In 1914 Forsythe, p. 177 noted that the name of Marpisa may be related to the name Marpesia in Sidney's Arcadia, Book III, but this suggestion hardly qualifies as a discovery of a source for The Politician and does not at all relate to the tale suggested by Huberman.

[85]Sir Philip Sidney, The Countess of Pembroke's Arcadia, The Original Quarto Edition (1590) in Photographic Facsimile, Edited by H. Oskar Sommer (London: Kegan Paul, Trench, Trubner and Co., Ltd., 1891), pp. 166-172.

with a superlative son, Plangus. In spite of his sterling
qualities Plangus is not immune to the frailities of youth
and is attracted to the wife of a commoner. The king hears
of the liaison and surprises them in their dalliance. The
prince, in an attempt to convince the king of the woman's
virtue, overdoes things and arouses a desire for her in the
king, who promptly orders Plangus off to the front lines so
that the royal father can have the lady to himself. She is
a clever woman, however, and refuses to succumb to the king
except on her terms, which are marriage and the queen's
crown (her husband has conveniently died). By the time
Plangus returns home he finds his father married to his
former mistress, who has borne two royal children, a boy and
a girl. Of course, the queen is not satisfied with a doting
old man even though he is king, and she immediately tries to
arouse Plangus to his former desires. Plangus, for various
reasons, refuses the queen's advances and leaves the woman
scorned and bitter. In revenge, she begins a long, subtle,
and successful plot to turn the king against his son.

First, alone she plants suspicions in her husband's
mind and then she is aided by a servant of the royal house-
hold who has ambitions himself. Together they convince the
king that Plangus plans, with the help of the common people
with whom he is extremely popular, to overthrow his father.
Finally, she directs the traitorous servant to go to the
prince and to entice him to her chambers by telling him that
the queen, the king, and his ministers are meeting to plot

the prince's demise. Having come to the appointed place, Plangus is discovered by the king, who has been deceived by the queen into thinking that the prince was there to violate her and kill the king.

Plangus is made prisoner, but to save the state from a rebellion which was developing on his behalf, he chooses to exile himself and goes to his cousin, Tiridates. The ambitious servant, under the king's orders to poison his son, is captured by Tiridates and before his execution confesses all. But the king, having all but given up governing, never sees the report from Tiridates as it was intercepted by the queen. To round out his hatred for his son, the king names Palladius, his son by the treacherous queen, as his successor. Plangus stays with Tiridates and fights with his cousin to bring home Tiridates' sister, Artaxia, a story detailed in another part of the Arcadia.

Clearly there are similarities between this tale and the plot and characters of The Politician. An essentially weak, but well-meaning king has a virtuous son; the king marries a scheming, clever widow who plots to turn father against son; the new queen is helped by an ambitious servant; the people love the prince; the prince is tricked into an ambush at the palace; the prince is aided by a loyal relative; the queen's son (also the king's in the Arcadian tale) is maneuvered into the position of heir; and at the end, the wicked servant dies because of his deeds. But the only similarity

between the Plangus story and The Politician not also found
in the Urania is that Plangus, like Turgesius, is sent off
to war by his father instead of being exiled as he is in the
Urania (though Plangus does exile himself later in the
story). No doubt Lady Mary knew of Sidney's work; the
Urania is a clear, if poor, imitation of the Arcadia. Nor
was Shirley ignorant of the Arcadia.[86] But the Arcadia
contains nothing of significance that is in The Politician
and not in the Urania, and the Urania contains much that is
in The Politician and not in the Arcadia. Practically,
then, there is no need to consider that Shirley went to the
Arcadia when he had the Urania, for to have done so would
have been an exercise in redundance. The influence of the
Plangus tale on The Politician is at best indirect and
should be considered no more of a source of Shirley's play
than the Hippolytus-Phaedra myth (through the Plangus tale)
is of the Antissius story in the Urania.[87]

Huberman admits that Lady Mary Wroth may have used the

---

[86]For years Shirley has been credited with the drama,
The Arcadia (London: John Williams and Francis Eglesfield,
1640) based on Sidney's romance. His authorship of this
dramatic pastoral has been seriously questioned by Alfred
Harbage, "The Authorship of the Dramatic Arcadia," MP 25
(1938), 233-237.

[87]T. P. Harrison, "A Source of Sidney's Arcadia,"
Studies in English, 6 (1926), 68.

story of Plangus to write her tale,[88] and notes that several
seventeenth-century literary figures used the Plangus story
as a source for some of their works. Beaumont and Fletcher
certainly used it in their Cupid's Revenge, printed in 1615;
J. S. (not James Shirley) clearly drew upon it in Andromana:
or the Merchant's Wife published in 1660, and perhaps even
Shakespeare used it in Cymbeline, first printed in the 1623
Folio.[89] Ethel Seaton, convinced that the story of Plangus
from Sidney's Arcadia is the source of The Politician,
notes that it "reappears with variations in Lady Mary
Wroth's Urania (1621), in the play of Andromana or the
Merchant's Wife, and later in Ingelo's allegorical romance
Bentivolia and Urania [1660]."[90] She even goes so far as to
suggest that because the Plangus tale "seems to have its
roots in Visigothic history . . . [i]t is . . . easy to see

---

[88]Huberman, "James Shirley's 'The Polititian,'" p. 16.
Huberman also raises the possibility that the Gotharus-
Marpisa political alliance and amour had its source in a
court scandal, perhaps even the rumor that Buckingham was
"over-familiar" with the consort of Charles I, Henrietta
Maria (p. 22).

[89]Huberman, "James Shirley's 'The Polititian,'" pp.
19-21. In Andromana (London: John Bellinger, (1660), the
scene is Iberia and the hero's name remains Plangus. J. M.
Nosworthy in the New Arden edition of Cymbeline (London:
Methueb and Co., Ltd., 1955) does not mention the Plangus-
story or any Arcadian tale as a possible source for this
Shakespearean play (pp. xvii-xxviii).

[90]Ethel Seaton, Literary Relations of England and Scandinavia in the Seventeenth Century (Oxford: The Clarendon
Press, 1935), p. 323.

. . . why Shirley put it in a northern dress."[91] Works

other than the Urania may provide prototypes for characters

found in The Politician,[92] but the overwhelming evidence

points to the Antissius tale from The Countess of Mont-

gomery's Urania as the major source for the plot and the

characters in The Politician.

The changes and selections Shirley makes in his use of

the Urania reveal a playwright attempting to provide effec-

tive drama by simplifying the plot and by creating veri-

similitude in character and action. For example,Shirley

extends without making hyperbolic, the king's proclivity to

the lascivious, making him all the more believably weak and

ineffectual as a proper ruler. The wicked queen in Shir-

ley's hands becomes a more plausible and more complex

character than her monstrous and grotesque, bogeywoman

prototype. Shirley tones down, while retaining, most of

the Romanian's characteristics, creating a multi-faceted

character in order to portray this essentially wicked per-

son as a more human figure.

Turgesius is the best example of Shirley's attempt to

simplify without losing anything essential. The single

prince in The Politician retains all the virtues of the

---

[91]Seaton, p. 323n. It is not likely, however, that
Shirley would have been aware of the possible Scandinavian
origins of a tale in Sidney's Arcadia.

[92]See the explanatory notes to the dramatis personae
and the discussion of characterization in the "Critical"
section for reference to some of these possibilities.

two Antissiuses in the Urania, and the naiveté of Antissius
the elder becomes perspicacity and wisdom in Turgesius, however late these qualities are revealed. The activities of
Turgesius combine those of the two princes of Romania.

Huberman points out that Seleucius and Olaus each
"exercises a cautious, watchful, and restraining hand over
his nephew."[93] Both uncles would warn the prince of dangers, but Olaus, while urging this kind of restraint on the
prince, erupts himself. While advising the prince to be
cautious, the old soldier speaks and acts imprudently before
the king. Retaining certain qualities found in Seleucius,
Shirley gives the uncle the additional dimension of the
blunt-soldier. Olaus becomes a more complex figure--the
guardian who needs a guide, the teacher who needs to be
taught--and thereby, a more interesting and real person.
Likewise, Shirley endows Aquinus, if his origin is found
in the honest Lisandrinus, with greater depth. Both are
loyal and honest, but Aquinus by the very nature of his
more significant role in the plot, becomes a much more capable and shrewd individual.

The basic figure of Haraldus, essentially Shirley's
creation, can be found in the Antissius tale as the son of
the wicked queen whom she would have king. But as Huberman
astutely observes: "Shirley's re-shaping of the plot

----

[93]Huberman, "James Shirley's 'The Polititian,'" p. 12.

demanded an entirely new treatment of Haraldus."[94] Haraldus'
character is the result of a dramaturgical necessity, and
Shirley could hardly be expected to retain the nameless son
in the Urania in his new plot.

Similarly, Albina becomes something that Lucenia was
not, primarily because Shirley changes the plot. Whether the
character is successful is perhaps not so pertinent a question as whether the role is successful. But her greater
prominence compared to Lucenia, and her impeccably honest and
often outspoken manner is an improvement on the conventional
and flat if virtuous and honorable fair lady of the romance.
Also an improvement is Albina's husband, Gotharus, who becomes a vigorous and complete figure in the play. The dim
character of the traitorous and ambitious favorite in the
Urania would not do for Shirley's titular character who
serves such an important role in the drama. More detailed
discussions of this villain and the other characters are
left for the critical commentary below.

The construction of the plot also shows Shirley's
skillful handling of his source. Huberman calls attention
to Shirley's use of time in the play as compared with the use
of time in the Urania. It is an important observation and,
therefore, I quote it:

> In the Urania there were practically no limitations of
> time; the wandering nature of the entire work made

---

[94]Huberman, "James Shirley's 'The Polititian,'" p. 13.

structural restrictions of almost any sort superfluous. Lady Mary, with two Antissius characters, was enabled to keep a young prince constantly in the story. But a play could not so easily ramble through the years it takes for an infant to grow into manhood without too appreciable an effect on the action and the remaining characters. It was a wise move, then, for Shirley to effect the amalgamation and condensation. The whole play consumes a day or two at most, and there is no need whatever for two generations of princes.[95]

Shirley adds the honest courtiers to balance the flatterers and parasites, and thereby gives a verisimilitude to the Norwegian court that is lacking in the cesspool of a court in the romance. The return of the prince to the court and the action surrounding his arrival are much more skillfully handled in The Politician than in the Urania. In fact, it is so skillfully worked out that some readers, used to seeing all explained on stage, are baffled by what happens in the play.[96] But the fault is theirs, not Shirley's. Everything is there--Aquinus' note to the prince, Olaus' doubts and warnings, the prince's trust, his feigned murder and Aquinus' "death"--but all is presented with a subtlety which reveals considerable skill on the part of the playwright.

---

[95]Huberman, "James Shirley's 'The Polititian,'" p. 12.

[96]One of these is John Genest, who in Some Account of the English Stage from the Restoration in 1660 to 1830, IX, 562, reveals that he cannot account for Turgesius' "escape" after being shot. Neither does J. Schipper, James Shirley: Sein Leben und Seine Werke (Wien and Leipzig: Wilhelm Braumüller, 1911) understand the prince's "recovery." Furthermore, Schipper admits that at least to him "wird das Verhalten und Vergehen des Aquinus nicht hinänglich aufgeklärt." (p. 250)

Shirley retains the rebels of the Urania but gives them a more prominent role. He clearly shares the judgment of Lady Mary that rebellion and revolution, no matter on whose behalf, is a socially and politically disruptive act. But by giving them a more significant role he provides an opportunity for many of them to speak and to reveal their character. Furthermore, their well-designed part in the swift moving climax is artistically integral to the play.

Perhaps the most significant change made by Shirley is in the denouement of the plot. The King of Norway, Turgesius, and Albina do not die. Only the evil characters, with the exception of the good and sickly Haraldus, meet their demise in the play. The effect of this important change on the play as tragedy is discussed in the critical commentary below.

An examination of Shirley's use of his source reveals the playwright to be a skillful and creative dramatist in the plot that he wrought and the characters that he drew. He condensed and pruned; he attempted to provide motivation for his characters and he tried to endow each with a personality. In spite of some of their slightly hyperbolic and typed characteristics, Shirley's attempt to make his characters and their actions credible is clearly the mark of a skilled dramatist.

Stage History

Support for believing that The Politician was first
performed in Ireland is provided by the great likelihood
that the play was composed when Shirley was writing for the
Werburgh-Street Theatre in Dublin during the years 1637-
1640, having arrived in that city late in 1636 in the company of Thomas Wentworth, Earl of Strafford, the Lord
Deputy of Ireland.[97] Apparently, Shirley went to Ireland
to help start the new theater on Werburgh-Street which
opened about Michaelmas in 1637. His trip appears to have
been the result of invitations from John Ogilby, the manager
of the new theater, and from the Lord Deputy.[98] If Ogilby,
appointed Master of Revels for Ireland by Strafford in
February, 1638, kept records about the theater and plays,
they are no longer extant. In fact, there are no records
of the Werburgh-Street Theatre of any sort available. But
aside from the coincidental dates of Shirley's stay in
Ireland and the probable composition of The Politician,

---

[97]Stevenson, p. 22.

[98]For a discussion of Shirley's career in Ireland see
Stevenson's article in RES; three additional articles by
Stevenson: "James Shirley and the Actors at the First Irish
Theater," MP, 40 (1942), 147-160; "Shirley's Publishers:
The Partnership of Crooke and Cooke," The Library, 25 (1945),
140-161; and "Shirley's Dedications and the Date of His Re-
turn to England," MLN, 41 (1946), 79-83; La Tourette Stock-
well, Dublin Theatres and Theatre Customs, 1637-1640 (Kings-
port, Tennessee: Kingsport Press, 1938), pp. 3-17; Peter
Kavanagh, The Irish Theatre (Tralee, Ireland: Kerryman
Limited, 1946), pp. 16-21; and William S. Clark, The Early
Irish Stage: The Beginnings to 1720 (Oxford: Clarendon
Press, 1955), pp. 32-37.

there are a few slight pieces of evidence that the play was
produced for the Irish stage.[99]

Turgesius, the name of the prince in The Politician,
not only has associations with Norwegian history, but is
found in Irish history as well. Centuries before, a Scandinavian of that name had invaded and conquered Ireland before
being killed by the Irish.[100] His name and feats appear in
Holinshed, in William Warner's Albion's England (1612), and
in Advertisement for Ireland (1623) by an anonymous Irish
historiographer.[101] Though the choice of this name does not
prove that Shirley had an Irish audience in mind while
writing the play, the name is singularly appropriate for a
play with a Norwegian setting that is being performed in
Ireland.

Additional evidence that The Politician was performed
on the Irish stage centers around an obscure Irish playwright, Henry Burnell, and his one extant, and very bad
play, Landgartha, printed 1641. Burnell was associated with
the new Werburgh-Street Theatre and wrote at least two plays

---

[99]No dramatic or literary historian who deals with The
Politician does not believe it very probable that the play
was written and performed in Ireland. Seldom, however, is
any evidence given to support this position.

[100]See The Dictionary of National Biography, XIX, 819
where this warrior is discussed under "Thurkill."

[101]See my explanatory note to line 6 (Turgesius) of "The
Names and Small Characters of the Persons" for the passages
in these works which deal with Turgesius.

for that stage. As Shirley was probably the chief dramatist of the company at that theater, each doubtless knew the other and his work.[102] Landgartha, an incredibly ridiculous play set in Norway, was first performed on St. Patrick's Day, March 17, 1640.[103] Its plot is taken from Saxo-Grammaticus[104] and very little about the play is Irish. Why, Burnell, an Irishman, writing for a struggling new Irish theater would ignore Irish history and turn to Scandinavian for a plot might be reasonably answered with the suggestion that he was trying to ride to popularity on some dramatic coattails.[105] For, as with most untalented writers, Burnell's work shows many imitative signs.

---

[102]For a discussion of Burnell's role in the Werburgh-Street Theatre see Stockwell, pp. 17-22; Kavanagh, pp. 40-45; and Clark, pp. 37-39. Alfred Harbage in Annals of English Drama (Philadelphia: University of Pennsylvania Press, 1940), p. 112 attributes two plays for which Shirley wrote prologues while in Ireland, The Toy and The Irish Gentleman to "possibly H. Burnell." Stockwell, p. 5 suggests the same thing. But G. E. Bentley in The Jacobean and Caroline Stage, III, 97, believes there is no evidence to support the attribution of these plays to Burnell. Samuel Schoenbaum, in his revision of Harbage's work (London: Methuen and Co., Ltd., 1964), p. 138, lists the plays as "anonymous."

[103]"This play was first Acted on S. Patricks day, 1639 [old style]. with the allowance of the Master of Revels [John Ogilby]." From the Harvard University Copy, Henry Burnell, Landgartha (Dublin [n.p.], 1641), sig. K1^v.

[104]Kavanagh, p. 41.

[105]Even Shirley, an Englishman, while in Ireland wrote a play with St. Patrick as the main figure, and he promised another about the same character.

Burnell had never been to England;[106] therefore, for models he had to rely on works in print available in Ireland or on those dramas which he had seen or, at least, had heard about. Peter Kavanagh goes so far as to say: "Burnell, who knew very little about drama, copied the manner of Ben Jonson. Even the prologue to Landgartha is in complete imitation of Jonson's prologue to The Poetaster where the author causes it to be spoken by one in armour."[107] A friend, addressing Burnell in commendatory verses in the 1641 edition of Landgartha underscores what Burnell may have thought was Jonsonian about himself:

> (Let others boast of their owne faculties,
> Or being Sonne to Iohnson) I dare say,
> That thou art farre more like to Ben, then they
> That lay clayme as heires to him, wrongfully:
> For he survives now only, but in thee
> And his owne lines; the rest degenerate.
> Nay, I can more affirme (and truly) that
> In some things thou do'st passe him; being more sweet,
> More modest, mylde, lesse tedious.[108]

Jonson's plays obviously were available to Burnell in print (having been published in 1616), and at least one, The Alchemist, was performed in the Werburgh-Street Theatre.[109] Little if anything about Landgartha, however, brings Jonson to mind.

---

[106]"Io. Bermingham," in his commendatory verses addressed to Burnell in Landgartha, sig. A3^V says: "And, though thou England never saw'st; . . ."

[107]Kavanagh, p. 41.

[108]Landgartha, sig. A3^V.

[109]Clark, p. 33.

The play is a tragicomedy, and perhaps Burnell is following still another dramatic tradition, Fletcherian tragicomedy. For more than one of Beaumont and Fletcher's plays were performed at the new theater,[110] and Burnell's statement at the end of his published play is an awkward attempt to explain the nature of tragicomedy, a statement vaguely reminiscent of Fletcher's famous defense of that genre in The Faithful Shepherdess.[111]

Burnell, faced with a lack of talent, apparently turned to imitation, and there existed a no more likely model than the famous court playwright from England, now

---

[110]Clark, p. 33.

[111]Burnell's statement reads:

"Some (but not of best judgments) were offended at the Conclusion of this Play, in regard Landgartha tooke not then, what she was perswaded to by so many, the Kings kind night-imbraces. To which kind of people (that know not what they say) I answer (omitting all other reasons:) that a Tragie-Comedy sho'd neither end Comically or Tragically, but betwixt both: which Decorum I did my best to observe, not to goe against Art, to please the ever-amorous. To the rest of bablers, I despise any answer." (Landgartha, sig. K1^V)

Fletcher's statement regarding tragicomedy is found in "To the Reader" of the first edition of The Faithfull Shepherdess, c. 1609/1610.

"A tragi-comedy is not so called in respect of mirth and killing, but in respect it wants deaths, which is enough to make it no tragedy, yet brings some near it, which is enough to make it no comedy, . . ."

W. W. Greg (ed.), "The Faithfull Shepherdess" in The Works of Francis Beaumont and John Fletcher. Variorum Edition. General Editor, A. H. Bullen. (London: George Bell and Sons and A. H. Bullen, 1908), III, 18, 11. 24-28.

the chief dramatist of the company. There are no striking verbal or plot similarities between Landgartha and The Politician. Surely, Burnell would be prudent enough to avoid simply repeating his superior's play. Nor is it likely that Shirley, in his influential position with Ogilby's company, would have encouraged an overly derivative work. But for Burnell, in an attempt for popularity, to pick up a few characteristics of a Shirley play, would not only be likely for that struggling playwright who had suffered one failure already, but it is reasonable that such an attempt would have the blessing of Ogilby and Shirley for the sake of the success of the company. Burnell's choice of a Scandinavian story and setting can, perhaps then, be explained by a previous, successful play with northern characteristics, The Politician. Furthermore, two of the characters in Landgartha are Gotar, a minor character, but an evil courtier and counsellor to the king, and Marfisa, a comic amazonian figure, who at least shares with Shirley's Marpisa some rather indelicate qualities.[112]

That such a play as Landgartha written by such a dramatist as Burnell for the same company and theater for whom Shirley was writing may have been patterned to some degree

---

[112]Of course, it is possible that both Burnell and Shirley just happened to choose these Scandinavian flavored names, but surely that would have been a miraculous coincidence. Other names in Burnell's play show he had little concern for authenticity and originality. Consider the names Scania and Elsinora, and what of Fatyma?

after The Politician provides some circumstantial evidence
that Shirley's tragedy was performed on the Irish stage. It
is possible, but certainly not probable, that James Shirley
wrote his play after Burnell wrote his. But even if Shirley's play were written at the unlikely time of spring or
summer, 1640, the only thing Burnell's play would have suggested to Shirley was to avoid Scandinavian characters,
stories and settings. Thus, these two items, (1) Shirley's
choice of the name, Turgesius, and (2) Burnell's 1640 play,
give some minor support for the long-held contention that
Shirley wrote The Politician for the Werburgh-Street Theatre and that it was actually performed there.

Unfortunately, except for the statement on the title
page of the 1655 edition, there is no evidence that The
Politician was performed in London. The statement "Presented at Salisbury Court BY HER MAJESTIES SERVANTS" on the
title-page of The Politician[113] would seem to provide clear
proof that the play was performed in London before the
interdiction of the stage, but seventeenth-century printers
were notoriously casual about the truth of the information
on the title-pages of the plays they printed. Often used
for advertisments, title-pages might very likely reflect a
printer's greater concern with sales than with informational
accuracy, and in any case, compositors quite often were

---

[113]James Shirley, The Polititian (London: Humphrey
Moseley, 1655), sig. [A1r].

careless about such matters. In spite of Humphrey Moseley's good reputation and in spite of the possibility that Shirley supervised the printing of his plays in the 1650's, the title-page statement would be considerably strengthened if there were corroborating evidence concerning the play's London performance. The Gentleman of Venice and The Politician were very close in the press, the former preceding the latter, and a statement regarding the performance of The Politician on its title-page might simply be a compositor's repetition of the same title-page information of The Gentleman of Venice.

Allan Stevenson in his examination of the relationship of Shirley to the actors in the first Irish Theatre, ingeniously and convincingly argues that when the Queen's Men at the Cockpit--for whom Shirley was the chief dramatist-- broke up as a result of the plague of 1636, some of the actors unaccounted for by extant theatrical records went to Dublin with Shirley to help form the new company at the Werburgh-Street Theatre.[114] Without question, others from the Cockpit formed the new Queen's Men at Salisbury Court in 1637. The likelihood that the new and sole theatrical company formed in Dublin at the same time, would be called the King's Men, would explain why Shirley, the former playwright for the Queen's Men, would reappear in London in

---

[114]Stevenson, MP, pp. 150-151.

1640 as the dramatist for the King's Men, and why several
actors, also formerly with the old Queen's Men, would also
reappear in London as players for the King's company.[115]
Such an explanation of the professional associations of the
various actors and Shirley would also explain why two of
Shirley's plays written in Ireland found their way to the
Salisbury Court Theatre and why other plays written in Ireland were performed by the King's Men at Blackfriars upon
Shirley's return to England. While in Dublin, the playwright
kept association with some of his old colleagues from the
Cockpit, then at Salisbury Court, by sending the group two
plays: The Gentleman of Venice and The Politician. As he
came to realize that he was going to leave the Irish theatri-
cal-desert, he held back other plays that had been performed
at the Werburgh-Street Theatre by other of his old associates
at the Cockpit and carried those to Blackfriars to be performed by the English veterans of the Irish stage who returned to England to join the King's Men with him.

F. G. Fleay says that Thomas Nabbes's The Unfortunate
Mother, though never acted, was written for Beeston's Boys
at the Cockpit as a rival piece to Shirley's The Politician
than being acted at Salisbury Court.[116] Bentley, demanding
evidence, says that none exists for believing the play was

---

[115]Stevenson, MP, pp. 159-160.

[116]F. G. Fleay, A Biographical Chronicle of the English
Drama, 1559-1642 (London: Reeves and Turner, 1891), II, 121.

written to rival The Politician or, in fact, that it was

written for Beeston's Boys. He does concede, however, that

Nabbes's "sneering" statement in the proem to the play

"sounds like a reference to the actions of Gotharus."[117]

The line reads:

> No Politician tells his plots unto
> These in the Pit, and what he meanes to doe.[118]

Bentley at least permits that these lines might be a "jeal-

ous dig at the tragedy which the Queen's Men had produced

in preference to The Unfortunate Mother,"[119] which seems to

have been written in the summer or early fall of 1639.[120]

Finally, if Thomas Killigrew in writing The Pilgrim,

printed in 1664, used The Politician as his source as ar-

gued by Alfred Harbage,[121] further evidence for a perfor-

mance of The Politician before the closing of the theatres

exists. Harbage believes that The Pilgrim was written in

1646 in Paris despite the date of 1651 as the composition

date on the title-page.[122] Killigrew was exiled from

---

[117]Bentley, IV, 943.

[118]Thomas Nabbes, The Unfortunate Mother: A Tragedie
(London: Daniell Frere, 1640), sig. A3^r.

[119]Bentley, IV, 943.

[120]Bentley, IV, 943 and Harbage and Schoenbaum, p. 138.
It was entered in the Stationers' Register, 4 November 1639.
Edward Arber (ed.), A Transcript of the Company of Stationers
of London, 1554-1640 A. D. (London: [n.p.], 1877), IV, 461.

[121]See the discussion on pp. lxiv-lxvii.

[122]Alfred Harbage, Thomas Killigrew, Cavalier Dramatist, 1612-83 (Philadelphia: University of Pennsylvania
Press, 1930), p. 193.

England in 1643 as a royalist but according to Harbage was
living in a fashionable Covent Garden section of London as
man-about-town until his exile.[123] More recently, J. W. Stoye
has demonstrated almost irrefutably that Killigrew was on
the continent from the summer or autumn of 1639 to June
1641.[124] If Killigrew based The Pilgrim on Shirley's The
Politician, and if the former was written in 1646 (or even
1651 for that matter) then Killigrew had to know of the
play from having seen one or more performances. For certainly Killigrew did not carry a manuscript of Shirley's
play to France, and The Politician was not printed until
1655. Of course, the argument that Shirley's play is the
source for Killigrew's is not without question, but if it
was the model for The Pilgrim, Killigrew must have seen a
performance of The Politician sometime before the fall of
1639 or between June, 1641 and the interdiction of the stage.

The information on the title-page of the 1655 first
edition of the play, Shirley's professional association
with various members of the Queen's players who were work-
ing at Salisbury Court while the playwright was living in Dublin, the possibility that Thomas Nabbes's play, The Unfortunate Mother, was a rejected rival of The Politician, and
the slight evidence that Thomas Killigrew saw one or more

---

[123]Harbage, p. 74.

[124]J. W. Stoye, "The Whereabouts of Thomas Killigrew
1639-1641," RES, 25 (1949), 246-247.

performances of Shirley's play in 1639 or 1641, altogether
indicate that The Politician was performed by the Queen's
Men at the Salisbury Court Theatre between 1639 and the
closing of the theaters.

There is no evidence, not even the circumstantial kind
presented above, that The Politician was ever performed
after its appearance at the Salisbury Court Theatre in
1639-1641. Allardyce Nicoll quotes from a warrant dated
August 19, 1678, which cites plays acted from May 31, 1677,
to May 28, 1678. For the year 1677 is found: "His Mates
Bill From His Royall Highnesse Theatre 1677 . . . Nov:
17th: At the Polititian [£] 10."[125] And this citation
has led some to consider the possibility of a later performance of Shirley's play.[126] This reference, however, is
not to Shirley's tragedy, for William Van Lennep identifies
the play in the warrant as the anonymous Sir Popular Wisdom; or The Politician, 1677, which was not printed.[127]

---

[125]Allardyce, Nicoll, A History of Restoration Drama
1660-1700, 2nd Edition (Cambridge: University Press, 1928),
pp. 310-311.

[126]See Huberman, "James Shirley's 'The Polititian,'"
p. 112n.

[127]William Van Lennep (ed.), The London Stage, 1660-
1800 . . . Part 1 1660-1700 (Carbondale, Illinois: Southern Illinois University Press, 1965), p. 65. Nor does it
seem possible that Sir Popular Wisdom; or the Politician is
a revival of Shirley's play with a different name. Van
Lennep cites a letter from Andrew Marvell to Sir Edw. Har-
ley dated November 17, 1677, the date of the performance,
which reads: "To-day is acted the first time Sir Popular
Wisdom or the Politician, where my Lord Shaftesbury and all
his gang are sufficiently personated. I conceive the King
will there. [from] (HMC, 14th Report, Appendix, Part II,
1894, Portland MSS. Volume III, p. 357)." p. 265.

In another warrant cited elsewhere by Nicoll is found:
"1677. [Nov.] 17 at Sr. Popler Wisdome 10."[128] It is obvious that the two citations quoted by Nicoll are two separate seventeenth-century references to a single play, Sir
Popular Wisdom: or The Politician.

The Play as a Source

Even if we could be positive about the priority of The
Politician over Landgartha, the minor similarities between
the two would hardly be sufficient evidence to call the former the source of the latter. There is, however, one play
for which it might be said that Shirley's tragedy was a
source.[129] Alfred Harbage first said in 1930 that Thomas
Killigrew based his play, The Pilgrim, on Shirley's The
Politician.[130] Because Harbage made some mistakes about
The Politician in comparing the play with Killigrew's, and

---

[128]Nicoll, p. 311.

[129]Perhaps it should be noted here that a tale in Nathaniel Ingleo's Bentivolio and Urania (London: T. Dring, J.
Starkey, and T. Basset, 1669), originally published in 1660,
which is a variation on the Plangus-tale of Sidney's Arcadia
(Seaton, p. 323), actually contains two incidents that are in
neither Sidney's story nor Lady Mary Wroth's Antissius-tale,
but are in The Politician. They are: (1) the ruse by which
the king is disaffected from his son (a forged letter by the
prince's former secretary), and (2) the king's belief that
causes the ruler to repent his actions and which, at that
time, has no basis in fact (see Ingelo, Book V, pp. 30-41).
But in spite of these similar incidents, I hesitate to say
that Ingelo found them in Shirley's play. There is much that
is dissimilar about the two plots, and neither of these variations is especially peculiar so as to require a specific source.

[130]Harbage, Killigrew, p. 194.

because no one has re-examined the relationship of the two
plays, a brief review of this source-theory is required.

Several general similarities exist between Killigrew's
and Shirley's plays. In The Pilgrim the King is a basically
good fellow who takes as his wife the widow of a nobleman.
Her reputation is something less than superlative; in fact,
she is called: "a bloody and an ambitious woman."[131] This
new queen has a favorite who was her paramour during her
first marriage and who, apparently, is continuing in the
role. The lovers have a son (in this case the young man
actually is their son) who is an innocent and a good fellow
whom they wish to succeed to the throne instead of the
true heir, the king's son by his former marriage. The only
deaths in the play, save for some completely insignificant
characters, are those of the false queen, her minion, and
their son. Except that the son actually is their issue, the
major story line in The Pilgrim, therefore, is remarkably
similar to the story in The Politician,[132] and many other
similarities exist as well.

The Pilgrim, like The Politician, opens with two
honest men" (Giovanni and Ferdinando in the former and
and Cortes and Hormenus in the latter) providing exposition
of plot and character (pp. 157-160). Forged letters from

---

[131]Thomas Killigrew, The Pilgrim (London: Henry Herringman, 1663), p. 159. All further references to this
play appear in the text.

[132]Harbage, p. 194, says that they are identical, but
he misreads Shirley's play in one important respect: He believes Haraldus to be the true son of Marpisa and Gotharus.

Martino (a Gotharus-like figure) and Julia (the plotting
queen) establish distrust between Sforza, the King's son,
and Cosmo, their son, just as Gotharus causes a breach between the King of Romania and Turgesius by the same ruse
(pp. 157-158). Julia and Martino plan to have Sforza killed
as he returns from Pavia where he has been acting as a kind
of governor and from where he had been called home (pp. 162-
163). The intent is the same as in The Politician; the
actual plan is more akin to the Antissius tale in the
Urania. Richardo, a loyal friend to Sforza, advises the
prince not to return, much as Olaus does Turgesius, but
Sforza, like the Prince of Norway, too trusting, returns
nevertheless (pp. 176-77). Cosmo also returns against the
counsel of friends (pp. 158-159), and accidentally over-
hears that his mother and Martino are lovers and that they
plot to kill Sforza. He is deeply disturbed and shocked
(pp. 192-194). This incident, of course, is reminiscent of
Haraldus' overhearing Hormenus and Cortes discuss the liaison between Marpisa and Gotharus and of the young man's
reaction to the discovery. Just as Marpisa turns on
Gotharus after Haraldus dies, Julia, falsely believing that
Cosmo is dead, blames Martino and vows revenge on him
(p. 196).

There are several other echoes of The Politician in The
Pilgrim, and two passages will serve as examples. Julia's
comment about Fidelia, her Albina-like daughter, "No child
of mine could be so unseasonably vertuous" (pp. 161-162)

reminds one of Gotharus' similar statement about Haraldus:

> But that I have Marpisa's faith, I could
> Suspect him not the issue of my blood;
> He is too tame and honest. At his years
> I was prodigiously in love with greatness.
> (I.i.278-281)

And Carlo, perhaps another imitation of Gotharus, in trying
to get Julia to betray Martino says: "'tis no time to express a fondness when Crowns and Lives are at stake" (p.
193). Similarly Gotharus says: "Who looks at crowns must
have no thought who bleeds" (I.i.335).

The almost identical basic plot, the similarities of
characters and incidents, and the verbal echoes emphasize
the strong possibility that Killigrew used Shirley's play
as a source for his. But as Harbage says, "In some respects The Pilgrim resembles the possible prototype [Hamlet]
of The Politician more than it does The Politician itself."[133] This comment is directed particularly at the
character difference between Haraldus and Cosmo and the two
plays' structural differences, but Harbage's observation
serves in general to emphasize that The Politician as the
source for The Pilgrim must remain only a "strong possibility."

The Publication of the Play

The period between the closing of the theaters in 1642
and the Restoration in 1660 was a time of official hostility

---

[133]Harbage, Killigrew, p. 195.

toward the drama.[134] Governmental suppression of books
stiffened as pamphlets and books attacking the Commonwealth
government were issued from the presses. In fact, Henry R.
Plomer notes that on September 20, 1649, following the rise
of virulent passions over the execution of Charles I on
January 30 of that same year, "Parliament passed the most
drastic Act against the book-trade that had been known since
the Star Chamber decree of 1637."[135] The published appearance of a play (especially one that has at least peripheral,
political implications and which had gone unpublished for
fifteen years) during this period unfavorable to drama in
particular and oppressive regarding printing in general may
seem something of an anomaly, and for that reason is worth
examination.

According to Plomer, printers with Royalist sympathies
found it difficult to enter works in the Stationers' Register. This inhibition was just one of the many ways that the
government could bring pressure upon those publishers not
in harmony with the Commonwealth. But there were some very
discreet men, Plomer calls them "neutral men," who avoided

---

[134]It was not a period of complete suppression of all
performances of plays as it was once thought. For a discussion of the sub rosa theater in England during the Interregnum see Leslie Hotson, The Commonwealth and Restoration
Stage (Cambridge, Mass.: Harvard University Press, 1928).

[135]Henry R. Plomer, A Dictionary of the Booksellers and
Printers . . . from 1641 to 1667 (London: Blades, East &
Blades, 1907), p. xvi.

partisan politics and thereby could enter just about anything they wished within reason and were not bothered by
either side. In a time of such passions, such printers were
rare, but one such "neutral man" was Humphrey Moseley.[136]

It is interesting to note that until 1646 not one of
Shirley's works was printed by Humphrey Moseley, a publisher
who entered his first book in the Stationers' Register on
May 29, 1630.[137] In 1646, Moseley printed Shirley's Poems,
the first of the writer's works to be printed since 1640,
and in 1647 he brought out Shirley's long poem, Narcissus,
or, The Self-Lover, and his masque, The Triumph of Beautie.
Until 1659, when the Puritan hold on England had all but
slipped away, no one printed Shirley's plays except Moseley.[138] In short, Shirley went to one of the few "neutral
men" in the printing business in the 1640's and 1650's to
publish what very likely could not have been published
elsewhere without considerable difficulty. Or to reverse
roles, Moseley went to Shirley to gain the publication

---

[136]Plomer, p. xiv. Plomer further describes Moseley:
"He became the chief publisher of the finer literature of
his age. He published the first collected edition of Mil-
ton's Poems, as well as the works of Cartwright, Crashaw,
D'Avenant, Denham, Donne, Fanshaw, Howell, Vaughan and
Waller," pp. 132-33.

[137]Plomer, p. 132. For a list of all dates and printers of Shirley's plays, see Nason, pp. 401-421.

[138]Two grammar studies by Shirley, Via ad Latinum Lin-
guam Complanata (1649) and The Rudiments of Grammar (1656)
were not printed by Moseley, nor was one masque, Cupid and
Death (1653). But eight plays of Shirley's including The
Politician, were printed in the 1650's all by Moseley.

rights to his plays for reasons described below.

All of Shirley's plays printed by Moseley were issued in the 1650's, a fact that reveals not only Shirley's wisdom in the choice of a printer but also reveals something about why Moseley was one of the "neutral men." The book-trade was improving in the 1650's; the war was almost over and passions were subsiding. Despite the strong Cavalier associations with the drama,[139] Moseley obviously sensed that the atmosphere of the 1650's was more favorable for printing plays than it had been a decade or so before. Perhaps the printers and the play-reading public were emboldened by the knowledge that what energy the government directed toward the suppression of publication was turned more and more toward a threat greater than plays: political pamphlets and tracts.[140] As the machinery of government focused on suppressing overtly political material, and as the public demand for dramatic literature grew, Humphrey Moseley, from all evidence a shrewd businessman, turned his presses to

---

[139] In fact, printing, purchasing, and even reading any pre-Cromwellian play--especially a thematically political play--were all likely to be considered Royalist expressions. See Louis B. Wright, "The Reading of Plays during the Puritan Revolution," The Huntington Library Bulletin, 6 (1934), passim, especially 86 and 107.

[140] Wright, p. 75.

meeting this demand.[141] Thus, the published The Politician
in 1655 apparently was the product of the following combination: Shirley's need for money--the theaters having been
closed for thirteen years--the rising demand for dramatic
literature, the greater government emphasis on restricting
those publications which were clearly and overtly seditious,
and a discreet, shrewd business man in the person of Humphrey Moseley.

The Play and the Critics

The little attention that has been given The Politician
by various critics over the years has not produced anything
resembling agreement on the play's artistic and dramatic
value. The earliest published critical judgment of the play
is by Charles Dibdin who, in 1800, thought the play "of
inconsiderable merit,[142] and as previously noted, the editors of the 1812 Biographia Dramatica considered the play
"not one of Shirley's best productions.[143] K. Q. X. in the

---

[141]Wright, p. 84. It is interesting to note that Moseley, although in the publishing business since 1627,
brought out only one play written by any Jacobean or Caroline dramatist (The Sophister [1639] by Richard Zouches, an
"academic" play according to Bentley, V, 1278-1279) until
1647 when he printed the collected works of Beaumont and
Fletcher, for which, coincidentally, Shirley wrote the pre-
face. See John Curtis Reed, "Humphrey Moseley, Publisher,"
Oxford Bibliographical Society: Proceedings and Papers, II
(1927-1930), 104-105 and Greg, A Bibliography of the English
Drama to the Restoration, III, 1530-1531.

[142]Charles Dibdin, the elder A Complete History of the
English Stage (London: Charles Dibdin, [1800]), IV, 46.

[143]Biographia Dramatica, III, 169.

July, 1820, issue of The London Magazine is slightly more
charitable than his predecessors when he says: "The Politician,--by no means a favourite with us, either in plot or
characters,--has a few striking passages."[144] John
Genest's 1832 laconic statement is favorable: "[The Politi-
cian] is on the whole a good T[ragedy]."[145] These critical
comments were made before the Gifford and Dyce edition of
Shirley's work was issued; possibly critics prior to 1833
made their observations without having read all of Shirley's
plays. The only reference to The Politician in an anonymous review of the edition in the Quarterly Review, 1833, is
less a critical evaluation of the play than an historical
judgment of the time in which the drama was written and
produced: "Who would go to witness the imaginary 'Politician' of the dramatist, when he might watch the unraveling
of the great plot in either House of Parliament?"[146] But if
the anonymous reviewer in the Quarterly Review essentially
ignored Shirley's tragedy, his counterpart in the American
Quarterly Review did not. The latter gave the play only
"passing notice," but there is nothing equivocal about his
judgment of the play:

> The Politician is nearly abandoned a reprobate in
> reality, as most of the persons of his class are
> affirmed to be by their opponents. He commits

---

[144]K. Q. X., The London Magazine, II (July, 1820), 39.

[145]Genest, IX, 561.

[146]Quarterly Review, 49 (April, 1833), 4.

atrocities enough to gratify the most insatiate ama-
teur of horrors; but such as are not particularly de-
lighted with these, will have slight reason to regret
that we accord him but a passing notice.[147]

If the writer in the American Quarterly Review was the

first to judge Shirley's seventeenth-century play with

nineteenth-century moral attitudes, S. A. Dunham was the

first to attack the play after having obviously misunder-

stood or misread it. He calls The Politician "one of the

worst of Shirley's tragedies," saying that the "plot is

spoiled by a cluster of incidents that choke each other up,

and give it something of the air of an extravagant melo-

drama on stilts."[148] But it seems that the critic created

some of the problems in the play with which he charges

Shirley, for Dunham believes that Turgesius actually rebels

against his father, thinks that there is "scarcely a scene"

without "inconsistencies of some sort," and somehow be-

lieves that "the deaths of nearly all the principal persons

concerned" brings about the resolution.[149]

G. Barnett Smith, in an 1880 issue of The Gentleman's

Magazine, does nothing more than give a thumbnail sketch of

the major characters, commenting that "the chief interest

centers in Gotharus, who, after a career famed for

---

[147]American Quarterly Review, 16 (September, 1834), 156.

[148]S. A. Dunham, Lives of the Most Eminent Literary and
Scientific Men of Great Britain (London: Longman, Orme,
Brown, Green, and Longmans, 1838), III, 57.

[149]Dunham, III, 57.

treacheries and bloody deeds, at length meets with his just

doom." [150] Edmund Gosse, in the introduction to his 1888

selection of Shirley's plays, lists The Politician with

several others as "less interesting than Shirley's earlier

works."[151] It is Swinburne who is first to turn away from

judging Shirley's play on moral grounds or from condemning

or praising the work as a whole without qualification.

Brief as his comment is, he is the first critic to comment

on The Politician with a certain discrimination and judi-

ciousness:

> The Politician, if not one of Shirley's best plays, is
> one of his liveliest and most effective; the pathos of
> the scene immortalized by insertion in Lamb's immortal
> volume of 'Specimens' is so simple and so pure as to
> remind us rather of Heywood than of Shirley; and if
> the attempt at a similar effect in the part of an in-
> jured and misused wife is not equally happy or impres-
> sive, it is not for lack of graceful and facile
> writing.[152]

A similar attempt at balanced criticism is made by A.

W. Ward in 1899. He says that The Politician is "an effort

of a very ambitious kind; some of its characters are cast

in a tragic mould which they can hardly be said to fill.

. . .The interest in the action is well sustained, but

---

[150]G. Barnett Smith, "Shirley," The Gentleman's Magazine, 246 (1880), 604.

[151]Edmond Gosse, James Shirley (London: Vizetelly and
Co., 1888), p. xxv.

[152]A. C. Swinburne, "James Shirley," Fortnightly Review, 53 (1890), 475.

the characters are designed without depth."[153] Nine years
later Ashley Thorndike also calls the play an "ambitious
effort," but says little more about it other than to associate the drama with the works of Beaumont and Fletcher and
others.[154] In the same year, 1908, Felix Schelling calls
The Politician "only half a tragedy" because only the wicked,
with one exception, die; thereby, the "moral struggle has
been supplanted by intrigue and counterintrigue."[155] Even
so, Schelling speaks of the "holding power in the last
scene of this tragedy into which is crowded the unexpected
discovery of the dead traitor, the pitiable lamentations of
his miserable wife, the splendid Marpisa at bay, and the
reconciliation of the Prince and his father."[156]

W. A. Neilsen says little more than that the play is
actually a tragicomedy because for those characters with
whom we identify the play ends happily.[157] J. Schipper in
1911, after discussing some particular weaknesses and

---

[153]A. W. Ward, A History of English Dramatic Literature
to the Death of Queen Anne, New Revised Edition (London:
MacMillan and Co., Ltd., 1899), III, 97-98.

[154]Ashley H. Thorndike, Tragedy (London: Constable and
Co., Ltd., [1908]., pp. 232-233.

[155]Felix E. Schelling, Elizabethan Drama (Boston:
Houghton Mifflin, 1908), II, 313.

[156]Schelling, II, 320.

[157]W. A. Neilson, "Ford and Shirley," in The Cambridge
History of English Literature (Cambridge: University Press,
1910), VI, 200.

strengths of Shirley's tragedy, finds it one of Shirley's better plays: "So gehört diese Tragödie trotz der ihr anhaftenden oben erwähnten Schwachen doch zu den hervorragenderen Dramen unseres Dichters."[158]

Arthur H. Nason, in the most comprehensive biographical and critical study of Shirley available, discusses some of the charges brought against The Politician. He admits that the play is at times a "repulsive tragedy" dealing as it does with intrigue, lust, and assassination,[159] but there is "power" in the play "from scene to scene" (p. 309). Furthermore, it is Gotharus and Marpisa who are the protagonists in the play; they are the tragic figures. And just because the King, Olaus, Albina, and Turgesius remain alive does not make it "less a tragedy" (p. 312). Though Nason directs the reader, perhaps for the first time, toward thinking about Marpisa and Gotharus as the tragic figures as opposed to stage-bogeymen, he keeps a balanced, critical eye. The play, Nason says, "impresses one . . . for its swift tense scenes, its gloom, its horror" (p. 312). It is "terrible, despite the survival of many innocent; effective, notwithstanding clap-trap and the absence of profound psychology; a romantic tragedy that is almost notable" (p. 312). Later, Nason reduces the protagonists to one and suggests that the play is more than merely "almost notable." "The Politician,

---

[158] J. Schipper, p. 251.

[159] Nason, p. 307.

however, somber in subject, powerful in scene, mighty in its protagonist, Marpisa, is a tragedy," Nason concludes, "worthy of any but the greatest dramatist" (p. 396).

Brief attention has been given to The Politician since Nason, but what passing comment has been made about the play can hardly be called eulogistic. Gebhard Josef Scherrer writes in 1951: "The Politician is eine Pseudo-Tragödie, zu deren Gunsten sich sehr wenig sagen lässt."[160] Although Richard Gerber in 1952 at one point in his work seems to recognize something of the complexity and, perhaps, sympathetic potential of the character of Marpisa,[161] his final judgment of the play lacks this insight. He calls the play a "Pseudotragödie . . . [eine] Tragödie mit dem Happy Ending, . . . wo nur die Vebrecher umkommen, die Guten jedoch gerettet werden. Dies geschieht im fruheren elisabethanischen Drama nicht, wenigstens nicht in diesem Ausmass."[162] One of but five tragedies composed by the last of the major writers for what is broadly called the Elizabethan stage, The Politician deserves greater attention than these two cursory comments.

---

[160]Gebhard Josef Scherrer, James Shirleys Nachruhm (Zurich: Juris-Verlag, 1951), p. 65.

[161]Richard Gerber, James Shirley: Dramatiker der Dekadenz (Bern: Friedrich Gegenbauer s, 1952), p. 50.

[162]Gerber, p. 83

III. CRITICAL

Asserting that Ford and Shirley were perhaps the first writers of "modern dramatic literature . . . in a special sense," W. A. Neilson emphasizes that not only could they read and digest their predecessors in print, they could also look forward to seeing their plays in print, not just on the stage. They belong to what Neilson calls the "'literary' stage."[163] John Eglinton, in what is perhaps an overstatement, writes: "No dramatists could have taken their art more seriously than Jonson, Massinger, or Shirley, who seem to have written less for an audience than with a view to ultimate publication of their collected works.[164] An examination of The Politician should, therefore, take into account both the literary and the theatrical craftsmanship of its author, keeping the critical eye in balance between the two.

Characterization

An examination of Shirley's characterization in The Politician should properly begin with a study of the character from whom the play takes its name, the politician, Gotharus. This titular character is a full-blooded figure,

---

[163]Neilson, p. 188. Gosse, pp. vii-viii says essentially the same thing: Shirley, "an essentially literary poet, took up the drama as literature."

[164]John Eglinton, Anglo-Irish Essays (New York: John Lane Co., 1918), p. 60. By the time Shirley wrote The Politician he had seen at least fifteen of his plays and masques in print.

Shirley's creation, who bears little resemblance to the source character in the Urania. In the "Names and Small Characters" Shirley identifies Gotharus as a politician concerned with his "pleasures and ambition" and a "great favorite of the Queen."[165] Long ago Mario Praz pointed out the sinister associations of the word politician in the sixteenth and seventeenth centuries. Other derivatives of the noun policy, such as politic, had also become associated with scheming and intrigue as a result of the identification of these words with a distorted view of Machiavelli as an unprincipled figure.[166] By simply calling Gotharus a politician, therefore, Shirley identifies him as the Machiavel who had been part of the English theatrical tradition since the early days of Marlowe and Kyd, a conflation of an unsympathetic portrayal of the author of The Prince with the more native strains of the medieval stage villain.

As a typical Machiavel, Gotharus is forever plotting and scheming. He is cruel, deceptive and unprincipled, and he adopts another characteristic of the Machiavel noted by Praz, avarice or miserliness,[167] forcing his wife, Albina,

---

[165]"The Names and Small Characters of the Persons," ll. 4-5. All references to the play are to this edition and hereafter will be cited in the text by act, scene, and line.

[166]Mario Praz, Machiavelli and the Elizabethans (London: Humphrey Milford Amen House, 1928), pp. 14-17.

[167]Praz, p. 5.

to keep account books to record all her expenditures (see
I.i.183-185). When he berates Albina for her infidelity, he
tells her to curtail her wardrobe and "train" (I.i.148-152)
and expresses no desire to pay a doctor's fee for her, re-
vealing his niggardliness as well as his suspicious nature
(I.i.160-163).

Like his villainous atheistic predecessors who stalked
the stage before him, the politician expresses nothing but
disdain for heaven and an afterworld; he is called a "pagan"
by the riotous mob (IV.iv.79) and in his description of an
ambitious, scheming figure, Gotharus accurately portrays
himself: "He that aspires hath no religion" (III.i.257).
To the biased, Satan and Machiavelli were "interchange-
able,"[168] and accordingly, Shirley's politician is identified with hell and the devil, sometimes obliquely (see I.i.
20-22, I.i.39-41, and I.i.316-317), but often quite directly. He is called an "incarnate fiend" (II.i.208) and
even the "devil" twice (IV.v.40 and V.ii.70). Marpisa, his
paramour and co-plotter, is called a "limb of Lucifer"
(V.ii.13).

In one major sense, however, Shirley's Machiavel must
be considered an embarrassment to his theatrical ancestors.
The Iagos and Barabases of early years are in the end, like
Gotharus, undone by their villainy, but until that end
their cunning rules. In spite of a surface cleverness and

---

[168]Praz, p. 37.

several adroit moves, Gotharus' cunning never actually
rules. The king's favorite never knows, for example, that
Marpisa has been using him for years, and he innocently--
a terrible adjective to be applied to a Machiavel--allows
Marpisa to murder him. Of all the courtiers available in
the Norwegian capital, Gotharus foolishly engages Sueno and
Helga, two fops at best, to be the "educators" of Haraldus.
And for no good reason, apart from the melodrama it provides, the politician admits to Haraldus what the boy believes to be true: he is Haraldus' father. By these two
acts, Gotharus becomes the cause of the death of the young
man he has been tricked into believing is his son. Fooled
by Marpisa, he deludes himself further by distorting Haraldus' true position, acting as if Haraldus were indeed a
prince (see I.i.266 ff.) and most damaging, he is tricked by
an ordinary Captain, Aquinus, all the while the politician
believes he is manipulating the soldier (see III.i.280 ff.).
Finally, when threatened by the mob, he throws himself on
the mercy of his enemies and asks the chief of them, Olaus,
for help. Had he not already been deceived and poisoned by
one of his friends, this trust of his enemy would have
proved as unfortunate as it was unworthy of a consummate
villain.

Praz notes that as the tragedy of Elizabeth's age gave
way to a more "sentimental" or romantic tragedy, the

Machiavel was less terrible than he was ridiculous.[169] Gotharus is rather a bugbear. He forces his wife to keep accounts, underlings scurry away at his frown (I.i.24 S.D.), his cruelty has all the subtlety of a side show ("I first / Practise at home my unkindness to Albina," I.i.202-201), he inveighs against conscience and laughs at hell (I.i.315-317), he believes his "son" should be corrupted for his own good (I.i.324-328), and parodying divine invocation, he calls on "malice [to] inspire my brain" (II.i.247). He has an exceptionally vulgar mind (see I.i.138-153 and 155-178) in which obscenities become curiously mixed with avaricious thoughts. But such excesses are not unique to late Caroline Machiavels. After all, Mankynde's Titivillus, Marlowe's Barabas, and Shakespeare's Aaron can hardly be described as subtle villains. Like so many of his predecessors, Gotharus' depravities are exaggerated, and he, like them, is just a little bit funny for it. He is less like Iago, the personification par excellence of human evil and the exceptional Machiavel, than he is like Herod of the medieval cyles, the archetypal bugbear and grandfather of comic English stage villains.

To Shirley's credit, however, there are subtle points to the characterization of Gotharus. He is a person concerned with the surface, with appearance and with superficial pleasures. He is a machinator, one who acts like a machine and treats the world as if all in it were designed for

---

[169]Praz, p. 48.

manipulation. His superficiality and his associations with the mechanical are closely related and complementary.

Gotharus' emphasis on the material and the monetary and his concern with the tangible and the extrinsic detach him from the more subtle pleasures, love and honor. For Albina, who is troubled by the king's overtures, Gotharus' only concern is that she drive a good bargain with the ruler and get a good return for her services (I.i.134-135). And in response to her tears brought forth by his berating, Gotharus reveals only an appreciation for tricks and machination, "Come," he says, "These are but painted tears; leave this. Have you / Prepared your last accounts?" (I.i.183-184).

Even his relations with Haraldus show him to be more concerned about self and plots, his plots, than about the person he believes to be his son and for whom, apparently, he is doing all he can to gain the throne. In response to the boy's request that he be granted leave to go to the university (I.i.248-287), Gotharus shows that he wants what he wants for the boy, not what Haraldus wishes. One can be forgiven for thinking that Gotharus has maneuvered Haraldus into his close position to the throne less for love of the young man than for love of the power he would achieve through Haraldus and Marpisa.

In keeping with this coldness, this self-centered detachment, Shirley provides Gotharus with a language of an impersonal, mechanical world. Speaking of his having persuaded the king to send Turgesius to war, Gotharus says that he "wrought / The king to send him forth to war" (I.i.

29-30). When talking to Albina about the possible issue of

an affair between her and the king, his reference to a child

is coldly mechanical: "the king shall give it / A name.

He'll name it master of a province" (I.i.136-137). When

soliloquizing about Haraldus' "tame and honest" nature and

about the need to make him more like himself, he speaks of

the boy in impersonal terms, as if Haraldus were an object,

not a human: "I must new-form the boy / Into more vice and

daring" (I.i.285-286). Life to Gotharus is stratagems and

engines, terms he uses several times (I.i.31-32, 304-305,

II.i.333, and IV.iv.5) in a manner associating him with a

mechanical and non-human world, and suggesting a coldness and

manipulation appropriate to his character.[170]

In the end the character of Gotharus, created with some

subtlety but with more heavy-handedness, arouses little sym-

pathy, and perhaps one might argue that in his character and

actions the comic possibilities are greater than the tragic.

But for all his faults, the character is dramatically and

theatrically effective and well wrought. The nameless, and

essentially faceless "favorite" Shirley found in his source,

the _Urania_, simply would not have worked in any drama worthy

of that name. Gotharus, essentially the playwright's crea-

tion, helps to give Shirley's play a life lacking in Lady

---

[170]Only two other times is the word _engine_ used: once
when Olaus refers to weapons (IV.ii.2) and again when he refers to a scaffold or the ax of the executioner (III.i.72).

Mary's romance even if he does not attain the tragic heights of earlier theatrical figures lost to ambition and to their own evil.

The source-character of Marpisa is definitely the Romanian queen in the _Urania_, but Shirley's queen is much more credible and complex than the monstrous and grotesque Romanian. Marpisa retains many of the characteristics of her prototype, but they are moderated, and, unlike her predecessor, she is not a static character. It is her complexity that allows this essentially wicked character to approach the level of sympathetic identification and to come nearer to the tragic role than does the politician himself.

Juliet McGrath, writing on Shirley's uses of language, says that Hormenus and Cortes describe Marpisa and several other characters at the beginning of The Politician and that thereafter "virtually no further characterizations of these figures are made."[171] As true as this statement may be regarding other chracters, it does not fully account for Marpisa. The two honest courtiers comment on her adultery (I.i.8-14) and on her ambition (I.i.4). However accurately Marpisa is described as an ambitious adulteress, that description does not take in account other charcteristics which are hers just as surely.

In the simplest moral terms, Marpisa is not a good

---

[171] Juliet McGrath, "James Shirley's Uses of Language," SEL, 6 (1966), 333.

person, but she has qualities which provide her with some
appeal. She is clever, capable of turning the unfavorable
to her advantage. She knows, for example, that Olaus and
Turgesius are going to express opposition to her marriage
and she uses their opposition to her advantage by playing
the role of the long-suffering woman who is willing to
sacrifice her position to keep peace between father and son
(II.i.119-156 and III.i.163-167).

She is perspicacious. She immediately perceives that
the letter that is supposed to be from the prince chiding
the king for her marriage to her is from Gotharus (see III.i.
168-169). She is superlative with language and wit. Olaus
is aware of this talent and though he tries to cut the
ground from under her by accusing her of being deceitfully
clever with words, her response is such a marvel of dissembling that anyone (save instinctively distrustful Olaus)
might wonder if she indeed does not wish the king to forgive the explosive duke for casting "black aspersions" on
her honor (III.i.21-39).

McGrath observes that Shirley invariably places "specious rhetoric" in the mouths of his "sinister schemers."[172]
But all of Shirley's schemers are not equal in their use of
this rhetoric. The entire time he believes he is deceiving
Aquinus with his sophistry, Gotharus is being deceived himself; Marpisa is never found at such a disadvantage. In

---

[172]McGrath, p. 236

fact, she deceives and poisons Gotharus when he ironically

believes she is providing him with a curative. Marpisa al-

ways ably employs the deceptive language; Gotharus is only

sometimes successful with his.

The queen is more than merely shrewd; she is a woman of

much will. As her son languishes in his last illness, with

an obvious belief in the power of determination, she says:

> Have but a will and live.
> Sink, with fever, into earth? Look up;
> Thou shalt not die.
> (IV.iii.41-43)

And when Haraldus in fact dies, she turns her strong will to

thoughts of revenge:

> I am resolv'd; my joys are all expir'd;
> Nor can ambition more concern me now.
> Gotharus has undone me in the death
> Of my loved son; his fate is next. While I
> Move resolute, I'll command his destiny.
> (IV.iii.125-129)

"Ambition," a characteristic first associated with Marpisa

by Hormenus and Cortes in the first scene is no longer the

queen's concern. Her interest now is revenge, which may

have been introduced as much for a "handy motivation," to

use Fredson Bowers' phrase,[173] as for psychological interest

in Marpisa. Nonetheless, this woman of strong will succeeds

with her plan of revenge as Gotharus fails in every one of

his plots.

Finally, this scene (IV.iii) reveals that Marpisa, un-

like her paramour, without question loves her son, and since

---

[173]Fredson Bowers, _Elizabethan Revenge Tragedy, 1587-1642_ (Gloucester, Mass.: Peter Smith, 1959), p. 217.

his birth has worked for him to gain an advantage not naturally his as the son of Lord Altomarus and a commoner with a
bad reputation. She is genuinely distraught at the boy's
death, and with Haraldus dead she has no reason to live even
though she is Queen. Her relationship with Gotharus has no
further purpose.

Jean E. Gagen in her book on the emergence of the new
woman in seventeenth-century drama says that this female
character in her variety of forms has "one distinguishing
trait. She does not consider herself merely an appendage
to man. She insists, however grotesquely, on the right to
study, to think, and above all to make decisions without the
constant surveillance of a male overlord."[174] Whether she is
one of Gagen's new women, Marpisa, without doubt, is inde-
pendent, clever, capable, and of great will. Her one depen-
dency is not connected with a lover or a husband, but with
her child for whom she has great, perhaps even sacrificial
love. Certainly, Marpisa is more than the simple ambitious
adulteress described by Hormenus and Cortes.

Still, to the other characters in the play she is what
the courtiers describe, and her unsavory reputation is singularly well known. Turgesius is obviously stunned almost
to disbelief that his father could marry such a woman:

---

[174]Jean E. Gagen, The New Woman: Her Emergence in English Drama, 1600-1730 (New York: Twayne Publishers, 1954),
p. 11.

TURGESIUS.
> Are all good women dead within the kingdom,
> There could be found none worth my father's love
> But one whose fame and honor are suspected?

OLAUS.
> Would they were but suspected.

TURGESIUS.   Marpisa!
>   (III.iii.23-26)

As Shirley associated Gotharus with Satan to underscore the politician's evil, he identifies Marpisa with
witchcraft and sorcery to help characterize her. Associating a character with witchcraft in 1639 would not be a
mere ornamental gesture. K. M. Briggs, in her investigation
of witchcraft and magic in the late sixteenth and seventeenth-century drama, argues that the belief in witches,
though not at its strongest point in the late 1630's and
early 1640's, was not without considerable subscription.[175]
Marpisa is repeatedly associated with special powers. Both
Gotharus and the king mention that she has the power to
bring life to that which is lifeless (I.i.309-314 and II.i.
39-40). Her beauty is referred to as "magic" twice (II.i.
332 and III.i.12), and according to Olaus she charms (III.i.
11) and uses tricks (III.i.15). Storms and clouds are repeatedly identified with her, sometimes in regard to her

---

[175]K. M. Briggs, *Pale Hecate's Team* (London: Routledge
and Kegan Paul, 1962), p. 219. Ethel Seaton, pp. 283-291,
writes that northern witches were extremely popular among
the English in seventeenth-century lore. Olaus Magnus, in
*A Compendious History of the Goths, Swedes, & Vandals, and
other Northern Nations* (London: J. Streater, 1658), pp. 46-
51, mentions the power of the witches of the north to raise
tempests, a power that is discussed as well by Heinrich
Kramer and James Sprenger in *Malleus Maleficarum*, trans.
Montague Summers (London: The Pushkin Press, 1948), pp.
147-149.

xc

power to disperse them (see I.i.292-293; II.i.39 and III.i.
135-137). The king refers to a storm that "hovers o'er my
kingdom" (III.i.274), apparently associating it with Turgesius, but shortly after Marpisa dies, he says: "A bright
day shines upon us" (V.ii.307).

More directly, Marpisa is called an "evil genius"
(III.i.8), and in the last act, the direct references mount
rapidly. The "sorcery" of her tongue is mentioned (V.i.8);
she is called a "limb of Lucifer" and must be "roasted"
(V.ii.13), a rather clear reference to burning at the stake.
This witch-devil relationship is appropriate to Marpisa and
the devil Gotharus and is played on when she is called the
"queen of hell" (V.ii.224) and a hellcat" (V.ii.230), when
she is said to have a lecherous devil reside in her eye
(V.ii.226), and when her facetious offer of poison to Olaus
is called "Devil's charity" (V.ii.261). Poisoning itself
was commonly associated with witches, for it demanded knowledge of herbs and various compounds thought to be available
only to witches.[176] And in this regard the inclusion, just
before she dies, of Marpisa's brief commentary on the effi-
cacy of her poison as compared with the usual painful type
(V.ii.262-264) is perhaps understood. Olaus believes he is
bewitched, for his mind becomes confused and short-circuited
when he thinks of her (V.ii.141-144), and, in fact, says

---

[176]Christina Hole, A Mirror of Witchcraft (London:
Chatto & Windus, 1957), p. 107.

that she had "bewitch'd" the king (V.ii.136). Aquinus
appropriately believes she is "shot-free" (V.ii.230), free,
that is, from being wounded by a rapier or a musket, a common characteristic of witches.[177] Finally, Olaus calls her
"my lady Circe" (V.ii.140), the most direct reference to her
powers as a sorceress.

Marpisa, then, is an evil person with great strength,
will, and a good measure of intelligence. But what makes
her a complex character is that her evil is tempered by her
love for her son, her strength and ability are balanced by a
singular lack of control (around Albina, a generally weak and
pale figure, this powerful, capable and forceful queen inex-
plicably loses control [III.i.170 ff., and IV.iv.51 ff.]), and her
intelligence and perspicacity are muted by her lack of in-
trospection. If things do not work out as they ought, this
otherwise perceptive woman seeks to find the blame anywhere
but within herself, with Gotharus, with the king, or with
Fate. Her perception is not turned inward until too late.
But even in defeat, unlike her son, unlike her lover, she
conveys character, and she also gains, before her death,
some introspective awareness of her own responsibility for
the unhappy conditions that exist. Before she makes her last
minute repentance, a repentance which is more charitably
attrituted to Shirley's concession to moral conventionality
than to his dramatic inventiveness, she pronounces such

---

[177]Robert Burton, The Anatomy of Melancholy, 5th ed.
(Oxford: Henry Cripps, 1638), p. 55.

passages as:

> I am mistress of my fate and do not fear
> Their [the army's] inundation. Their army coming,
> It does prepare my triumph. They shall give
> Me liberty and punish thee [the king] to live.
>   (V.i.42-45)

In her last scene (V.ii.223 ff.), when she turns back the taunts of lesser figures who in victory appear less in authority than she does in defeat, the queen has been described by Felix Schelling with the felicitous phrase, "the splendid Marpisa at bay."[178] She is especially "splendid" in her scorn and disdain of Olaus before, for the first time, admitting her guilt and responsibility for her present state. Though she asks them all to "forgive, forgive" (V.ii.277), the king has known her too well to be sure that her pride and will have actually given way to softer qualities. "Those accents yet may be repentance" he says (V.ii.278). He is not sure, and his doubts are just as well, for her character is not dependent on, indeed would have fared better without, the deathbed repentance.

Of all the characters in The Politician, Marpisa alone seems to approach a struggle that matters, to come near what could be called serious reflections on her actions, and to rise towards a suffering that evokes both a modicum of sympathy and some measure of admiration, if not awe. But this reaction is only relative to the other characters in the play, and any final judgment about Marpisa as a tragic

---

[178]Schelling, II, 320.

figure awaits additional examination of Shirley's dramaturgical method.

The remaining characters, all fundamentally secondary
and tertiary figures, have no special order of importance,
but it would seem appropriate to begin with the king. In
the second act, when the king is especially doting upon Marpisa and happily hearing absurdly flattering remarks from
Sueno and Helga, Cortes, speaking to Hormenus says of the
king, "His judgment's, I fear, stupified" (II.i.69). It is
as succinct and accurate a description of any character as
is found in the play. Not very bright, the king is credulous and easily manipulated. He is irresponsible, not only
in familial and governmental relationships, but also in human
relationships. His actions toward Albina (I.i.67-123) are
nothing less than depraved. By expanding the lustful nature
of his source character, however, Shirley helps to make the
king of Norway more credible as the weak, preoccupied, ineffectual ruler that he had to be to be so easily turned a-
gainst his son. The more we realize how correct his statements are about the demands upon and the responsibilities of a
ruler, reflected upon by him rather conventionally in V.ii.
84-105, the more we realize that the king simply is incapable
of meeting those demands or of fulfilling those responsibilities. As if to prove that judgment, he tries to abdicate in
favor of Turgesius. Refusing the crown, Turgesius is given an
opportunity to provide the king with a lecture on becoming
an example of a "king's power and duty" (V.ii.280-294).

Perhaps the answer to Turgesius' earlier rhetorical question

> For what sins
> Hath angry heaven decreed to punish Norway
> And lay the scene of wrath in her own bowels?
> (III.iii.13-15)

simply lies in the character and actions of his father, Norway's king. But this is not a political play; it is not seriously concerned with political matters. If it were, the role of the king would have far more importance in a play first performed in 1639 and first printed in 1655 than with justification can be ascribed to it here.

If Shirley needed a prototype for Olaus, the blunt soldier, uncomfortable at court, a stock character of the seventeenth-century stage, he found him in the person of Seleucius in the Urania. Shirley's gruff fellow, a wise counselor and cautious guardian who nonetheless requires restraint, has both comic and serious potential and helps to provide some of the more dramatically effective scenes in the play.

The character exposition of Olaus provided in the Hormenus-Cortes conversation (I.i.41-42) is quite meager. All we discover from their comments is that Olaus is not going to like the king's marriage to Marpisa. And Marpisa's comments to the king (II.i.137-144) give us no additional information, nor do additional statements by Hormenus and Cortes in II.i.202-203. But late in the second act Shirley creates the character quickly and effectively. When Gotharus calls to him, the duke brusquely replies: "I am too stiff for complement, my lord; / I have rid hard--" (II.i.236-237) and quickly departs, clearly a man with no sympathy for the world of the court.

Olaus is a man of few words. To an inquiry concerning the prince's well-being, he replies: "Well. Where's the king?" (II.i.233). In her study of Shirley's use of language, McGrath says that "'Good' language would seem to be plain unpretentious language, in which sense is never obscured by specious figures or deceptive rhetoric.[179] Furthermore, good characters refuse to employ "deceptive language"[180] and character is indicated by how one uses language.[181] Olaus' simple statement "I am plain" (III.i.20), then, conveys linguistically the virtue of the man as does his laconic comment to Gotharus, who with a florid statement had greeted Olaus, Turgesius and the army at the gates of the city: "Leave rhetoric, and to'th'point" (IV.ii.41).

He is a choleric old fellow. The king calls him a ruffian" and an "incendiary" (IV.i.43-44), and Turgesius chides him with "Passion will not let you see" (III.iii.82). The comic potential of such a character, a kind of blunderbuss, does not always remain beneath the surface. At lighter moments in the play, it shows its head, as when the duke

---

[179]McGrath, p. 330.   [180]McGrath, p. 334.
[181]McGrath, pp. 327-328.

continues to demand conditions from the king and the prince
before he will agree to relinquish control of the army
(V.ii.120 and 138).

The Duke Olaus, an appealing character, provides tension in the more somber moments of the play and a kind of
comedy in brighter sections. As an extremely explosive and
passionate man he acts as a foil for the prince, the paragon
of reason and restraint.

Turgesius combines two characters in the Urania, Antissius and his son of the same name. Like the two Romanian
princes he is a superlative figure, but unlike the elder
Antissius, Turgesius is wise and perspicacious instead of
naive. As with Olaus, the earliest references to the prince
by Hormenus and Cortes are not very enlightening; they simply reveal that he is not going to be happy to hear of the
royal marriage. In the early part of the third act, though
he has yet to appear, we learn more about Turgesius. Olaus'
description of a paragon:

> . . . . the good prince, your son, the hope of war
> And peace's darling, honor of our blood
> And worth a better kingdom than he's born to--
> (III.i.46-48)

And shortly after, the duke compares him with another, more
famous, and great young warrior, the victorious young Augustus (III.i.56-58). The distortion of the prince's character
by Gotharus in his conversation with Aquinus (III.i.340-362)
can only make us think more of Turgesius.

When we encounter the Prince in the third scene of the

third act no character has been better prepared for. He is
shocked that his father should think him disloyal and should
threaten his uncle (III.iii.3-9). He is obliquely compared
with Alexander the Great (III.iii.73-79); he is respectful
to his uncle even though Olaus is acting impudently by implying that the prince is being foolish (III.iii.82-84); and
he is without a doubt an extraordinarily dutiful son, a son
who would even give up his life if his father desired it
(III.iii.86-87). He modestly expresses little concern for
the importance of his "single life" (III.iii.85). McGrath,
using her linguistic analysis of character, concludes that
"Prince Turgesius . . . reveals his innate goodness when he
apparently walks to his death in an effort to speak openly
and sincerely with his scheming opponents."[182]

Later we see that he is not only a dutiful son, but as
a firm opponent to civil war, a dutiful subject, both of
which he expresses in his refusal, despite Olaus' urging, to
attack his father's city (IV.ii.3-15). The young man is
forever optimistic. At what should be one of his darkest
moments, after he has escaped a murderous plot to which he
has much reason to believe his father has been privy, the
young man expresses confidently that his father will repent
(V.ii.8-10). A magnanimous person, he even shows compassion for the body of Gotharus, his deadly enemy, by ordering the rebels who would tear it apart to leave the corpse

---

[182]McGrath, p. 334.

alone (V.ii.82).

Turgesius is indeed a very fine person and as a human being he would be very much admired. But a character who is always right, intelligent, responsible, dutiful, courageous, humble, magnanimous, correctly optimistic and just plain good is not in fact very human and, therefore, provides little interest. If it is true as someone once said that nothing is more boring on the stage than a virtuous woman, a completely virtuous man must run a close second.

The other son in the play, Haraldus, is similar to Turgesius in his quality of virtue, but much more inexperienced, and certainly less dynamic and forceful. Curiously, however, he has received a great deal of critical attention, perhaps as much as the protagonists of the play, Marpisa and Gotharus. The section of the play reprinted by Charles Lamb in his Specimens of English Dramatic Poets is the death scene of Haraldus. A. W. Ward comments on the manner by which Haraldus' death is caused ("undignified"[183]), and both E. A. Peers[184] and Lawrence Babb[185] discuss Marpisa's son as a victim of melancholy.

---

[183]Ward, III, 98n.

[184]Edgar A. Peers, Elizabethan Drama and Its Mad Folk (Cambridge, Mass.: W. Heffer and Sons, Ltd., 1914), p. 149n.

[185]Lawrence Babb, The Elizabethan Malady: A Study of Melancholia in English Literature from 1580 to 1642 (East Lansing: Michigan State College Press, 1951), p. 104.

The almost faceless son of the Romanian queen in the
Urania is but a shadow of Shirley's character and because
the creation of Haraldus apparently was demanded by the
playwright's plot, the character suffers from being more a
dramaturgical device than a person. Haraldus provides the
motivation for the ambition of Marpisa, and to a lesser degree, of Gotharus. Edward Huberman correctly notes that
Haraldus' death is the turning point in the play.[186] For it
is Haraldus' demise that provides the motivation for Marpisa's revenge and suicide, and it also enables us to see
the one unequivocally good quality in Marpisa, her love for
her son. Additionally, as a son faced with some unfortunate
revelations about his parents, he acts as a foil to Turgesius, who is similarly confronted with the sins of his father.

As a character, he can be readily described as a young,
inexperienced, properly modest person whose personal innocence and virtue are made abundantly clear. A bit too pure
and with an unattractive propensity toward the grave, he is
too somber to be really likeable. Once, however, he does
show some spunk, if but for a moment. Shocked by Gotharus'
talk of his becoming king with the attendant implication
that the king and Turgesius should be dispatched to make the
crown accessible, Haraldus does not wilt. Rather he assumes
the princely demeanor that Gotharus has been insisting

---

[186]Huberman, 'The Polititian,' p. 56.

c

should be his, interrupts the politician and brusquely lec-
tures the evil minister on the proper attitude (I.i.270-
277).

His natural sobriety does aid in explaining what some
readers have found difficult to accept: his death. The
cause of Haraldus' death would have been understood by Shirley's audience as melancholy brought on by excessive grief
and by drink, aided by the boy's natural disposition toward
melancholy. Robert Burton wrote, "For many times the drinking of wine alone causeth [melancholy], especially if it be
immoderately used . . . [especially] to such as are hot, or
of a sanguine, cholerick complexion, young, or inclined to
head melancholy."[187] Furthermore, Burton noted that melancholy could be caused by shame and disgrace (p. 99) and by
sorrow (p. 96), both of which Haraldus feels immediately
before getting drunk. Thus, it was quite understandable to
a seventeenth-century audience that an extremely sensitive
young man with a predisposition toward gravity, who believes
he is a bastard and his mother a whore, who is made excessively drunk the first time he drinks wine, should become
melancholy, contract a fever and die.

Haraldus, as a character, is not entirely without
interest, but in his creation of Haraldus, Shirley apparently was more concerned with plot than with character. In
fact with the exception of Aquinus, no character is so

---

[187]Burton, p. 70.

central to the plotting of The Politician as Haraldus.   That
he becomes such a weak character as a result is unfortunate.

Robert R. Reed, Jr., argues that in a "large majority
of Shirley's plays" one finds a stock character usually
found in realistic comedies: the "virtuous but sorely
tempted wife.[188]   And if McGrath is correct that Shirley
uses "emblematic names . . . [that] are indicative of the
essential qualities of [his] characters,"[189] then Albina is
certainly meant to be virtuous.   Albina has obvious association with the Latin, albus or white, a color traditionally
signifying purity.   Furthermore, the application of Mc-
Grath's linguistic criteria of character, identifies the
plain-speaking and undeceptive Albina as a "good" character,
and a cursory examination of her actions and statements confirms her to be a virtuous heroine indeed.

Though she is never "sorely tempted" she has several
opportunities to be tried.   The King of Norway wishes to be
her lover, and her husband cares not if he is; in fact, Gotharus appears to be attracted to the idea as another way to
gain royal favor.   But she is the loyal, loving wife and she
definitely and promptly rejects the king's propositions, re-
minding him of his dignity as king and his responsibilities
as a husband (I.i.67-187).

---

[188]Robert R. Reed, Jr., "James Shirley and the Sentimental Comedy, Anglia, 73 (1955), 159-161.

[189]McGrath, p. 334.

Why she is so loyal to and so much in love with such a horror as Gotharus, Shirley explains as fate or destiny (I.i.53-54 and I.i.73-78). A rather weak explanation, the dramatist includes it twice in the play indicating that he was aware of the incredible nature of this marriage and felt the need to provide some justification. As a woman of compassion, understanding, and forgiveness--necessary attributes for one married to Gotharus--she even wishes Marpisa saved from the rebellious mob (IV.iv.98-99).

Yet Albina has mettle. In fact, some of the most dramatic scenes of the play are the result of her pluck. She turns on Marpisa, telling the queen in perfectly clear terms what she thinks of her (III.i.200-230). Later, in the face of a wild mob, to give Gotharus and Marpisa time to escape she picks up the pistol that her husband has dropped and greets the rebels with a stern warning (IV.iv.74-76 and 87-89). One of the most effective displays of honest and direct expression is her monologue in V.ii.146 ff. She speaks to others who have not the courage to speak to her about her husband's death, and for that she chides them. With timidity, Aquinus finally provides the information, and Albina, unlike the simpering female that she could have been, vows revenge on her husband's murderer in a manner that is nothing if not determined.

The role of the virtuous heroine, the long-suffering weeping-willow whose roots are in the romances, is hardly effective in any play, and to the extent that Albina plays this role she is not a successful character. Still, the character of Albina differs from the stock character, for Shirley, recognizing the inherent weakness and boredom of the virtuous heroine, endowed Albina with a spirit, a mettle, to make her more interesting and more dramatically effective, if perhaps slightly inconsistent as a character.

It is natural to see a similarity between Sueno and Helga in The Politician and Rosenkrantz and Guildenstern in Hamlet; both pairs are tools of an intriguer. If comparisons are of any value, one must not forget Osric, the court fop in Shakespeare's play. For Sueno and Helga are more interesting, perhaps, as comic figures of the court than as hired villains. They are thorough-going flatterers and parasites, fools and fops, often toyed with and deceived by others. Their attempts at cleverness are disasters, always bettered by their betters and looking the fools for trying.

Generally, they do provide humor, but it is a humor that causes us to laugh at, never with them, and in no way does it interfere with the tone of the play. For the humor that derives from them is sardonic, macabre, or depraved, providing a dark humor to fit a dark play. This fundamental gravity is perhaps also underlined by a twist on their characters introduced by Shirley. His court toadies know what they are, and Helga's chastisement of Hormenus even provides another view of these sycophants. In reply to Hormenus' question, "Which of you can resolve what serpent spawn'd you?" Helga says:

> My good lord, it hurts not you;
> There is necessity of some knaves, and so
> Your lordship be exempted, why should you
> Trouble yourself and murmur at our courses?
> (II.i.70-74)

Aquinus, the one remaining character of importance dif-

fers fundamentally from his possible prototype in the Urania,

the loyal and devoted Lisandrinus, in that he has a consider-

ably larger role in the action. Aquinus' function as a

dramaturgical device is so important to his character that

he is discussed in the more appropriate section on form.

It has been tempting for critics to summarize Shirley's

characterization by emphasizing his dependence upon earlier

dramatists and his tendency to rely upon stock characters.

Richard Gerber, who believes The Politician to be a "Pseudo-

tragödie" because only the evil suffer and the good live

happily ever after, refers to Gotharus as the "Bösewicht"

or miscreant, to the king as the "Lüstling" or the debau-

chee, to Albina or Turgesius as a "Tugenheld" or rigid

moralist.[190] The characters of Shirley's play are in many

respects conventional figures, but he has given each greater

complexity than Gerber's classification would allow. Also

it is clear that Shirley often becomes preoccupied with

plotting and concerned less with character. Nonetheless,

the characters in The Politician are faceted, some, admit-

tedly, a good deal less than others.

---

[190]Gerber, pp. 39-44.

<u>Form</u>

In general, critics have tended to praise Shirley's
ability at plotting and dramatic construction rather than
his talent at characterization. For example, Ashley Thorndike says that in Shirley's plays "the real interest is in
the plot."[191] A. W. Ward emphasizes Shirley's inventiveness
and originality in plots and then says that the dramatist's
"general skillfulness in construction is on a par with his
facility of invention."[192] A discussion of Shirley's alteration and simplification of the plot found in his source,
Lady Mary Wroth's <u>The Countess of Montgomery's Urania</u>, which
bears on this topic, is found elsewhere.[193] Shirley's construction of this play, from an examination of the most
obvious techniques to the more subtle methods of dramaturgy,
is discussed here.

Forsythe, in his study of the relationship between
Shirley's plays and the dramas of other playwrights, notes
that the first scene of <u>The Politician</u> is very much like
that in Jonson's <u>Sejanus</u>. The exposition is presented the
same way in both plays by having two characters comment on
the other characters and give background to the action about
to begin.[194] Much information is provided by Cortes and

[191]Thorndike, p. 231.

[192]Ward, III, 121.

[193]See above, pp.

[194]Forsythe, p. 179.

Hormenus in the first sixty-five lines of the play (see I.i.
1-65). Aside from commenting on the major characters of the
play, some of whom come on the stage while the two courtiers
are speaking, they raise questions around which Shirley con-
structs his play. For example: How will the prince react
to the marriage of his father and Marpisa? Is Haraldus the
bastard of Gotharus? Is Albina faithful to Gotharus? What
is wrong with a country whose king is deceived by his coun-
selors and who busies himself with other men's wives? These
questions, which arouse interest, are raised clearly but
unobtrusively, and answers to them provide the action of the
play which unfolds in great part along contrasts, contrasts
which frequently lead to conflict, the core of drama.

Felix Schelling states of The Politician: "No other
play of Shirley's is constructed so frankly on the method
of contrasts,"[195] and characters are at the center of this
method. Both sons are fundamentally good young men, but the
manner in which they face up to problems separates them.
Haraldus, the younger of the two, when confronted with
unfortunate circumstances, simply folds. Turgesius, a more
courageous person, faces his problems head-on with optimism,
faith, and trust. Marpisa and Albina provide two starkly
different examples of a wife's responsibility in marriage.
Olaus seems to contrast with Gotharus; both are counsellors,
but one is devious; the other forthright. The honest

---

[195]Schelling, II, 319.

courtiers, Hormenus and Cortes, contrast with the syco-
phantic courtiers, Sueno and Helga. Much of the drama of
the play is derived from character contrast, whether it is
revealed in actual conflict as with Marpisa and Albina or
only inferred by the auditor as with Turgesius and Haraldus.

The dual organization of the play with its single plot
also relies on contrasts and comparisons in action. Perhaps
the most dramatic is the conflict between the court and the
army. With the exception of Albina, who is obviously out of
place, and Hormenus and Cortes who end up in the army camp,
the court is fundamentally corrupt, and the camp is honest
and virtuous. Whenever the two are brought together, tension arises, from the first confrontation of Olaus and the
king, to the climax and actual conflict in the fourth act,
to the denouement in the fifth act when the honesty of
Turgesius' side is victorious over the corruption of the
court.

There are moments in The Politician when Shirley succeeds in creating superb dramatic scenes through tension
caused by character conflict and lively dialogue. The
scene in which the king and Olaus confront one another
(III.i.1-94) is charged with excitement, first because of
the temperament of Olaus and second because of the conflict
between the duke and Marpisa. Dramatically the scene is
very satisfactory. Less explosive, but just as successful,
is Albina's exchange with various persons in the last act
before and after she is informed of her husband's death.

And an example of Shirley's utilizing character and situation
to create dramatic tension is found in the exchange between
Gotharus and Olaus outside the city gates (IV.ii.38-85). In
his statements to Turgesius, Gotharus constantly refers to
some unruly force that has misguided the prince. The politician is obviously alluding to Olaus, and he hopes to provoke the cantankerous duke into some rash act. The duke, not
insensitive to Gotharus' insinuations, does not act imprudently, and in fact, resists lashing out at the politician
directly. He merely tells him to "Leave rhetoric" and get to
the point. Throughout the scene, Olaus is hard-pressed to
control himself, and the reader is aware of his slipping
restraint and Gotharus' goading. The scene is masterfully
constructed, and its success derives from Shirley's deft
handling of conflict.

When Turgesius is "murdered" and Aquinus is "killed" by
Olaus, the scene and the play have reached their climax.
This climactic moment is the result of more than the oblique
Olaus-Gotharus exchange that precedes it. It is the result
of a long, intricate and subtle web of actions that Shirley
has skillfully wrought, actions that have at their center an
otherwise minor character, Aquinus.

Aquinus is a loyal and devoted captain of the prince's
army, quiet and self-effacing. But he becomes much more
than a mere trusty soldier when he is revealed as the one

who "counterplotted" against Gotharus. Aquinus is not mentioned by Hormenus and Cortes in the exposition scene of the
first act, and when he first enters (II.i.75 ff.). He
cozens Sueno and Helga. Thus, we know little about him
other than that he can fool two court fops, not an extra-
ordinary achievement. In his conversation with Gotharus
(II.i.181-195), he becomes suspect as a possible intriguer
primarily because of what Hormenus and Cortes say about him.
Aquinus says very little himself save "I am your lordship's
creature" to Gotharus, his first step, as it turns out, to
gain the confidence of the politician. To the reader, however, who is never allowed to know the mind of Aquinus, his
actions bespeak other things just as his dealings with Olaus
in Act III which result in Olaus' beating him also only become maneuverings in retrospect. Shirley does not let us in
on his plan from the outset. He carefully prepares what
some have called the deus ex machina at the end, but with
such preparation, the ending should not be considered a true
deus ex machina.

Shirley's thorough preparation includes the conversation in which Gotharus and Aquinus plot the murder of the
prince, Gotharus appearing to lead Aquinus. But Aquinus is
aware of Gotharus' game, and an examination of the dialogue
reveals that the captain actually leads the politician. The
statement by Aquinus "Let him be the prince--" (III.i.353)
is not just a lucky guess about the identity of the person
whom Gotharus wishes murdered.

Furthermore, Shirley does not simply spring a surprise
ending. Aquinus' letter that is sent to the prince via
Cortes tells Turgesius of the plot to kill him (III.iii.56-
57) and relates to the prince how the captain plans to
counterplot Gotharus. The counterplot is clearly implied by
Olaus' statement: "But now you know the plot, you wo'not
trust / Your life as he directs" (III.iii.61-62). Though the
plan is not revealed, it is clear that from this point Turgesius, Olaus and Aquinus are engaged in a plot of their
own. Olaus is not as trustful as Turgesius, but that skep-
ticism is in character and helps to maintain the suspense
that had been necessarily diminished by Aquinus' letter.
Thus, the entire exchange between Turgesius and Aquinus and
the "deaths" in IV.ii are an act, but as Olaus remains
skeptical ("I do not like things yet" IV.ii.116) it is not
surprising that others, who know less than he, should also
wonder about the outcome. Of course, after the feigned murders, the explanations are numerous. Olaus explains (IV.vi.
22-23) and Turgesius explains (V.ii.1-3 and 115-116).
Aquinus' comment that Turgesius should thank the duke for
"Breaking o'my pate" (V.ii.4) not only refers the reader to
that incident in III.i, but provides evidence that the captain was searching for something to gain the confidence of
Gotharus.

Though the plotting is intricate, there is no inconsistency regarding Aquinus' aid to Turgesius nor any dramaturgical dishonesty regarding the two counterfeit deaths.

Shirley takes great care to prepare for the surprise ending, providing the play with a surprising kind of realism: the auditor sees the action as he would see life--as a spectator or as a participant with partial knowledge, not as a member of an audience who enjoys omniscience.

The only contradiction or inconsistency in the play that cannot be readily explained has not previously been noted, but neither is it very important. Marpisa states that she gave Gotharus the poison when he was in a state of anxiety stemming from a fear of the rebels when, in fact, it was administered when he was grieving over the death of Haraldus. He did not become aware of the rebels until after he had taken the poison cordial (V.ii.240-241). Elizabethan dramas are certainly not devoid of contradictions and improbabilities. That The Politician contains but one is hardly reason to condemn the playwright's construction of the play.

Shirley's emphasis in the drama on external rather than internal conflicts and on plotting leaves the reader, and surely the auditor, little concerned with ideas or thought. This emphasis does not make for a bad play, but it does have a detrimental effect on the drama as tragedy. Writing about The Cardinal, another of Shirley's tragedies, Fredson Bowers says that we see only the resultant action of the characters' thoughts, not the thinking on stage. He comments that this makes for a "brisker play but a more shallow one."[196] His statement is equally applicable to The Politician.

---

[196]Bowers, pp. 229-230.

Poetry

With Shirley's image of Helga as a "kind of pendant /
To the king's ear" (I.i.64-65), the truckling flatterer
becomes a mere bauble, a piece of decoration, nothing of
substance, appropriately hanging on the king's ear. This
figure, imaginatively rich but isolated in its use, is typical
of a good deal of the poetic language in The Politician.
Shirley also occasionally incorporates classical and historical references in this same manner, heightening an incident
or detailing a character. Thus Marpisa is compared to
Niobe, Turgesius to Augustus, and Albina to a "poor deer"
pursued by a "fierce hound," the lustful king (I.i.125-130),
calling to mind those figures in the Tereus and Philomela
myth.

Shirley, however, also creates patterns of figurative
language to serve characterizations. Gotharus' identification with Satanic forces and Marpisa's with witchcraft,
previously described, inform us of Gotharus' complete
reprobacy and Marpisa's power and exceptional cleverness.
Gotharus' associations with the mechanical help to characterize him as cold-hearted and lacking in humanity.

Aside from helping to shape characters, Shirley's patterns of figurative language also serve to underscore
themes or recurring ideas. Typical of these are the varied
references to the sun, metaphorically the king or the throne.
When Gotharus urges Haraldus to be more ambitious and strive
for the crown, the politician says:

> Catch at the sun, divest him of his beams
> And in your eye wear his proud rays. Let day
> Be when you smile, and when your anger points,
> Shoot death in every frown. Covet a shade, . . .
>   and forfeit
> So brave an expectation?

(I.i.253-258)

The clouds and tempests associated with the bewitching Marpisa obscure the sun; indeed, the throne sits in darkness throughout most of the play. Gotharus creates a kind of anti-sun when he says: "Now to the king with whom / If the queen's beauty keep her magic, then / Our engines mount and day grows bright again" (II.i.331-333). Their light rises like the sun, but it is achieved by magic and by engines, unnatural plots, quite unlike the natural sun announced by the king at the end of the play: "A bright day shines upon us" (V.ii.307). With such references to sun and clouds, Shirley sets proper authority against the insidious threat of grasping ambition.

Figurative references to disease are associated by Shirley with the unnatural and the corrupt, especially at court. Gotharus speaks of his wife's "longing for disease" or more prosaically, visits from court physicians for illicit sexual activities. He falsely tries to convince Aquinus that Turgesius is a "disease" in the king (III.i.344-348), and he does convince the king that the prince is a "canker" (IV.i.6) and a "gangrene" (IV.i.30) and that the politician is the king's "honest chirurgeon" (IV.i.29). Haraldus comes to Gotharus to be "cured" and he is sent to Sueno and Helga. Haraldus ironically calls the two courtiers his "physicians"

(III.ii.59); and they, while drinking repeatedly to Haraldus' health, cause his death, thereby corrupting the innocent. Before the arrival of Turgesius, the court indeed is
a "hospital," a place of disease despite Olaus' hope to the
contrary (III.i.61).

Contributing to this idea of corruption and depravity
in the play's world is Shirley's use of animal imagery.
Though some of the good characters are now and again identified with animals (Albina with a deer and Turgesius with a
sacrificial animal), figurative language associated with
animals is almost entirely identified with evil characters.
Gotharus is a wolf (I.i.20 and IV.ii.92), a serpent
(III.iii.33-35), a cur and a dog (IV.v.32-33), a goat
(V.i.24) and a stallion (V.ii.232), all of which are used in
an opprobrious manner. Gotharus himself employs references
to animals in his speech, and by their distasteful use he
reveals more about himself than about those he is trying to
deprecate. He compares Albina with an animal in heat
(I.i.176-178), calls Aquinus his creature (IV.i.37), and refers to the soldiers who counsel Turgesius as insects.

Sueno and Helga are described as a drawing team or
beasts of burden (I.i.63), "wretched parasites" (II.i.66 and
III.i.149), serpents (II.i.70), rats (II.i.102), and squirrels (II.i.225). Marpisa is a lioness (III.i.220), a basilisk (V.i.14), a dragon (V.i.17), a cockatrice (V.ii.122), a
monkey (V.ii.136), and a hell-cat (V.ii.250). The rebels
are identified with the hunt and become hounds in pursuit by

their repetitious call "Follow, follow." They are called

mastiffs (IV.vi.13 and V.ii.50) and bloodhounds (IV.vi.28);

they "scent" things (V.ii.48) and "whet their teeth" (V.ii.

53). They are a "devouring multitude" (IV.vi.30) that will

"inhumanly" tear at limbs (IV.vi.32). They seek their

"prey" (V.i.14) and are identified as "cannibals" (V.ii.61).

There is a kind of imaginative ordering of this animal

imagery as used by Shirley. Except to their advantage, the

good characters are not identified with animals, and the

evil and wicked are opprobriously associated with animals

carefully chosen to reflect the characters' natures. The

beasts identified with Gotharus, for example, are vicious, of

low estate and of immoderate sexuality. Marpisa's bestial

associations stress her dignity, wickedness, sexuality and

special power. The rebels are savages, and the creatures

associated with them are appropriately blood-thirsty,

destructive wild beings.

Shirley's figurative language in The Politician is not

unusual, and its employment is rarely striking. At times

images are introduced in the most perfunctory manner and

allowed simply to decorate the piece. Yet Shirley seems

concerned with artistic integration, frequently employing

figurative language in support of action and character and,

on occasion, evoking an imaginative response in the reader

which momentarily lifts the character or incident above the

limits of the world of the play. Generally, however, his

use of poetic language, though fitting, comes off as

slightly artificial, even predictable. In the end, the
author of The Politician impresses a reader as more the
poetic craftsman than the imaginative poet.

Themes

The Politician is not a play which is invested with
profound ideas, but one must not conclude that the drama is
without substance at all. The ideas that Shirley incorporates in his plot are not unusual for the seventeenth century; nor can it be said that they are presented in such a
manner that refreshes them. But the craftsman in Shirley
presents them with a clarity and an effectiveness that one
would expect of a playwright who had previously constructed
over twenty plays for the Caroline theatre.

One of the subjects which Shirley treats in The Politician is ambition. The two lovers, Gotharus and Marpisa, are
differently motivated in their ambition (one works for himself, the other for her son), but both motivations are variations of an unacceptable climb to power. Gotharus' comment
"Who looks at crowns must have no thought who bleeds" (I.i.
335) succinctly summarizes the evil manifestation of that
climb. Other variations on this theme treat the subject of
ambition from another perspective. Turgesius, accused of
ambition by Gotharus (III.i.246-258) is perhaps the least
politically ambitious man ever known. Albina reveals her
lack of desire for personal glory and power by refusing the
king's advances both before and after she is married to

Gotharus. But the queen and especially the politician,
"prodigiously in love with greatness" in his tender years
(I.i.280-281), are the central figures in Shirley's handling
of ambition.

Another subject that recurs throughout the play is the
prevalence of corruption in the court. At the court
Gotharus and Marpisa rule and Sueno and Helga thrive, and
the chief member of the court, the king, is far from the
paragon of virtue that he should be. Albina, to be sure,
exists there also, but only with great difficulty. Haraldus
is finally destroyed both literally and figuratively by the
corruption surrounding him, and Hormenus and Cortes, though
they survive, know the world they live in and are on constant guard. At court, values are in need of transvaluation;
vice is virtue. One rises by pandering his wife (I.i.96-
100), and goodness is considered a defect. Gotharus says of
Haraldus and his good nature:

> I must new-form the boy
> Into more vice and daring. Strange, we must
> Study at court how to corrupt our children.
> (I.i.285-287)

Even the most virtuous, because they are in the court, become suspect as the exchange between Hormenus and Cortes
about Albina's honesty reveals (I.i.49-51).

As conventional as such a treatment of the court is,
that unflattering portrayal by the chief court dramatist,
especially in the late 1630's, is worth considering. Perhaps at this time Shirley's feelings about the court were

different from his usual favorable bias. Marvin Morillo, discussing Shirley's loss of court preferment, believes that the playwright "became less and less tolerant of the moral laxity, the triviality, and the sometimes humiliating injustice of court life" from 1629 to 1636.[197] He argues that this disenchantment is revealed in his Grateful Servant, The Humorous Courtier and especially The Ball. Perhaps the playwright, who went to Ireland in 1636, had not shaken his disenchantment by the time he wrote The Politician there in 1639.[198] Yet Shirley's handling of this matter of corruption is directly related to the people in the court. It is their misuse of power and their refusal of responsibility that distorts the court, a court which is salvageable given the right people. Accordingly, Turgesius returns and "A bright day shines upon" the court and nation. Shirley's treatment of corruption in the court is not to be separated from his treatment of ambition, which turns on the motives and natures of individuals, not places.

The matter of chaos and disorder, on the other hand, is a subject to which the Royalist Shirley can warm without any problem. The rebels most clearly and directly convey the idea of disorder, and despite the mob's support of the prince and dislike of Gotharus, the dramatist makes clear

[197]Marvin Morillo, "Shirley's 'Preferment' and the Court of Charles I," SEL, 1 (1961), 109.

[198]The famous statement about the loss of preferment at court is found in the 1639 publication of The Maid's Revenge

that rebellion contains a threat to peace and stability equal to whatever horrors Gotharus and Marpisa represent.

Through the savage and gross animal imagery he chooses to associate with the rebels, and with their timely introduction in IV.iv at the climactic point of the play when the center no longer holds, Shirley condemns the rebels no matter with whom their sympathies lie. Everyone is properly afraid of them and what they represent: chaos. Indiscriminately, they would eat Gotharus' heart and knock down Albina who scolds them for it (IV.iv.84-85). Olaus considers them rabble (IV.vi.10) as does Turgesius (V.ii.18). They are uncontrollable and must be allowed to go where they wish (IV.vi.40-41). They would violate the church as well as the orders of their king ("We'll pull the church down / But we'll have our will," IV.vi.69-70). Cortes' belief that Gotharus would fare better were he buried alive than discovered by the mob (V.ii.26-27), and Aquinus' belief that the politician would choose to cut his own throat rather than be placed in the hands of the mob (V.ii.39-40) carry hints of sympathy for the villain whose dreadfulness takes on a relative quality after the spectre of the mob rushes on stage. Though this distaste for mobs and rebels is found in the playwright's source,[199] there is no reason to believe that Shirley's presentation of social disruption was dependent upon Lady Mary Wroth's views. He was no democrat, and

----

[199]See pp.xxxvii & xlii

cxx

his political bias is rather specifically directed in this
play in which he identifies his rebels with a particular
class: the craftsman. They are shoemakers, tailors, and
shopkeepers (V.ii.62-80) in keeping with what Charles W.
Camp in The Artisan in Elizabethan Literature says was a
changing attitude toward craftsmen reflected in sixteenth
and seventeenth-century literature. The idealistic treatment of Deloney and Dekker in the later sixteenth century
shifted to a satiric and harsh treatment by Fletcher,
Middleton, and Shirley.[200] That Shirley in 1639 should
associate craftsmen, perhaps Puritans, with a threat to
order and stability is understandable.

    But one could argue that disorder, whether brought on
by a wild mob, corrupt courtiers, or ambition-driven men
and women, is only a manifestation of larger problems such
as the loss of reason to passion or the ancient and timeless
struggle of good with evil. To identify such philosophical
ideas in a serious way with Shirley's play, however, is
probably to engage in an unprofitable attempt to find more
in The Politician than it readily offers. Even the most
theatrical plays require substance on which to build a plot,
and Shirley's subjects--ambition, corruption, chaos and disorder, and perhaps even the more general loss of reason--
provide that substance, not for serious examination and
thought but for a basis on which to construct a play.

---

[200]Charles W. Camp, The Artisan in Elizabethan Literature (New York: Columbia University Press, 1924), p. 12.

though Shirley is a moralist in The Politician, politically
and ethically, little in it compels one to believe that his
concern is with moral issues, and even less is in it to im-
press one with Shirley's interest in the nature of man, good
and evil, beyond that knowledge required of a playwright to
put together a piece of good theatre.

The Play as Tragedy

On the title page of the 1655 edition, The Politician
is called a tragedy, though for the last two hundred years
critics have questioned the appropriateness of that classification. Clearly, the drama was properly categorized for
the seventeenth century when a play was not thought to have
failed as a tragedy merely because the evil characters die
and the good live. Fredson Bowers succinctly summarizes an
earlier, the Elizabethan, view of tragedy: "[T]ragedy portrayed violent action--deeds of lust, villainy, and murder--
but these deeds were always punished at the close. The firm
object of Elizabethan tragedy, therefore, was the enacting
not only of poetic but, more important, of divine justice."[201] No one can argue that The Politician does not
meet these requirements perfectly.

But Shirley was not an Elizabethan, and though he
treats subjects that Shakespeare and Marlowe wrote about,
touching on matters that provide the seeds of tragedy, he
treats these matters differently. Alfred Harbage is right

---

[201]Bowers, p. 263.

when he says that Shirley did not give into the "cavalier mode" entirely, that he did not use "gilded manikins for characters, sensibilities for emotions, heroic posturing for dramatic action."[201] Perhaps that is why he is considered the last of the "Elizabethan" dramatists. But he did write for an age and a society that Samuel Schoenbaum, so aptly described as "not particularly stirred by tragedy. It wished to be amused rather than moved; . . . above all, it craved novelty."[203] To achieve this amusement, one could say that Shirley imitated the successful theatricality of the drama of Beaumont and Fletcher with its emotional structure, and in his plays anticipated the complicated but skillfully wrought plotting emphasized in Restoration drama. The effect of this emphasis on plotting, which existed as early as the first decade of the seventeenth century, resulted, as Cyrus Hoy says, in a "breakdown of conventional distinctions between comic and tragic modes."[204] Of the "notoriously bizarre" tragedy that developed between the times of Shakespeare and Shirley, Hoy suggests that a

> principal explanation for some . . . of its odder effects lies in its expropriation of a number of devices traditionally associated with comedy . . . [including] plots and character types . . . . In

---

[202]Alfred Harbage, _Cavalier Drama_ (London: Oxford University Press, 1936), p. 164.

[203]Samuel Schoenbaum, _Middleton's Tragedies: A Critical Study_ (New York: Columbia University Press, 1955), p. 55.

[204]Cyrus Hoy, "Renaissance and Restoration Dramatic Plotting," _Renaissance Drama_, 9 (1966), 249.

the degree of complexity which the typical Jacobean
tragic plot entails, with its layers of disguises
and its deceptive ruses and its air of unabashed
contrivance, there is nothing to distinguish it
from the typical Jacobean comic plot; the premium
placed on intrigue is on par in both. And such
plots are regularly engineered by an ingenious
manipulator who as often as not reminds us of nothing so much as the wily servant of Roman comedy
schooled in the precepts of the English Machiavelli
. . . . [T]he exclusive preoccupation of this
tragedy with sexual passion--its frustration and
satisfaction--reminds us of all the hilarious and
bawdy mileage which comedy has always gotten out of
just this subject . . . . [S]exual passion is
never viewed as sublime; on the contrary, it is
always conceived of as degrading, and the surrender
to it is the infallible measure of man's creaturalness . . . . [Man's] enslavement to creatural in-
stinct makes a travesty of all the higher stirrings
of the spirit."205

have quoted this passage at length because Hoy's observa-

ions about Jacobean tragedy seem, with some minor qualifi-

ations, to account so well for what must be agreed is The

olitician's failure as tragedy. Present in Shirley's play

s the same dramaturgical emphasis on plotting, on intri-

ate dramatic devices. The presentation of the human

orld as fundamentally ignoble despite obviously good, over-

y good, characters--a presentation that itself seems to be

ore for theatrical rather than for any weightier purpose--

lso harks back to the drama of Middleton and Ford which Hoy

escribes. The "ingenious manipulator" of the play's title

ust share his role with Aquinus and with Marpisa, but the

ocus remains on manipulation and on ingenuity. And if

an's sexuality must make room for his ambition in The

205Cyrus Hoy, The Hyacinth Room (New York: Alfred A.
nopf, 1964), pp. 220-221.

Politician, the treatment of the latter does no more for the "higher stirrings of the spirit" than the presentation of the former. There is an appropriateness, then, to the sole potentially tragic figure in this play, Marpisa, being denied her titular place just as she was denied her truly tragic role. Shirley's focus and emphasis were never really on her, never on what Bradley calls "human actions producing exceptional calamity," but elsewhere, on plotting and on what Hoy calls "man's creaturalness."

The Politician, despite this judgment, can be described as an arresting play, not because it is profound, but because it is good drama. It captures attention because of its tense conflicts, because of its intricacies, and perhaps because of man's interest in his own creaturalness. Our attention to the play is primarily held, then, for the same reasons we remain riveted to a well-constructed mystery story that treats the slightly bizarre: to discover how all will work out and to experience the attendant excitement and the occasional thrill. Shirley's achievement, then, should properly be measured in how well the play attains these limited ends with which good drama is by no means incompatible. Great drama, admittedly, is something else. But Shirley need not be faulted for not attempting to carry in his play the more profound weight that English dramatists had some years before ceased to take up.

THE
POLITITIAN,
A
TRAGEDY,

Prefented at *Salisbury* Court
BY HER
MAJESTIES SERVANTS;

WRITTEN
By JAMES SHIRLEY.

LONDON,

Printed for *H umphrey* *Moseley* and are to be
fold at his Shop at the *Princes Armes* in St.
Pauls Church-yard. 1655.

THE

POLITICIAN

A

TRAGEDY

Presented at Salisbury Court   5

BY HER

MAJESTY'S SERVANTS

WRITTEN

By JAMES SHIRLEY

LONDON   10

Printed for Humphrey Moseley and are to be
sold at his shop at the Prince's Arms in St.
Paul's Churchyard. 1655.

---

5. Salisbury Court] a private or enclosed theatre
built in 1629 and destroyed in the great fire of 1666.

6-7. HER MAJESTY'S SERVANTS] the Queen's Men who performed under the patronage of Queen Henrietta Maria.

11. Humphrey Moseley] A London bookseller from about
1630 until his death in 1661. For more about this seventeenth-century publisher of English letters, see pp.
lxvii-lxi.

1

To the very much honored

WALTER MOYLE, Esq.

Sir,

Though the severity of the times took away those dramatic recreations (whose language so much glorified the   5
English scene), and perhaps looking at some abuses of the
common theaters, which were not so happily purg'd from
scurrility and under-wit (the only entertainment of vulgar
capacities), they have outed the more noble and ingenious
actions of the eminent stages. The rage yet hath not been   10
epidemical; there are left many lovers of this exiled
posie who are great masters of reason and that dare con-
scientiously own this musical part of humane learning

---

2. WALTER MOYLE] See Appendix II.

4. severity of the times] doubtless a reference to the
restrictions during the Cromwellian period that detrimentally
affected dramatic literature, particularly the official
closing of the theaters in 1642.

7. common theaters] public theaters.

8. under-wit] "a poor or inferior kind of wit" (OED).

8. vulgar] common, ordinary; though coarse or obscene
might be implied.

9. outed] "driven out" (OED).

12. posie] poetical form of literature, in this case,
verse drama.

when it is presented without the stains of impudence and   15

profanation.

Among these persons, sir, you deserve an honorable

inscription. For my own part, this is the last which is

like to salute the public view in this kind, and I have

only to say that I congratulate my own happiness to con-   20

clude with so judicious a patron.

To make a doubt of your fair receiving this piece

were to dishonor your character and make myself undeserv-

ing. Read at your leisure what is humbly presented to

15-16. stains of impudence and profanation] Though Shirley seems here to have in mind "scurrility and under-wit,"
he could hardly have forgotten his own first-hand experience
with what others considered "impudence" on the seventeenth-
century stage. Sir Henry Herbert, Master of Revels, wrote
in his office-book on 18 November 1632:

> In the play of The Ball, written by Sherley, and acted
> by the Queens, ther were divers personated so natur-
> ally, both of lords and others of the court, that I
> took it ill, and would have forbidden the play, but
> that Biston promiste many things which I found faulte
> withall should be left out, and that he would not suf-
> fer it to be done by the poett any more, who deserves
> to be punisht; and the first that offends in this
> kind, of poets or players, shall be sure of publique
> punishment. (Adams, p. 19)

18-19. this . . . kind] In 1658 Shirley's Honoria and
Mammon and The Contention of Ajax and Ulysses were first
printed and Huberman believes, therefore, that "this kind"
must refer to tragedy. He is probably right, but as
Honoria and Mammon is almost certainly a closet-drama, and
The Contention of Ajax and Ulysses is at best, an inter-
lude, "this kind" could refer to those of his old plays
performed prior to the closing of the theatres.

your eye and judgment while I preserve my confidence in   25

your virtue and good thoughts upon

    Sir,

      The most humble honorer of your worth

        JAMES SHIRLEY

The Names and Small Characters of the Persons

KING of Norway: easy and credulous in his nature and pas-

sionately doting upon Queen Marpisa.

GOTHARUS, the politician: active to serve his pleasures

and ambition, a great favorite of the Queen.   5

---

1. Small Characters] Characters are brief descriptions
of types and individuals. Larger characters of a paragraph
or more had become very popular in the seventeenth century,
especially those of Nicholas Breton, Thomas Overbury, John
Earle, and Thomas Fuller.

2. easy] easily deceived.

2-3. passionately doting] This exact phrase, describing
the King of Romania, appears in the Antissius-tale in Lady
Mary Wroth's Urania.

4. Gotharus] a name surely to be identified by seventeenth-century Englishmen with the Goths, a group generally
considered by Shirley's contemporaries as northern, probably
bellicose and barbaric, and certainly unenlightened and
uneducated. Shirley, himself, uses the word Goth in this
last pejorative manner in The Lady of Pleasure, The Humorous
Courtier, and Honoria and Mammon. E. H. Sugden, A Topographical Dictionary to the Works of Shakespeare and His
Fellow Dramatists (Manchester: University of Manchester
Press, 1925), pp. 228-229.

4. politician] "a politic person, chiefly in the
sinister sense, a shrewd schemer; a crafty plotter or intriguer" (OED). See also the discussion of the sixteenth-
seventeenth century English attitude toward the word policy
and its derivatives on p. lxxix.

6

TURGESIUS, the prince: of a gallant disposition and honored

by the soldier.

---

6. Turgesius] Turgesius has associations both with
Norway and with Ireland where The Politician probably was
written and first performed. William Warner wrote:

Five Kings at once did rule that Ile [Ireland], in
civil strife that droopes,
When fierce Turgesius landed with his misbeleeving
Troopes.
This proud Norwegan Rover so by aides and armes did
thrive,
As he became sole Monarke of the Irish Kingdomes
five, . . .
And thirtie yeeres, tyrannizing did keepe that ile
in awe.

William Warner, Albion's England (London: R. Moore, 1612),
Book 5, Chapter 26, pp. 126-127. In Advertisements For
Ireland, a manuscript in the Library of Trinity College,
Dublin, and printed anonymously about 1623, there is found:

And first of all Egfride King of Northumberland in
anno 64, Norwegians a little after for 30 years together made it their prey under the leading of their
Captain Turgesse.

George O'Brien (ed.), Advertisements for Ireland (Dublin:
The Royal Society of Antiquaries of Ireland, 1923), p. 2.
This same story of the conquest and rule of Ireland by the
Norwegian, Turgesius, is found in Holinshed's Chronicles.
Raphaell Holinshed, The Chronicles of England, Scotland,
and Ireland (London: Lucas Harrison and George Bishop,
1577), I, Part 3, 14-15.

7. soldier] The OED does not list this form as a
plural. The modern equivalent probably would be "the military."

DUKE OLAUS, the king's uncle: old, choleric and distast'd
with the court proceedings, disaffected to Gotharus
and the queen, but resolute and faithful to the   10
prince.

HARALDUS, son to Marpisa: young, of a sweet and noble
disposition, whom Gotharus would form more bold and
ambitious for the greatness he had design'd.

REGINALDUS   15
                    Captains
AQUINUS

HORMENUS
                    two honest courtiers
CORTES   20

SUENO
                    a couple of court-parasites
HELGA

17. AQUINUS] Gifford; Aquinas Q.

---

8. Olaus] the Latin form of Anlaff or Olaf, one of the
noblest Scandinavian names.

8. distast'd] disgusted, offended.

10. resolute] constant, loyal. Another meaning of
resolute, "decided with regard to matters or opinion" (OED),
is also appropriate to the inflexible duke.

17. Aquinus] the Latinized form of the Scandinavian
name, Hakon (Seaton, p. 323).

21. Sueno] Holinshed refers to a Sueno, King of Norway
who invaded Scotland and was defeated by Macbeth (I, Part 2,
241-242), an event also related in Shakespeare's Macbeth
(I.ii).

MARPISA, the queen: a proud, subtle, and revengeful lady,

    from the widow of Count Altomarus advanc'd to royal   25

    condition by the practise of her creature and confi-

    dant, Gotharus.

ALBINA, wife to Gotharus: a virtuous but suffering lady,

    under the tyranny of an imperious and disloyal

    husband.   30

---

    24. Marpisa] There seems to be no definite source for
the queen's name. A Marpessa who chose the mortal Idas over
Apollo when given this opportunity by Zeus, appears in the
writings of Apollodorus. Apollodorus, The Library, Sir
James G. Frazer (trans.), (London: William Heinemann, 1921).
I, Book I, 63. Pausanias also refers to this mythical tale.
Pausanias, Description of Greece, W. H. S. Jones (trans.),
(London: William Heinemann, 1926), II, Book V. Elsewhere
Pausanias writes of another Marpessa, a warrior "surnamed
Choera [who] surpassed, they say, the other women in dar-
ing." Pausanias, IV, Book VIII, 139. Ethel Seaton says
that "Marpisa is classical" and identifies her as an amazon.
She notes that Belleforest in Histoires Tragiques writes
that amazon women were believed to have existed in the
Scandinavian countries   (Seaton, p. 323). Shirley's con-
temporary, Thomas Heywood, writes:

> There were of them Amazons two queens . . . Marthesia
> and Lampedo; . . . and being grown potent both in
> power and riches they went to warre by turnes, . . .
> they proclaimed themselves to be derived from Mars.
> [But] Marthesia (or as some write, Marpesia) [was]
> defeated and slaine [in Asia].

Thomas Heywood, Γunaikeion . . . History Concerninge Women
(London: Adam Islip, 1624), p. 221. Finally, Robert Forsythe suggests that Shirley may have derived the queen's
name from Marpesia in Sidney's Arcadia, Book III (Forsythe,
p. 177).

    28. Albina] doubtless the name was chosen to suggest
purity and virtue (Latin albus, white).

Soldiers, Rebels, [Physicians, Petitioners, Servants,]

    and Attendants.

              Scene, Norway

31.   Physicians, Petitioners, Servants] <u>Gifford</u>.

---

    33. <u>Scene</u>, <u>Norway</u>] There is little, if anything, in the play to suggest the atmosphere and locale of Norway except the names which tend to have a Scandinavian flavor.

THE POLITICIAN

[I.i]

<u>Enter</u> Cortes <u>and</u> Hormenus.

CORTES.

It was a strange and sudden marriage.

HORMENUS.

Could he not love her for the game and so forth,

But he must thus exalt her? No less title

Than Queen to satisfy her ambition?

CORTES.

'Tis a brave rise!

HORMENUS.   I did not prophesy   5

When the honest count, her husband, Altomarus

Liv'd, she would bring us on our knees.

---

2. <u>the game</u>] "promiscuous sexuality, or addiction to sexual intercourse." Eric Partridge, <u>Shakespeare's Bawdy</u>: <u>A</u> <u>Literary</u> <u>and</u> <u>Psychological</u> <u>Essay</u> (London: Routledge & Kegan Paul, 1955), p. 119.

5. <u>brave</u>] excellent, admirable, probably spoken with sarcasm.

5-7. <u>I</u> . . . <u>knees</u>] Hormenus did not anticipate that Marpisa would attain a rank requiring the courtiers to kneel before her.

CORTES.   I hope

She'll love the king for't.

HORMENUS.   And in his absence,

Gotharus, the king's minion, her old friend.

He has done this royal service beside what   10

Rests on accounts in her old husband's days.

I do suspect her son, Haraldus, was

Got with more heat and blood than Altomarus'

Age could assure her; but he's dead.

CORTES.   God be

    with him.

Although I wo'not make oath for her chastity,   15

That boy's good nature is an argument

To me, Gotharus had no share in him.

He's honest, of a gentle disposition,

And, on my conscience, does pray sometimes.

              Enter Gotharus reading a letter

11.   accounts] accompts Q.

14.   God be] Gifford; --Be Q.

---

10.   service] "sexual attention" (Partridge, p. 185).

13.   heat and blood] amorous passion (Partridge,
p. 126 and pp. 75-76).

14.   God] This word is represented by dashes (--) in
the seventeenth-century texts.

HORMENUS [to Cortes].

    No more. We have a wolf by th'ear. What news   20

    From hell? He cannot want intelligence, he has

    So many friends there. He's displeas'd. There is

    Some goodness in that letter, I will pawn

    My head, that makes him angry.

          Enter some with petitions. Gotharus frowns

              upon them, they return hastily.

                        How his frown

    Hath scatter'd 'em like leaves. They fly from him   25

    As nimbly as their bodies had no more weight

    Than their petitions. I would give an eye-tooth

    To read but three lines.

GOTHARUS [aside].   Curse upon his victory!

    I meant him not this safety when I wrought

    The king to send him forth to war, but hop'd   30

    His active spirit would have met some engine

---

    20. We have a wolf by th'ear] a perilous situation, for it is dangerous to continue to hold a wolf by the ears and equally as dangerous to release him. Proverbial. See Morris Palmer Tilley, A Dictionary of the Proverbs in England in the Sixteenth and Seventeenth Centuries (Ann Arbor: University of Michigan Press, 1950), p. 739 (W603).

    21. want intelligence] lack information.

    23-24. I will pawn my head] A modern equivalent might be the hyperbolic, "I'll bet my life." Pawn here means "to stake, wager; to risk" (OED). Huberman suggests that it is a mild oath (p. 210).

    29. wrought] manipulated.

    31. engine] instrument or device, especially an instrument of war. Huberman notes that there is a double-entendre here: "(1) plot; (2) machine use in warfare" (p. 211).

To have translated him to another world.

He's now upon return.   *Exit*.

HORMENUS.   Would I had but

The harrowing of your skull. My genius gives me

That paper is some good news of the prince;   35

I would I knew it but concern'd him.

CORTES.   'Twas

My wonder the king would send his son abroad

To wars, the only pledge of his succession.

HORMENUS.

He had a counselor, this politician,

That would prefer the prince to heaven, a place   40

His lordship has no hope to be acquainted with.

The prince and his great uncle, Duke Olaus,

Would not allow these pranks of state, nor see

The king betrayed to a concubine.

---

32.   translated] transported.

33-34.   Would . . . skull] The statement is made in reference to Gotharus and made, as it were, to the politician,
but after he has left the stage. Hormenus wished he knew
what was in Gotharus' mind, especially in regard to the
letter.

34.   genius] intuition.

38.   pledge] security, referring to Turgesius as the
king's only heir.

39.   politician] See the note to Gotharus' character on
p. 5.

43.   pranks] not mischievous acts in the humorous sense;
rather, pernicious deeds.

Therefore, it was thought fit they should be engag'd 45

To foreign dangers.

Enter Albina <u>and</u> <u>her</u> <u>waiting</u> <u>woman</u>.

'Tis Madam Albina,

Our great man's wife.

CORTES.   The king did seem to affect her

Before he married her to his favorite.

HORMENUS.

Dost think she's honest?

CORTES.   I'll not stake my soul on't

But I believe she is too good for him   50

Although the king and she have private conference.

HORMENUS.

She looks as she were discontent.

Ex[eunt] Albina [<u>and</u> <u>her</u> <u>waiting</u> <u>woman</u>].

CORTES.   She has cause.

In being Gotharus' wife. Some say she lov'd him

Most passionately.

HORMENUS.   'Twas her destiny.

She has him now, and if she love him still,   55

---

47. <u>affect</u>] fancy.

49. <u>honest</u>] respectable, in general, and sexually virtuous, <u>in</u> particular.

51. <u>private conference</u>] meeting, probably implying a lovers' rendezvous or assignation.

54. <u>'Twas her destiny</u>] Perhaps the playwright's justification for having such a virtuous woman love a villain of long-standing.

'Tis not impossible she may be a martyr;

His proud and rugged nature will advance

Her patience to't.

                              Enter Helga and Sueno.

HELGA.   Avoid the gallery.

SUENO.

The king is coming.--Oh, my lord, your pardon.

HORMENUS.

Nay, we must all obey.

CORTES.   I ne'er lik'd   60

This fellow.

HORMENUS.   He is one of fortune's minions,

The love of the choice ladies of the laundry.

That's one that draws in the same team but more

Inclin'd to'th knave; he is a kind of pendant

To the king's ear, an everlasting parasite.   65

60. ne'er] never Gifford; near Q.

---

58. Avoid] quit, leave.

58. gallery] a room, not a passageway, both of which
were called "galleries."

61. fortune's minions] one relies on fortune for his
well-being. Moreover, a favorite of Fortune was proverbially
considered a fool. See Tilley, pp. 236-237 (F600).

62. choice of ladies of the laundry] "In the seventeenth century regarded as women of easy virtue" (Huberman).

63. That's . . . team] Helga. He and Sueno are a pair.

64-65. he . . . ear] a good image. He is a mere bauble, a
piece of decoration, nothing of substance and by implication,
a "hanger-on" to the king. Also it is an apt metaphor, for
a flatterer would be at the king's ear.

The king! Albina return'd with him.

               Ex[eunt Cortes and Hormenus].

           Enter King and Albina.

KING.   Leave us.

           [Exeunt Sueno and Helga.]

Y'are most unkind to yourself in my opinion;

You know well who I am and what I have

Advanc'd you to. Neither in virgin state

Nor marriage to allow your king a favor?   70

ALBINA.

Sir, let the humble duty of a subject

Who shall with zealous prayers solicit heaven

For you and your fair queen--

KING.   Had you been wise,

That might have been your title; but the god

Of love had with his arrow so engraven   75

Gotharus in your heart, you had no language

But what concern'd his praise, scarce any thought

At liberty. I did imagine, when

66.   S.D. Exeunt Cortes and Hormenus.] Gifford; Exit. Q.

66.1.   S.D. Exeunt Sueno and Helga.] Gifford

---

70.   favor] double-entendre: female sexual parts as
well as an indulgence or privilege. See Partridge, pp. 66
and 111.

78.   liberty] sexual promiscuity as well as freedom.
See Partridge, p. 142.

I had compassion of your sufferings

And gave thee a fair bride to my Gotharus,   80

You would not lose the memory of my benefit,

But--now in state and nature to reward it--

Consent to return me love.

ALBINA.   Be pleas'd

To excuse the boldness of one question.

KING.

Be free, Albina.

ALBINA.   Do not you love my husband?   85

KING.

There wants no testimony. Beside the rest,

My giving thee to him, dear to my thoughts,

Is argument I love him.

ALBINA.   Would you take

Me back again? You but betrayed his faith

And you own gift to tempt me to forsake him.   90

KING.

You are more apprehensive. If you please,

88.   Consent] Consented Q.

78-83. I . . . love] The sense is: Having arranged your
marriage to Gotharus out of sympathy for you, I had hoped
that you would not have forgotten my kindness and, especially
now that your marriage protects you, would return my favor
by loving me.

88.   argument] evidence, proof.

91.   You are more apprehensive] You have unnecessary
fears.

He shall possess you still. I but desire

Sometimes a near and loving conversation.

Though he should know't, considering how much

I may deserve, he would be wise enough   95

To love thee ne'er the worse. He's not the first

Lord that hath purchas'd offices by the free

Surrender of his wife to the king's use;

'Tis frequent in all commonwealths to lend

Their play-fellows to a friend.

ALBINA.   Oh, do not think   100

Gotharus can be worth your love to be

So most degenerate and lost to honor.

You have a queen to whom your vow is sacred;

Be just to her. The blessing is yet warm

Pronounc'd by holy priest; stain not a passion   105

To wander from that beauty, richer far

Than mine. Let your souls meet and kiss each other

That while you live the examples of chaste love,

Most glorious in a king and queen, we may

Grow up in virtue by the spring of yours,   110

93. near] Gifford; neere Q.

96. ne'er] Gifford; near Q.

---

92. possess] double-entendre, "To have . . . a woman, by way of sexual intercourse" (Partridge, p. 169).

93. conversation] double-entendre, "sexual intimacy" (Partridge, p. 93).

100. play-fellows] "sharer[s] in sexual pleasures" (Partridge, p. 167).

    Till our top-boughs reach heaven.

KING.   You are resolved

        then;

    We must be strangers. Should my life depend

    On the possession of your bosom, I

    Should languish and expire, I see.

ALBINA.   Good Heaven

    Will not permit the king want so much goodness   115

    To think the enjoying of forbidden pleasure

    Could benefit his life. Rather let mine

    Ebb at some wound and wander with my blood

    By your command ta'en from me. On my knees--

            [Kneels.]

KING.

    Rise. [Albina rises.] I may kiss Albina--

                            Enter Gotharus [,unseen].

GOTHARUS.   Ha!

KING.

    'T has shot   120

    Another flame into me. Come you must--

_____

119. S.D. Kneels.] Gifford.

----

    115. want] lack.

    121. flame] associated with lust (Partridge, pp. 113-
114).

ALBINA.

What?

KING.   Be a woman; do't or I'll complain.

ALBINA.

To whom?

KING.   Thy husband.

[ALBINA].   Horror!

KING.   Think upon't. Exit.

ALBINA.

What will become of miserable Albina?

Like a poor deer pursu'd to a steep precipice   125

That overlooks the sea by some fierce hound,

The lust of a wild king doth threaten here.

Before me, the neglects of him I love,

Gotharus, my unkind lord, like the waves

And full as deaf affright me.

GOTHARUS [cóming forward].   How now madam?   130

---

123. S.P. Albina Horror!] Go. Horror! Q. It is possible
that Gotharus would make this statement but only with the
utmost sarcasm, certainly without any serious fear or of-
fense. It is much more likely that Albina would be both
shocked and frightened by the King's threat.

130. S.D. coming forward] Gifford.

---

122. Be a woman] serve your sexual function.

125-130. Like . . . me] Appropriate similarities exist between this metaphorical description and the lustful pursuit
of Philomela by Tereus in Ovid's Metamorphoses.

130. And full as deaf] so loud as to be deafening.

Come can you kiss?

ALBINA.   Kiss, sir?

GOTHARUS.   What difference

Between his touch and mine now? His perhaps

Was with more heat, but mine was soft enough.

What has he promis'd thee? But that's no matter;

Thou wo't be wise enough to make thy bargain   135

I father all; only the king shall give it

A name, He'll make it master of a province.

ALBINA.

What means my lord?

GOTHARUS.   Thou thinkst I am jealous now.

Not I. I knew before he doted on thee,

And it is to be presum'd having a veil   140

To hide thy blushes, I do mean our marriage,

Thou mayst find out some time to meet and mingle

---

133. heat] lust (Partridge, p. 126).

135. Thou . . . bargain] You would be shrewd enough to strike a good bargain.

136-137. I . . . province] To the confusion of Albina, Gotharus here refers to both Haraldus and any child that Albina bears. Gotharus publicly will be thought the father, but the king, knowing or believing it his, will give it a "name" or title. Compare Gotharus' statement with the king's, 11. 82-83 above.

139. before he] before our marriage that he.

Stories and limbs; it may be necessary.

And 'cause I will be dutiful to the king,

We will converse no more abed. I'll be   145

Thy husband still, Albina, and wear my buds

Under my hair close like a prudent statesman;

But 'twere not much amiss, as I advis'd

Before, and these new premises consider'd

You appear abroad with a less train. Your

    wardrobe   150

Will make you more suspected if it be

Too rich. And some whole days to keep your

    chamber.

140-143. <u>And</u> . . . <u>necessary</u>] Gotharus' ideas about the
use of marriage as a cloak to cover up affairs, and the use
of one's wife to rise in the court, are the same as the
king's. See 11. 82-83, 96-100, and 136-137.

142-143. <u>mingle</u> . . . <u>limbs</u>] (1) to concoct and make up
stories, but to unite and mix limbs in sexual intercourse;
(2) to be sexually aroused by certain books; cf. 11. 164-
169.

145. <u>We</u> <u>will</u> <u>converse</u> <u>no</u> <u>more</u> <u>abed</u>] We will no longer
have sexual intercourse. See Partridge, p. 93. Cf. the
king's comment, 11. 92-93.

146-147. <u>wear</u> . . . <u>statesman</u>] Like a good courtier,
Gotharus will refrain from making a public outcry against
the king and Albina; he will hide his cuckold's horns.

148-153. <u>But</u> . . . <u>certain</u>] In a very business-like way,
Gotharus proceeds to give Albina advice as how best to carry
off the assignations of the king. The instructions are
given in a matter-of-fact style, but doubtless there is
irony and anger in the long speech. In fact, the politician works himself into an angry, obscene frenzy in 11.
155-178.

149. <u>premises</u>] facts, information.

Will make the king know where to find you certain.

ALBINA.

Will you have patience, my lord, to hear me?

GOTHARUS.

The world doth partly think thee honest too;   155

That will help much, if you observe good rules

And diet, without tedious progresses

And visiting of ladies expert in

Night revels, masks, and twenty other torments

To an estate. Your doctors must be left too;   160

I wo'not pay a fee to have your pulse

Felt and your hand roll'd up like wax by one

Whose footcloth must attend while he makes legs,

---

155. honest] chaste.

156-160. if . . . estate] Be prudent and moderate in your
actions; do not become involved in various sorts of profli-
gacies that will cause people to suspect you.

160. estate] physical and mental condition (OED).

161-162. I . . . Felt] one of the first indications of
Gotharus' miserliness, a characteristic that is revealed
several times in this scene.

162. footcloth . . . legs] There are at least two possible interpretations of the reference to footcloth. (1)
According to OED a footcloth was "a large richly-ornamented
cloth laid over the back of a horse and hanging down to the
ground on each side. It was considered as a mark of dignity
and state." Perhaps Gotharus believes the physician would
travel pompously and opulently, a manner sure to arouse the
miser's contempt. (2) Footcloth might also refer to a rug
or carpet which the physician must ostentatiously bring with
him to kneel on while he takes the pulse of his patient.
To Gotharus, the image of the physician on his knees before
Albina, taking her pulse, probably suggests wooing, not
medical attention.

And every other morning comes to tell

Your ladyship a story out of Aretine   165

That can set you a longing for diseases

That he may cure you and your waiting-woman,

Whose curiosity would taste your glister,

Commend the operation from her stomach

Should you be sick, and sick to death, I wo'd   170

Not counsel you to physic; women are

160-167. Your . . . you] Gotharus apparently feels that once fallen, Albina's sexual desire will grow compulsive and she will arrange affairs with any man who is able to have secret access to her. In addition, physicians in the Renaissance were often depicted as rascals.

165. Aretine] Pietro Aretino, the sixteenth-century Italian poet whose work, especially I Sonnetti Lussuriosi, was famed for its sexual explicitness, and conventionally considered lewd and pornographic. See 11. 142-143 above.

166. longing for diseases] i.e., in order to have visits from the physician. Diseases might also refer to syphilis, and though Albina would hardly desire a venereal disease, she could long for what brings the affliction. Diseases, in this sense then, functions metonymically.

168. taste] "to have sexual enjoyment." Partridge, op. cit. p. 201.

168. glister] The modern word is clyster or enema. As a reference to the pipe used for the injection, the phrase is a coarse allusion to male genitalia. Furthermore, glister was "a contemptuous name for a medical practitioner" (OED). Whatever the particular interpretations of specific words, the meaning of this line and the next is that Albina's waiting-woman, aroused by Albina's and the physician's sexual activity, would likewise make herself available to the doctor.

169. Commend . . . stomach] Recommend, present or offer her stomach ("sexual appetite and its organ of satisfaction" Partridge, p. 195) for the operation of the physician.

171. physic] medicine or medical treatment.

Frail things, and should a cordial miscarry,

My conscience would be arraign'd, and I

Might be suspected for your poisoner.

No, no, I thank you; y'are in a fine course   175

To ease me, wife; or if you must be loose

I'th spring and fall, let the king bear the charges.

He will, if you apply yourself.

ALBINA.   I am wretched.

Why do you without hearing, thus condemn me?

The lady lives not with a purer faith   180

To her lov'd lord than I have; nor shall

    greatness

Nor death itself, have power to break it.

GOTHARUS.   Come,

---

172. cordial] medicine.

173. My . . . arraign'd] my motives would be questioned.

175. course] position.

176. to ease me] to give me assistance.

176. loose] lascivious.

177. I'th . . . charges] Albina is further humiliated
by Gotharus as he compares her to animals who are in heat in
the spring and the fall. The king is identified with a stud
by Gotharus, for as one who bears the charges he is the one
who inseminates the female. See Partridge, p. 86. Of
course, as one who bears the charges he is also the one
responsible for the issue, a circumstance to which the politician has already referred; cf ll. 136-137 above.

> These are but painted tears; leave this. Have you
>
> Prepar'd your last accounts?

ALBINA.   They are ready, sir.

> Never was lady slav'd thus like Albina,   185
>
> A stipendiary, worse, a servile steward,
>
> To give him an account of all my expenses.

GOTHARUS.

> I'll have it so in spite of custom's heart
>
> While you are mine. Accountless liberty
>
> Is ruin of whole families. Now leave me;   190
>
> We may talk more anon.

Exit Albina.

> I have observ'd
>
> This privacy before. Search here, Gotharus;

184.   accounts] accompts Q.

187.   account] accompt Q.

191.   S.D. Exit Albina.] Gifford; after leave me (1. 190)
Q.

---

183.   painted] fake.

183.   leave this] cease this particular discussion.

186.   stipendiary] one who serves for pay.

188.   custom's heart] the feelings and customs that nor
mally exist in the relationship between man and wife.

189.   accountless] irresponsible (OED).

189.   liberty] to Gotharus, license with implications
of wantonness.

192.   privacy] Albina's expressed opposition to reveal
ing all her expenditures.

'Tis here from whence mutinous thoughts conspiring

With witty melancholy shall beget

A strong-born mischief. I'll admit she be   195

Honest; I love her not, and if he tempt her

To sin, that's paid him back in his wife's

    looseness

From whom I took my first ambition

And must go on till we can sway the kingdom

Though we climb to't o'er many deaths. I first   200

Practise at home my unkindness to Albina;

If she do love me, must needs break her heart.

Enter Haraldus

HARALDUS.

My honor'd lord.

GOTHARUS.   Most dear Haraldus, welcome.

Preciously welcome to Gotharus' heart.

197. wife's] Gifford; wives Q.

192-195. Search . . . mischief] Gotharus is always sus-
pecting intrigues and plots. Note also how Gotharus'
thoughts of money often become subtly mixed with thoughts
of sex. Cf. ll. 189-190, 192-197, and 150-177.

194. witty melancholy] cunningly feigned depression.

196. he] the king.

198. From . . . ambition] 1) with whom I first began
to climb, and 2) with whom I satisfied my first great desire.

200-201. I . . . Albina] A sardonic bit of humor in which
Gotharus plays upon the proverbial "charity begins at home."

HARALDUS.

The queen, my mother, sir, would speak with you.   205

GOTHARUS.

How excellently do those words become thee.

'Tis fit Haraldus' mother be a queen;

Th'art worth a princely fate. I will attend her.

HARALDUS.

I'll tell her so.

GOTHARUS.   'Tis not an office for you.

HARALDUS.

It is my duty, sir, to wait upon   210

My mother.

GOTHARUS.   Who i'th court is not your servant?

You do not exercise command enough;

You are too gentle in your fortunes, sir,

And wear your greatness as you were not born

To be a prince.

HARALDUS.   My birth sure gave me not   215

That title; I was born with the condition

To obey, not govern.

GOTHARUS.   Do not wrong those stars

Which, early as you did salute the world,

Design'd this glorious fate. I did consult,

And in the happy minute of thy birth,   220

---

215. sure] surely.

Collect what was decreed in heaven about thee.

ARALDUS.

Those books are 'bove my reading, but whate'er

My stars determine of me, 'tis but late

I heard my mother say, you are on earth,

To whom I am most bound for what I am.   225

OTHARUS [aside].

'Tis a shrewd truth if thou knew'st all.

ARALDUS.   You have

Been more a father than a friend to us.

OTHARUS [aside].

Friend to thy mother, I confess, in private;

The other follows by a consequence.--[To Haraldus.]

A father, my Haraldus? I confess   230

I was from thy nativity inclin'd

By a most strange and secret force of nature

22.   whate'er] Gifford; what (1. 222) and E're (1. 223) Q.

26.   S.D. aside] Gifford.

29.   S.D. To Haraldus.] aside. Q.

---

221.   Collect] deduce, conclude (OED).

227.   us] Marpisa and Haraldus, for the modest boy
would not refer to himself in the royal manner.

228.   Friend] paramour, lover.

229.   the other] father.

232.   secret] mysterious.

Or sympathy to love thee like my own.

And let me tell thee, though thy mother had

Merit enough to engage my services,   235

Yet there was something more in thee consider'd

That rais'd my thoughts and study to advance

Thee to these pregnant hopes of state.   Methinks

I see thee a king already.

HARALDUS.   Good sir, do not

Prompt me to that ambition.   I possess   240

Too much already and I could, so pleas'd

My mother, travel where I should not hear

Of these great titles.   And it comes now aptly,

I should entreat your lordship to assist me

In a request to her.   I know she loves you   245

And will deny you nothing; I would fain

Visit the university for study;

247.   Visit the] Q and O (corrected); Visit 't the O (uncorrected).

---

235.   services] double-entendre, sexual services.   See
Partridge, p. 185.

236.   consider'd] held in esteem or regard (OED).

237.   study] endeavor.

243.   And . . . aptly] i.e., this is an appropriate
time for me to raise the subject.   Haraldus has just mentioned traveling, but also, as Gotharus has expressed his
devotion and his desire to help Haraldus, the boy believes
the present is an appropriate time to request Gotharus' aid
in persuading Marpisa to allow him to go to the university.

I do lose time, methinks.

GOTHARUS.   Fie, Haraldus,

And leave the court? How you forget yourself!

Study to be king. I shall half repent my care   250

If you permit these dull and phlegmatic

Thoughts to usurp. They'll stifle your whole

    reason;

Catch at the sun, divest him of his beams,

And in your eye wear his proud rays. Let day

Be when you smile, and when your anger points,   255

Shoot death in every frown. Covet a shade,

Affect a solitude and books, and forfeit

So brave an expectation?

HARALDUS.   Of what?

GOTHARUS.

Of Norway's crown.

---

248. I . . . methinks] i.e., I am running out of time.
"The usual age [for young Englishmen to attend the univer-
sity in the seventeenth century] was from fourteen to six-
teen, but they were frequently sent as early as twelve."
Elizabeth Godfrey, Home Life Under the Stuarts (New York:
E. P. Dutton and Co., 1903), p. 77.

250. repent my care] regret my past concern for you.

253. sun] metaphorically (1) greatness, (2) the king,
or the throne, and (3) the king's "son," Turgesius.

255. points] sharpens or comes to a peak (OED), with
obvious metaphorical comparisons to arrows.

256. Shoot] send forth swiftly, continuing the archery
metaphor.

257. Affect] show a preference for (OED).

HARALDUS.   Could there be any thought

Within me so ambitious, with what hope   260

Could it be cherished when I have no title?

GOTHARUS.

I that have thus far studied thy fortune

May find a way.

HARALDUS.   The king--

GOTHARUS.

Is not immortal while he has physicians.

HARALDUS [aside].

What's that he said?--[To Gotharus.] The King is

    happy,   265

And the whole nation treasure up their hopes

In Prince Turgesius, who with his great uncle,

Valiant Olaus--

GOTHARUS.   Are sent to'th wars where 'twill

    concern 'em

To think of fame and how to march to honor

Through death.

HARALDUS [aside]. I dare not hear him.

GOTHARUS.   Or if they   270

270. S.D. aside] Gifford.

---

    264. Is . . . physicians] "Poison is frequently sup-
plied by physicians in Elizabethan drama." (Huberman, p.
221.) As true as that may be (see IV.iii.18-19 below), it
seems that the meaning of this line is that a person who is
still attended by physicians is mortal and subject to death;
and therefore, Haraldus should not give up hope of being
king simply because the king presently lives.

Return--

HARALDUS.   They will be welcome to all good

Men's hearts, and next the king, none with more joy

Congratulate their safeties than yourself.

I am confident, my lord, you will remember

To see my mother and excuse me if   275

To finish something else I had in charge.

I take my leave; all good dwell with your lordship.

    Exit.

GOTHARUS.

But that I have Marpisa's faith, I could

Suspect him not the issue of my blood;

He is too tame and honest. At his years   280

I was prodigiously in love with greatness;

Or if not mine, let him inherit but

His mother's soul; she has pride enough and spirit

To catch at flames. His education

---

272. next the] next to the.

276. had in charge] was instructed to do, or had
responsibility for.

278. faith] assurance.

280. tame and honest] meet (OED) and virtuous.

283. pride] double-entendre, "sexual desire" (OED).
See also Partridge, p. 172.

284. To . . . flames] (1) to reach into fire, therefore, showing courage; and (2) figuratively, Marpisa has
such spirit that she could burst into fire (OED, "to catch
a fire . . . to become inflamed or inspired"). Both flames
and fire carry sexual implications. See Partridge, pp.
113-114.

Has been too soft; I must new-form the boy   285

Into more vice and daring. Strange, we must

Study at court how to corrupt our children.

Enter Marpisa.

The queen!

MARPISA.   My expectation to speak

With thee, Gotharus, was too painful to me.

I fear we are all undone; dost hear the news?   290

The prince is coming back with victory;

Our day will be o'ercast.

GOTHARUS.   These eyes will force

A brighter from those clouds. Are not you queen?

MARPISA.

But how Turgesius and his bold uncle

Will look upon me.

GOTHARUS.   Let 'em stare out   295

Their eyeballs. Be you mistress still of the

King's heart, and let their gall spout in their

    stomach;

We'll be secure.

MARPISA.   Thou art my fate.

GOTHARUS.   I must confess

---

285. soft] gentle, and probably "effeminate, unmanly"
(OED).

288-289. My . . . me] i.e., I could not bear to wait any
longer to speak with you.

293. a brighter] a brighter day.

298. fate] the power that guides and controls individuals.

I was troubled when I heard it first. Seem not

You pale at their return, but put on smiles   300

To grace their triumph. Now you have most need

Of woman's art; dissemble cunningly.

MARPISA.

My best Gotharus.

GOTHARUS.

They shall find strategems in peace more fatal

Than all the engines of the war; what mischief   305

Will not Gotharus fly to to assure

The fair Marpisa's greatness and his own

In being hers, an Empire 'bove the world.

There is a heaven in either eye that calls

My adoration; such Promethean fire   310

As were I struck dead in my works, shouldst thou

But dart one look upon me, it would quicken

My cold dust and inform it with a soul

More daring than the first.

MARPISA.   Still my resolv'd

     Gotharus.

GOTHARUS.

Let weak statesmen think of conscience;   315

---

304. stratagems] "an artifice or trick" (OED), and an
obvious play on military terminology.

310-314. such . . . soul] Prometheus was to have made
images (men) and given them life and the gift of fire stolen
from the gods.

313. inform] animate.

I am arm'd against a thousand stings and laugh at

The tales of hell and other worlds. We must

Possess our joys in this and know no other

But what our fancy every minute shall

Create to please us.

MARPISA.   This is harmony;   320

How dull is the king's language. I could dwell

Upon thy lips; why should not we engender

At every sense?

GOTHARUS.   Now you put me in mind;

The pledge of both our hopes and blood, Haraldus,

Is not well-bred; he talks too morally.   325

He must have other discipline and be fashion'd

For our great aims upon him; a crown never

Became a stoic. Pray let me commend

Some conversation to his youth.

---

319. fancy] imaginative desire, "amorous inclination"
(OED).

320. harmony] beauty.

321. dull] cacophonous.

323. At every sense] each of the five senses.

323. Now . . . mind] Now you bring me to a purpose.

326. discipline] teaching (OED).

328. stoic] here used in the sense of an austere and
unambitious person.

329. conversation] way of life, perhaps, as specific
as some acquaintances.

MARPISA.   He is thine.

Enter Helga.

GOTHARUS.

He shall be every way my own.   330

HELGA.

The king desires your presence, madam.

MARPISA.

I attend, you'll follow--   Ex[eunt Marpisa and

Helga]

GOTHARUS.   Thee to death, and

triumph in

My ruins for thy sake. A thousand forms

Throng in my brain; that is the best which speeds.

Who looks at crowns must have no thought who

bleeds.   335

Exit

[II.i]

Enter King, Hormenus, Cortes, [and] Sueno [playing an

instrument].

[II.i]

0.1. S.D. and] Gifford.

---

333. forms] shapes, probably in the sense of plans and
ideas.

334. speeds] succeeds (OED).

335. looks] aspires to.

KING.

> This music doth but add to melancholy;
>
> I'll hear no more.

CORTES.

> He's strangely mov'd.

HORMENUS.   I cannot think a cause--

> You were wont to fool him into mirth; where's Helga,
>
> Your dear companion? No device between you   5
>
> To raise his thoughts?

SUENO.   I am nothing without

> My fellow; music is best in consort.

HORMENUS.

> Your buffoonery is musical belike.

CORTES.

> Your jugglers cannot do some o'their tricks
>
> Without confederacy.

SUENO.   I'll try alone.--   10

> If please your majesty, there is--

1-16. This . . . parts] Puns relating to music are found throughout this section.

7. music . . . consort] Sueno tries to be poetic and clever and attempts to compare his and Helga's form of entertainment to a more sophisticated mode, music. Hormenus and Cortes, far more clever than Sueno, pick up the metaphor and tease the fop.

7. consort] in partnership, suggesting harmony and punning on the word concert.

10. confederacy] cooperation.

KING.   Strikes him   That

For your unseasonable and saucy fooling.

HORMENUS.

That was a musical box o'th'ear.

KING.

Leave us.

CORTES.   'Tis nothing without a fellow;

He knows music is best in consort.   15

SUENO.

Would you had your parts!

KING.   Hormenus, you may stay.

Ex[eunt Cortes and Sueno].

HORMENUS.

Your pleasure, sir.

KING.   Men do account thee honest--

HORMENUS [aside].

'Tis possible I may fare the worse.

11.   S.D. Strikes him.] after fooling (l. 12) Q.

16.1 S.D. Exeunt Cortes and Sueno.] after consort (l. 15)
Q.

18.   S.D. aside.] Gifford.

---

12.   unseasonable] untimely, inopportune (OED).

16.   parts] share, just deserts. Perhaps the whole
phrase is a double-entendre, a petulant and spiteful attack
upon Cortes' and Hormenus' masculinity. It is, of course,
a musical pun as well.

17.   honest] candid, truthful.

18.   'Tis . . . worse] From the direction the conversation is leading, Hormenus thinks that perhaps he would have
been better off had he been allowed to leave with Cortes and
Sueno.

KING.   And wise.

  Canst tell the cause why I am sad?

HORMENUS.   Not I, sir.

KING.

  Nor I myself; 'tis strange I should be subject   20

  To a dull passion and no reason for it.

HORMENUS.

  These things are frequent.

KING.   Sometimes ominous,

  And do portend.

HORMENUS.   If you enjoy a health,

  What is in fate?

KING.   I am king still, am I not?

HORMENUS.

  We are all happy in't.   25

  And when time shall, with the consent of nature,

  Call you an old man from this world to heaven,

  May he that shall succeed you, Prince Turgesius,

  The glory of our hope, be no less fortunate.

KING.

  My son; I was too rash to part with him.   30

24. am I not] Gifford; and I not Q.

---

  21. dull passion] depression, gloominess.

  22. frequent] common, usual, nothing to worry about.

  23-24. If . . . fate] The sense is probably: If you enjoy good health, why worry about the future or matters you
cannot control?

HORMENUS.

    We should have thought his stay a blessing, and

       did wish

    You would not have expos'd such tender years

    To the rough war, but your commands met with

    His duty and our obedience.

KING.   It is very

    Strange, we of late hear no success; I hope   35

    This sadness is not for his loss. He has

    A kinsman with him, loves him dearly--

    'Tis the queen.

                 <u>Enter</u> Marpisa <u>and</u> Helga.

           I feel my drooping thoughts fall

    off,

    And my clouds fly before the wind; her presence

    Hath an infusion to restore dead nature.--   40

    My sweet, my dear Marpisa.

MARPISA.   You sent for me?

KING.

    I am but the shadow of myself without thee.

35-36. <u>I</u> . . . <u>loss</u>] The king continues to fear that his
depression is portentous.

    37. <u>kinsman</u>] Olaus.

39-40. <u>her</u> . . . <u>nature</u>] Cf. with Gotharus' statement
about Marpīsa's life-giving powers (I.i.310-314).

    42. <u>I</u> . . . <u>thee</u>] Cf. with Marpisa's statement, V.i.
36, about the then pathetic king.

Enter Cortes [*and*] Sueno.

No wonder I was sad; my soul had plac'd

All her delight in these fair eyes and could not

But think itself an exile in thy absence.   45

Why should we ever part, but chain ourselves

Together thus?

SUENO.   He's in a better humor, I hope.

I do not think but his majesty would cuff well;

His hand carries a princely weight.

HELGA.   A favor.

SUENO.

Would you might wear such another in your ear!   50

KING.

Come hither--on this side.

SUENO [*aside*].

You were on that side before.

KING.

Wo'dst not thou lose thy life to do a service

My queen would smile upon?

SUENO.   Alas, my life

Is the least thing to be imagin'd. He   55

42.1. S.D. *and*] <u>Gifford</u>.

---

48. <u>cuff</u>] box, fight.

49. <u>favor</u>] Helga, having a little fun at the expense of his fellow, says that this talent of the king is something to be admired, a handsome quality.

52. <u>You . . . before</u>] A reference to the king's earlier <u>striking of Sueno</u>.

Is not a faithful subject would refuse

To kill his wife and children, after that

To hang himself, to do the queen a service.

KING.

Come hither, Helga.

HELGA.   Royal sir.

KING.

What would affright thy undertaking to deserve   60

The least grace from my queen?

HELGA.   I cannot tell,

But I've an opinion, the devil could not.

My life is nothing, sir, to obtain her favor;

I would hazard more. I have heard talk of hell;

So far she should command me.

HORMENUS [to Cortes].   Bless me, goodness!   65

What wretched parasites are these; how can

The king be patient at 'em? Here is flattery

So thick and gross, it would endure a handsaw.

CORTES.

His judgment's, I fear, stupified.

HORMENUS [to Sueno and Helga].   Come hither.

60-61. What . . . queen] What would frighten you from doing anything that might bring you even the smallest favor
from the queen?

68. gross] heavy, dense.

Which of you can resolve what serpent spawn'd you?   70

SUENO.

You are pleasant.

HELGA.   My good Lord, it hurts not you;

There is necessity of some knaves, and so

Your lordship be exempted, why should you

Trouble yourself and murmur at our courses?

Enter Aquinus hastily.

AQUINUS.

The king!

HELGA.   Peace!

SUENO.   Your business?

AQUINUS.   News from the field.   75

SUENO.

Good?

AQUINUS.   Good.

HELGA.   How?

SUENO.   How, prithee?

AQUINUS.

The day, the field, the safety, O the glory

Of war is Norway's. Letters to the king--

HELGA.

---

70. resolve] explain.

70. spawn'd] Aside from the obvious opprobrious reference to serpent, Huberman notes that spawn'd means "gave
birth to in a contemptuous sense."

71. You are pleasant] (1) a sarcastic statement, or
(2) "you jest" (Huberman).

Give 'em to me.

SUENO.   Or me.

HELGA.

Trust not a fool with things of consequence;   80

He's the king's mirth. Let me present the news.

SUENO.

Sir, I should know you; this is a knave,

Would take to his all the glory of your report.

If please you, let me present the letters.

HELGA.

My leige!

SUENO.   My sovereign!

HELGA.   News!

SUENO.   Good news!   85

HELGA.

Excellent news!

SUENO.   The prince--

HELGA.   The prince is--

SUENO.

The enemy is--o'erthrown.

HELGA.

They have lost the day.

SUENO.   Defeated utterly.

HELGA.

And all are slain.

---

81. mirth] jester, fool.

SUENO [to Marpisa].   Madam, will you hear the news?
KING.

    Say on, what is't you would relate?   90
HELGA.

    One of my creatures, sir, hath brought you letters.

               Aquinus delivers the letters.

    My servant, sir; one strengthened to your service

    Out of my maintenance, an instrument of mine.

    So please you to consider my duty in his service.
AQUINUS [aside to Helga and Sueno].

    Why, hark you, gentlemen; I have but mock'd   95

    Your greedy zeals. There's no such matter in

    Those letters as you have told; we have lost all,

    And the prince taken prisoner. Will you not

    Stay for the reward? You know I'm but your

        creature;

    I look for nothing but your courtly faces   100

    To pay my travel.
HELGA.   We wo'not appear yet.

               Ex[eunt Helga and Sueno].

---

101. S.D. Exeunt Helga and Sueno.] Gifford; Exit. Q.

    91. creatures] instruments, servants.

    95. mock'd] toyed with.

    101. travel] journey and labor.

    101. yet] henceforth.

AQUINUS [aside]. How the rats vanish.

KING.

>   Read here, my best Marpisa, news that makes
>
>   A triumph in my heart great as the conquest
>
>   Upon our enemies.--Hormenus, Cortes,   105
>
>   Our son will prove a soldier! Was my sadness
>
>   Omen to this good fate? Or nature fear'd
>
>   The ecstasy of my joy would else o'ercome me?
>
>   They are return'd victorious.

HORMENUS.   Thanks to heaven!

KING.

>   And some reward is due to thee [Gives Aquinus a
>
>   ring.] Wear that   110
>
>   For the king's sake.

AQUINUS.   You too much honor me.

KING.

>   But something in Marpisa's face shows not
>
>   So clear a joy as we express.--Forbear.
>
>   Wait till we call.

>   Exeunt [Cortes, Hormenus, and Aquinus].
>
>   Can this offend my queen
>
>   To hear of happiness to my son? O, let   115

110.   S.D. Gives Aquinus a ring.] Gives him a ring.   after
sake (1. 111) Gifford.

114.   S.D. Exeunt Cortes, Hormenus, and Aquinus.] Gifford:
Exeunt.   after Forbear (1. 113) Q.

---

104.   triumph] joy (OED).

113.   Forbear] leave (the room).

Thy eyes look bright; their shine hath force to make

The wreath of laurel grow upon his temples.

Why dost thou weep? This dew will kill the victory

And turn his bay to cypress.

MARPISA.   Witness, heaven,

There's not a tear that mourns for him; his safety   120

And conquest are most welcome, and he shall

Have still my prayers. He may grow up in fame

And all the glorious fortunes of a prince,

But while my wishes fly to heaven for blessings

Upon his head, at the same time, I must   125

Remember in what miserable condition

My stars have plac'd me.

KING.   What can make thy state

116.   their] Gifford; there Q.

121.   are] is Q.

---

117.   wreath of laurel] a symbol of victory.

118.   dew] tears.

119.   bay] laurel, i.e., victory (see 1. 117).

119.   cypress] funereal symbol, mourning.

119.   Witness, heaven] Let heaven be a witness, a mild oath.

Guilty of such a name and so deject

Thy nobler thoughts? Am not I still the king?

And is not fair Marpisa mine by marriage?   130

Crown'd here my queen immortally?

MARPISA.   Though I be

By royal bounty of your love, posses'd

Of that great title, sir, I have some fears.

KING.

You amaze me; speak thy doubts at large.

MARPISA.   The

prince,

Dear to your love, and I still wish him so,   135

Dear to your people's hearts, I fear will think

Our marriage, his dishonor. And Olaus,

Your passionate uncle, no good friend of mine,

When he shall see to what a height your love

And holy vow hath rais'd me, most unworthy,   140

Will but salute Marpisa with his scorn,

And by his counsel, or some ways of force,

Unchain our hearts and throw me from your bosom

To death, or worse, to shame. Oh, think upon me,

And if you have one fear that's kin to mine,   145

Prevent their tyranny and give me doom

---

128. such a name] "miserable," l. 126.

134. at large] openly.

138. passionate] irascible.

Of exile ere their cruelty arrive.

I'll take my sentence kindly from your lips

Though it be killing.

KING.   Let my son or uncle

Dare but affront thee in a look; I shall   150

Forget the ties of nature and discharge 'em

Like the corruption in my blood.

MARPISA.   I can

Submit myself to them, and would you please

To allow my humbleness no stain to what

You have advanc'd me to, I can be their servant,   155

And with as true a duty wait upon 'em.

KING.

Thou are all goodness; twenty kingdoms are

Too little for thy dowry.--Who attends?

                  Enter Hormenus, [Aquinus,] and Cortes.

Thus every minute I will marry thee

And wear thee in my heart. Vanish the thought   160

Of all thy sex beside, and what can else

158.1. S.D. Aquinus] Gifford.

151-152. discharge . . . blood] "In the old surgery, corruption in the blood was discharged by blood-letting. Is
the king implying that he would have knives used on his son
and uncle?" (Huberman, pp. 226-227).

154. no stain to what] no reflection on what.

Attempt our separation? Th'art obscure

And liv'st in court but like a masking star

Shut from us by the unkindness of a cloud

When Cynthia goes to revels. I will have   165

A chariot for my queen richer than e'er

Was shown in Roman triumph, and thou shalt

Be drawn with horses white as Venus' doves

Till heaven itself in envy of our bliss

Snatch thee from earth to place thee in his orb,   170

The brightest constellation.

CORTES [to Hormenus].   He dotes strangely.

KING.

Hormenus! Cortes! I would have you all

Search your inventions to advance new joys;

Proclaim all pleasures free! And while my fair

Queen smiles, it shall be death for any man   175

I'th court to frown. Exeunt [King and Marpisa].

166. e'er] Gifford; e're Q.

176. S.D. King and Marpisa.] Gifford.

160-162. Vanish . . . separation] an obscure passage. The
sense, however, is probably: "Rid yourself of the anxious
thoughts that seem to be natural to your sex; nothing else
threatens to separate us."

162. obscure] humble.

163-165. like . . . revels] a difficult passage, but it
appears as if the king compares Marpisa 1) with a "star that is
obscured by an ordinary cloud when the heavens, led by Cynthia, or the moon, take to revels or masquing, and 2) by
association, with the virtuous Cynthia herself.

173. inventions] imagination, creativity.

HORMENUS.

    You ha' not so much love i'th court, Aquinus.

CORTES.

    How do you like the queen?

AQUINUS.

    Why she's not married? He does but call her so.

HORMENUS.

    And lies with her.

AQUINUS.   The prince yet knows it not.   180

HORMENUS.

    He'll meet it coming home.

                    Enter Gotharus.

GOTHARUS.   Aquinus? [Takes

        Aquinus aside.]

AQUINUS.   Sir.

GOTHARUS.

    You brought letters from the camp?

AQUINUS.   I did, my lord.

HORMENUS [to Cortes].

    What in the name of policy is now hatching?

    I do not like those fawning postures in him;

181. S.D. Enter Gotharus.] Gifford; after Aquinus? Q.

181. S.D. Takes Aquinus aside.] Gifford.

---

    181. it] the news of the marriage.

    183. policy] intrigue, plotting.

    184. him] Aquinus.

How kind they are.

[CORTES].   That soldier is thought honest.   185

HORMENUS.

But if he cringe once more I shall suspect him;

That leg confirms he is corrupt already.

GOTHARUS.

How does he like his father's marriage?

AQUINUS.

We had no fame on't there when I set forth.

GOTHARUS.

'Twas strange and sudden, but we are all happy   190

In the good prince's health and victory.

The Duke Olaus, too, I hope is well.

AQUINUS.

He was design'd at my departure to

Be here before the Army.

185. S.P. Cortes.] Gifford; Go. Q.

---

185. How . . . are] The proper interpretation of this
line depends on the meaning of kind (1) If kind means "inti-
mate" or "fond" (OED), then the phrase means: "How friendly
they are."   (2) If kind means "keeping to nature, natural"
(Huberman), then the adjective probably refers to "fawning
postures" in 1. 184, and the phrase means: "How natural the
fawning postures are to Aquinus."

186. cringe] "bow servilely" (OED).

186-187. But . . . already] Apparently Aquinus bows and
nods to Gotharus in their conversation and Hormenus inter-
prets these actions as "fawning" to Gotharus.

189. fame on't] knowledge of it.

193. design'd] instructed, "designated" (OED).

GOTHARUS.   He will be welcome.

You shall accept the price of a new armor,   195

And wherein any power of mine can serve you

I'th court, command.

AQUINUS.   I am your lordship's creature.

Exeunt [Gotharus and Aquinus].

HORMENUS.

They are gone; I long to see the prince.

How do you think his highness will

Behave himself to his new mother-queen?   200

Will it be treason not to ask her blessing?

CORTES.

I am confident his uncle, brave Olaus

Enter [behind,] Haraldus.

Wo'not run mad for joy of the king's marriage.

HORMENUS.

Let them look to't; there may be alterations.

HARALDUS.

They talk sure of my mother and the king.   205

197.1 S.D. Gotharus and Aquinus.] Gifford.

202.1 S.D. behind] Gifford.

---

195. You . . . armor] as a reward for bringing the
good news of victory, but, of course, the gift is designed
by Gotharus to compromise Aquinus and to make the captain
believe Gotharus is his friend.

197. I . . . creature] a phrase certainly to raise
additional suspicions in Hormenus and the audience.

HORMENUS.

>Secure as they account themselves, the prince

>Must be receiv'd spite of Marpisa's greatness,

>And all the tricks of her incarnate fiend,

>Gotharus, who both plot, I fear, to raise

>That composition of their blood,   210

>Haraldus,--

HARALDUS.   How was that?

HORMENUS.   --the strange effect

>Of their luxurious appetites, though in him,

>Poor innocence, suspecting not their sin,

>We read no such ambition.

HARALDUS.   Oh my shame!

>What have my ears receiv'd? Am I a bastard?   215

>'Tis malice that doth wound my mother's honor.

>How many bleed at once? Yet now I call

>To memory, Gotharus at our loving

205-223. They . . . me] Haraldus, unseen by Hormenus and
Cortes but not out of ear-shot, makes his comments to pass
unheard by the two courtiers.

>206. they] Marpisa and Gotharus.

>207. spite of] despite.

>211. effect] result.

>212. luxurious appetites] lascivious desires.

>217. How . . . once] How many suffer by this attack
on one person's honor.

Late conference did much insult upon

The name of a father, and his care of me   220

By some strange force of nature. Ha! my fears

Shoot an ice through me; I must know the truth

Although it kill me.   _Exit_.

CORTES.   Who was that, Haraldus?

HORMENUS.

I hope he did not hear us. Again, Gotharus

And the two squirrels; more devices, yet.   225

              Enter Gotharus, Sueno _and_ Helga

SUENO.

Let us alone, my lord; we'll quicken him.

GOTHARUS.

You must use all your art to win him to't.

HELGA.

Let us alone to make him drink;

We are the credit of the court for that;

He's but a child, alas; we'll take our time.   230

              Enter Olaus _attended_ _with_ _Captains_.

OLAUS.

Hormenus!

---

219. insult upon] Haraldus probably means by _insult_
upon Gotharus' loose and slightly improper use of the word
father during their conversation. Huberman's comment is
interesting: "insult: boast, exult, The word might also
be taken to mean 'insinuate', but such a meaning is not
recorded in the N. E. D. [_New_ _English_ _Dictionary_]" (Huberman, p. 229).

225. _devices_] plots.

HORMENUS.   My good lord, Olaus, I

    Joy in your safe return; how fares the prince?

OLAUS.

    Well. Where's the king?

HORMENUS.   Kissing his new-made

      queen, Marpisa.

OLAUS.   Ha! The king is married, then.

GOTHARUS [to Sueno and Helga]. Away, the Duke Olaus!

                Ex[eunt] Sueno and [Helga].

                        --[To Olaus.] Sir--   235

OLAUS.

    I am too stiff for complement, my lord;

    I have rid hard--

              Ex[eunt] Olaus, Hormenus, Cortes,

      and Captains].

GOTHARUS.   He has met the intelligence

    And is displeas'd with the state of things at home;

    This marriage stings him. Let it. We must have

    No trembling hearts, not fall into an ague   240

    Like children at the sight of a portent;

235. S.D. Exeunt Sueno and Helga.] Gifford; Exit. Su. & Ho.
after married then (l. 234) Q.

237. S.D. Exeunt Olaus, Hormenus, Cortes and Captains.]
Exit. Q.

---

    236. I . . . complement] I am too tired for social
formalities (especially those smacking of flattery).

    240. ague] quaking.

But like a rock when wind and waves go highest

And the insulting billows dash against

Her ribs, be unmov'd. The king must be saluted

With other letters which must counterfeit   245

The prince's character. I was his secretary

And know the art; malice inspire my brain

To poison his opinion of his son;

I'll form it cunningly.

>   Enter Haraldus.

>   Ha! 'tis Haraldus.

He looks sad.

HARALDUS [aside].   I dare not ask   250

My mother; 'twere a crime but one degree

Beneath the sinful act that gave me life

To question her, and yet to have this fright

Dwell in my apprehension without

The knowledge of some truth must needs distract   255

My poor wits quite.

>   [Discovering Gotharus.]

>   'Tis he! I will take boldness

And know the worst of him. If I be what

249. S.D. Enter Haraldus.] Gifford; after 'tis Haraldus. Q.

245-246. counterfeit . . . character] (1) falsely portray
the character of Turgesius, or (2) forge letters in the
prince's hand.

247. art] the prince's style of writing.

254. apprehension] thoughts.

I am already character'd, he can

Resolve my shame too well.

GOTHARUS.   How is't, my lord?

HARALDUS.

Never so ill, sir.

GOTHARUS.   Art sick?

HARALDUS.   Most dangerously.   260

GOTHARUS.

Where?

HARALDUS.   Here, at heart, which bleeds with such a
        wound

As none but you can cure.

GOTHARUS.   I'll drop my soul

Into it; show me how I may

Be thy physician.   To restore thy blood

I will lose all mine; speak, child.

HARALDUS.   This very
        love   265

Is a fresh suffering, and your readiness

To cure my sorrow is another wound.

---

258.   character'd] portrayed.

259.   Resolve] make clear.

262-265.   I'll . . . mine] Gotharus expresses his devotion
to Haraldus in terms that would disturb the boy further, for
the speech contains some contemporary ideas about begetting
a child: (1) dropping a soul, or infusing with life; and
(2) losing blood, a condition often connected with the sex
act.

You are too kind. Why are you so? What is

Or can be thought in me fit to deserve it?

GOTHARUS.

Thou dost talk wildly to accuse me thus   270

For loving thee. Could the world tempt me here

And court me with her glories to forsake thee,

Thus I would dwell about thy neck and not

Be bought from kissing thee for all her provinces.

There is a charm upon my soul to love thee,   275

And I must do't.

HARALDUS.   Then I must die.

GOTHARUS.

Forbid it, gentler fates.

HARALDUS.   If I could hear you

        wish

Me dead, I should have hope to live; although

I would not willingly deserve your anger,

By any impious deed, you do not know   280

What comfort it would be to hear you curse me.

GOTHARUS [aside].

He's mad.--Haraldus, prithee, do not talk so.

HARALDUS.

Or if you think a curse too much to help me,

---

268. kind] solicitous and sympathetic, but also suggesting kinship.

271-274. Could . . . provinces] Cf. Luke 4:1-13 and the
temptations of Christ.

Yet rail upon me, but do't heartily

And call me--

OTHARUS.   What?

ARALDUS.   Villain, or bastard, sir;   285

The worst is best from you.

OTHARUS.

Thou dost amaze me.

ARALDUS.   Will you not for me?

Then for my mother's sake if you do love her

Or ever did esteem her worth your friendship.

Let me entreat you draw your sword and give me   290

Something to wear in blood upon my bosom;

Write but one letter of your name upon

My breast, I'll call you father. By your love,

Do something that may make me bleed a little.

OTHARUS.

By that, I dare not, thou hast nam'd, Haraldus: 295

A father.

ARALDUS.   I but call you so. I know

You are a stranger to my blood although

Indeed to me your great affection

Appears a wonder; nor can nature show

More in a parent to a child. But if   300

I be--

OTHARUS.   What?

ARALDUS.   I shall blush, sir, to pronounce it.

There's something that concerns my mother, will

  not

Give it a name; yet I would be resolv'd

That I might place my duty right. If I

Must answer to your son, you may imagine   305

I shall no more ask you a reason why

You have been so kind to me and to my mother.

GOTHARUS.

Thou hast said it. Th'art mine own. 'Twas nature

  in me

That could not hide the actions of a father.

HARALDUS.

I am your base seed then.

GOTHARUS.   Stain not thyself   310

With such a name, but look upon thy mother

Now made a queen.

HARALDUS.   You made her first a strumpet,

And it would ask the piety of her son

To die upon that man that stole her honor.

Why did you so undo us? Why did you   315

---

303. <u>I</u> . . . <u>resolv'd</u>] I would have this cleared up.

305. <u>imagine</u>] assume (<u>OED</u>).

313-314. <u>And</u> . . . <u>honor</u>.] The base act would demand revenge of her son upon the man who dishonored his mother, maybe through a suicide-murder. "To die on one's enemies is equivalent to 'falling dead above them'" (Huberman, p. 231). Thus, Haraldus perhaps considers it appropriate to kill Gotharus and then kill himself, falling on his "father's" murdered body.

Betray my mother to this shame? Or when

She had consented, why should both your lust

Curse my unsinning heart. Oh, I must be

For your vice scorn'd, though innocent.

GOTHARUS.   None

    dare--

HARALDUS.

I should not by your virtue have been sav'd   320

Where shall I hide my life? I must no more

Converse with men--

GOTHARUS.   Thou art too passionate.

HARALDUS.

I will entreat my mother we may go

Into some wilderness where we may find

Some creatures that are spotted like ourselves   325

And live and die there, be companion

To the wild panther and the leopard; yet

316-318. Or . . . heart] a rhetorical question: Why did
your sinful act have to be fruitful and produce one who must
be cursed?

They are too good for our converse. We are

By ours, defil'd; their spots do make them fair.

   Exit.

GOTHARUS.

   'Tis time that Sueno and his companion   330

Dispers'd these clouds. Now to the king with whom

If the queen's beauty keep her magic, then

Our engines mount and day grows bright again.

   Ex[it].

[III.i]

Enter King, Marpisa, Olaus, Reginaldus, Aquinus,

   [Sueno,] and Helga.

KING.

   Uncle, I am glad to see you.

328. our] Gifford; their Q. Huberman disagrees with this
emendation: "Gifford reads 'our' for 'their'. The original
is easily understood, and should be retained. Besides, the
contrast offered by the word 'our' [sic] in the next line is
lost if Gifford's emendation be accepted" (Huberman, p. 231).
The contrast with ours in l. 329, however, is not with their
[Q.] converse in l. 328 but with their spots in l. 329. Of
greater significance is the contrast introduced by the con-
junction "yet" (l. 327), which emphasizes the difference
between the two groups of "spotted" creatures: defiled man
and the wild animals, the latter being too good to associate
with the former, not too good for themselves.

333. S.D. Exit.] Gifford; Exeunt. Q.

---

   328. converse] perhaps "manner of life" (OED), but
more likely intercourse.

   331. dispers'd these clouds] got rid of this melancholy in Haraldus.

   333. engines] plots.

OLAUS.   I am not glad

    To see you, sir,--

KING.   Not me?

OLAUS.   -- consorted thus.

KING.

    If Olaus be forgetful of good manners,

    I shall forget his years and blood; be temperate.

OLAUS.

    There's something in your blood that will undo   5

    Your state and fame eternally; purge that.

    You know I never flatter'd you; that woman

    Will prove thy evil genius.

KING.   Y'are too saucy.

OLAUS.

    Do not I know her? Was she not wife

    To the Count Altomarus, a weak lord,   10

    But too good for her, charm'd by the flattery

    And magic of her face and tongue, to dote

---

2. consorted] married, but with sexual overtones (OED).

4. blood] familial relationship.

5-6. There's . . . that] Olaus picks up the word blood, by which he means (1) disposition, (2) heredity, and possibly (3) the king's sexual relations. The king and Marpisa mix blood in marriage; therefore, the exhortation to purge has several meanings.

8. evil genius] i.e., your downfall, for an evil genius was an evil spirit that was one of two (the other being good) that attended each person throughout his life and governed his actions (OED). "Cf. I.[i.]34., where Hormenus is probably referring to his 'good' genius" (Huberman, p. 232).

And marry her? Born of a private family,

Advanc'd thus, she grew insolent, and I fear,

By pride and liberty and some trick she had,   15

Broke her good husband's heart.

MARPISA.   Sir, you much

   wrong me

And now exceed the priviledge of your birth

To injure mine.

OLAUS.   We all know you can plead

Your own defense; you have a woman's wit.

Heaven send you equal modesty; I am plain.   20

MARPISA.

It would be held an insolence in others

And saucy boldness in the sacred presence

Thus of the king to accuse whom he hath pleas'd

To take companion of his bed. And though

It would become the justice of my cause   25

And honor to desire these black aspersions

May be examin'd further, and the author

Call'd to make proof of such a passionate

   language,

---

   13. private family] common family, as opposed to a
public family, one that is of royal blood.

   15. By . . . had] Certainly there are strong implications of illicit sexual acts here. Pride suggests the
"heat" of animals and liberty suggests sexual looseness.
See Partridge, pp. 142 and 172. Trick, according to Partridge, could mean "a bout of love-making; a sexual strata-
gem" (p. 208).

   19. wit] cunning.

Which will betray his accusation was

But envy of my fortunes, I remember   30

Y'are the king's uncle, and 'tis possible

You may be abus'd by some malicious tale

Fram'd to dishonor me.--[To the king.] And,

   therefore,

I beseech you humbly, sir, to let this pass

But as an act in him of honest freedom.--   35

[To Olaus.] Beside what else may give you

   privilege.

Being a soldier and not us'd to file

His language, blunt and rugged ways of speech

Becoming your profession.

OLAUS.   Very good!

Although we ha'not the device of tongue   40

And soft phrase, madam, which you make an idol

At court and use it to disguise your heart,

We can speak truth in our unpolish'd words.

Thou art--

MARPISA.   What am I?

OLAUS.   Not the queen.

KING.   She is

---

32.   abus'd] deceived, misguided (OED).

37.   file] polish.

42.   heart] true feelings.

My wife, Olaus.

OLAUS.   I must never kneel to her,   45

Nor the good prince, your son, the hope of war

And peace's darling, honor of our blood

And worth a better kingdom than he's born to--

KING.

What of him?

OLAUS.   Must never call her mother.

KING.

Dare you instruct him against his duty?   50

Leave us!

OLAUS.   You have lost

More honor in those minutes you were married

Than we have gain'd in months abroad with all

Our triumph purchas'd for you with our blood.

Is this the payment, the reward for all   55

Our faith? When thy young son, whose springing

  valor

And name already make the confines tremble,

Returns like young Augustus crown'd with victories,

Must a stepdame first salute him

And tread upon his laurel?

57. make] Gifford; makes Q.

---

56. springing] first appearing and growing (OED).

56. confines] (1) region, territory, and (2) neighbors
(OED).

58. Returns . . . victories] The great Roman emperor,
Augustus, was famous for the victories of his youth.

KING.   Leave the court!   60

OLAUS.

    May it not prove an hospital. 'Tis i'th way

    To change a title; lust and all the riots

    Of license reeling in it by th'example

    Of one should least prophane it. I am still

    Olaus and your father's brother.   65

AQUINUS [to Olaus].

    My lord.

KING.   Take heed.

    You do not talk your head off; we have scaffolds.

    But the old man raves.--Come, my Marpisa.

OLAUS.

    Then I will talk! Threaten my head;

    Command that parasite that dares do most   70

    In wickedness to show himself you servant;

    Give him his engine and his fee for hangman;

    Let him take boldness but to move one hair

---

    60. laurel] bay laurel, signifying victory.

    61. May . . . hospital] May the court not become a
place of disease and madness.

    61-64. 'Tis . . . it] A vague passage, but one which prob-
ably means: "For one of your rank and responsibility to foul
his title in the manner in which you have, through lust and
excessive liberty, is the manner of a madman and [by exten-
sion] might cause others to imitate your actions and change
all titles, that is to rebel."

    72. engine] instrument of execution.

That withers on my head out of its posture,

He shall have more hope to o'ercome the devil   75

In single duel than to escape my fury!

AQUINUS [to Olaus].

Sir--

KING.   Our guard.   [Enter soldiers.]

OLAUS.

Look you, I'll bring no danger to your person;

I love you too well. I did always use

To speak; your father lik'd me ne'er the worse.   80

And now I am cool again.

You say you are married.

KING.   We are.

OLAUS [aside to the king].

Then between you and I, and let none hear us,

To make yourself, you son, and kingdom prosper,

Be counsel'd to a divorce.

KING.   No, not   85

To save thy soul. My son's life added

To thine and lives of all the army shall

Be divorc'd from this world first. Your are my

    father's

74. its] his Q.

80. ne'er] Gifford; near Q.

---

83. between you and I] Not an unusual construction in the seventeenth century.

        Brother, and if you love my son, your pupil,

        So hopeful in your thoughts, teach him to come   90

        More humbly to us, without thought to question

        Our marriage, or I'll find a chastisement

        For his rebellious heart, we will.

                    Ex[eunt King and Marpisa with soldiers].
OLAUS.

        You must not; I wo'not leave him yet.   Exit.
REGINALDUS.

        This freedom may engage his life to danger;   95

        He is too passionate.
AQUINUS.   He has said too much;

        I'll venture speaking to him.   Exit.
HELGA [aside to Sueno].

        He's alone; now to him.
SUENO [to Reginaldus].

        Noble sir, I have a suit to you.
REGINALDUS.

        A courtier asks a suit of a soldier?   100

85. No] not Q.

100. asks] ask Q.

_____

    89.   pupil] ward.

    95.   freedom] free and blunt speech.

    95.   engage] expose, risk.

You'll wear no buff nor iron.

SUENO.

> I come very impudently, and I hope to thrive
>
> The better for't. This gentleman, my friend,
>
> A man of quality, and in some grace with
>
> The king, hath laid a wager with me of   105
>
> Two hundred crowns, I dare not pull a hair
>
> From your most reverend beard. Now, if you
>
>> please
>
> To give me leave, I'll win the crowns, laugh at
>
>> him,
>
> And drink your health at supper.

REGINALDUS.   A hair from my

>> beard?

SUENO.

> But one hair, if shall please you.

REGINALDUS.   Come, take it.   110

[Sueno <u>plucks</u> <u>his</u> <u>beard</u>.]

SUENO.

> I have pull'd three, noble sir.

REGINALDUS.

> 'Twas more than your commission.

[<u>Kicks</u> <u>him</u>.]

There's one.

---

101. <u>You'll</u> . . . <u>iron</u>] a play on the word <u>suit</u>. Soldiers wore <u>buff-leather</u> <u>and</u> iron armor.

Kicks him [again.]

That's another.

Strikes him.

And that will make you

An upright courtier.

HELGA.   Ha! Ha!

SUENO [to Reginaldus].   Sir, I beseech

you--

REGINALDUS.

Beg modestly hereafter; take within your bounds.   115

You have small beard to play upon; 'tis fit.

My fist should make an answer to your wit.

SUENO.

I have it to a hair.   The choleric duke again!

I am gone.

[Reginaldus and Sueno] exeunt

[separately].

Enter Olaus and Aquinus.

AQUINUS [to Olaus].   Sir, you have been to blame.

OLAUS.

How dare you talk to me, sir?   120

AQUINUS.

'Tis my duty, and I must tell you,

Y'ave built too much upon him as a kinsman

113.   S.D. Strikes him] after courtier (1. 114) Q.

---

118.   to a hair] "to a nicety, with the utmost exact-
ness" (OED).

And have forgot the king.

OLAUS   Strikes him with his cane.

Take that for your impudence.   Exit.

AQUINUS.

I have it, and I thank you.   [Exit.]   125

Enter King, reading letters, Marpisa [and

Sueno].

HELGA.

They are gone, sir, but have left prints of

their fury;

The angry duke has broke Aquinus' head

For speaking dutifully on your behalf;

T'other mute man of war stroke Sueno, sir.

SUENO.

I hear his language humming in my head still.   130

KING.

Aquinus struck so near our presence?

124.   S.D. Strikes him with his cane] after Exit.   Q.

125.   S.D. Exit.] Gifford.

125.1 S.D. and Sueno] Gifford.

129.   T'other] Gifford; To'ther Q.

131.   struck] strike Q.

122-123.   Y'ave . . . king] You have relied too heavily on
family ties and have ignored your duties as a subject.

131.   Aquinus . . . presence] It was considered an affront, and perhaps even treason, to draw a weapon or to engage in physical combat before a king. This ban extended to
the royal palace as well.

SUENO.

    Nay, these soldiers will strike a man if he do not

    Carry himself to a hair's breadth; I know that.

KING.

    They shall repent this impudence.--Look up

    My dear Marpisa; there's no tempest shall   135

    Approach to hurt thee. They have rais'd a storm

    To their own ruins.

                    Enter a soldier.

SOLDIER [*to* Helga].   Sir, if you'll bring me

    To'th'king, you shall do an office worth your

        labor;

    I have letters will be welcome.

                              You must give

    Me leave, sir, to present 'em from the prince.   140

        Soldier gives Helga *the letters and exit.*

    --[*to the king.*] Most excellent sir, my sovereign.

SUENO.

    Letters?--[*To the king.*] If you have a chain of

        gold--

HELGA [*to* Sueno].

    Go hang thyself.

_____

140.1 S.D. *Soldier gives* Helga *the letters and exits.*]
after thyself (1. 143) Q.

_____

    132-33. *if* . . . *breadth*] "Within a hair's breadth," a
proverbial phrase meaning "within certain strict limits"
(Tilley, p. 281 [H29], is an appropriate metaphor for Sueno
in light of his recent encounter with Reginaldus.

SUENO.   We will divide.

HELGA [to the king].

    I am most fortunate to present you, sir.

    With letters from the prince.

      [Helga gives the king the letters; the king

        reads.]

                    And if your majesty   145

    Knew with what zeal I tender these--

KING.   Ha!

HELGA [aside to Sueno].

    He frowns; where's the soldade? You'll go my

      half.

KING.

    Who brought these letters? Where's the messenger?

HELGA.

    He was here, but now he's vanished.

KING.   Vanish

    Thee too and creep into the earth.

                    I shall, sir.   150

      [Exeunt Helga and Sueno.]

KING.

---

    147. soldade] Soldade is the anglicized form of sol-
dado, Spanish and Portugese for soldier. The only examples
of soldade listed in the OED are from Shirley's The Example
and The Doubtful Heir.

    147. You'll . . . half] "To go halves" is to share
equally (OED). Helga, now that he sees the king is dis-
pleased by the letters, is willing to share with Sueno the
reward his companion had been so eager to receive a few
lines earlier.

The impudence of children. Read Marpisa;

More letters from the proud, ambitious boy.

He dares to give us precepts and writes here,

We have too much forgot ourself and honor

In making thee our queen; puts on his grace   155

A discontent and says the triumph he

Expected, the reward of his young merit,

Will be ungloried in our sudden match

And weak election.

MARPISA.   This was my fear.

KING.

He threatens us, if we proceed, with his   160

Command and power i'th' army.--Raise new forces

To oppose 'em and proclaim 'em rebels, traitors--

MARPISA.

Sir, I beseech you, for the general good,

Temper your rage. These are but words of passion;

The prince will soon be sorry for't; suspect not   165

His duty. Rather than disgrace your son,

Divide me from your heart; the people love him.

KING.

I'll hate him for't.--Gotharus! Where's Gotharus!

    Exit.

MARPISA.

---

159. weak election] (1) poor choice, or (2) a choice
made by an "easily deceived, credulous" person (OED).

This letter tastes of his invention.

He's active; it concerns us both.

Enter Albina.

                                        --Albina.   170

Nay, you may forward, madam.

ALBINA.   I beseech

Your pardon; I did hope to have found my

Lord, Gotharus, here.

MARPISA.   The king ask'd for him

And is but new retir'd, who, I presume,

If he had known of your approach, w'od not   175

Have gone so soon.

ALBINA.   I have no business, madam,

With king.

MARPISA.   Come, do not disguise it thus.

I am covetous to know your suit,

But I am confident he will deny

You nothing, and your husband is of my   180

Opinion lately.

ALBINA.   By your goodness, madam,

Let me not suffer in your thoughts. I see

There is some poison thrown upon my innocence,

And 'tis not well done of my lord, Gotharus,

170. S.D. Enter Albina.] after Albina! Q.

---

169.   invention] creation or falsehood.

171.   forward] come forward.

    To render me to your suspicion   185

    So unhappy.   'Tis too much he has withdrawn

    His own heart; he will show no seeds of charity

    To make all others scorn me.

MARPISA.   If he do,

    You can return it, but take heed your ways

    Be straight to your revenge; let not my fame   190

    And honor be concern'd with the least wound.

ALBINA.

    I understand not what you mean.

MARPISA.   I cannot

    Be patient to hear the king commend your lip.

ALBINA.

    I am betray'd.

MARPISA.   My phrase is modest;

    Do not you love the king?

ALBINA.   Yes, with the duty--   195

MARPISA.

    Of one that wants no cunning to dissemble

188-191. If . . . wound] If Gotharus injures you, take revenge on him; but leave me and my name out of your revenge.

194. betray'd] Though Albina does not respond as the
king would like to his advances, she is aware that "improper"
conversations have taken place between the two. To this extent, then, betray'd means "discovered." But in so far as
she has been the innocent party and has done all she could
to deny the king, betray'd takes on the meaning of "maligned."

194. modest] straightforward, not elaborate.

196. wants] lacks.

Her pride and loose desires.

ALBINA.   You are the queen.

MARPISA.

What then?

ALBINA.   I should else tell you 'tis ill done

To oppress one that groans beneath the weight

Of grief already, and I durst take boldness   200

To say, you were unjust.

MARPISA.   So, so,--

ALBINA.   I can

Contain no longer. Take from my sad heart

What hitherto I have conceal'd, in that

You may call me dissembler of my sorrows;

I am weary of my life and fear not what   205

Your power and rage can execute. Would you

Had no more guilt upon your blood than I

Have sin in my accounts that way, my lord,

Gotharus, would not be so unkind to me.

MARPISA.

What's that you said so impudently, Albina?   210

ALBINA.

What I did think should have consum'd me here

In silence; but your injuries are mighty,

---

197. pride] sexual overtones are present. See Partridge, p. 172 and OED.

197. loose] lascivious.

And though I do expect to have my name

In your black register design'd for death,

To which my husband will I know consent,   215

I cannot thus provok'd but speak what wounds me.

Yet here again I shut the casket up,

Never to let this secret forth to spread

So wide a shame hereafter.

MARPISA.   Thou hast wak'd

A lioness!

ALBINA.   Death cannot more undo me.   220

And since I live an exile from my husband,

I will not doubt but you may soon prevail

To give my weary soul a full discharge

Some way or other; and i'th' minute when

It takes her flight to an eternal dwelling,   225

I will forgive you both and pray for you.

But let not your revenge be too long idle

Least the unmeasur'd pile of my affections

Weigh me to death before your anger comes

---

217. casket] mouth.

219-220. Thou . . . lioness] "Wake not a sleeping Lion," a
proverbial phrase. Tilley, pp. 383-384 (L317). Also, Edward
Topsell wrote in the Historie of Foure-Footed Beasts in 1607
"There is no Beast more vehement then a shee or Female-lyon."
Muriel St. Clare Byrne (ed.), The Elizabethan Zoo (London:
Frederick Etchells and Hugh MacDonald, 1926), p. 39.

228. affections] mental and emotional state (OED).

And so you lose the triumph of your envies.   230

   [Exit.]

MARPISA.

You sha'not be forgotten, fear it not;

And but that something nearer doth concern us,

You should soon find a punishment.

   Enter King, Gotharus, with letter[s, and

     servants].

                       The king!

   Ex[it].

KING.

He struck Aquinus! Helga saw him bleed.

GOTHARUS.

These are strange insolencies.-- [To a servant.]

   One go for Aquinus.--   [Exit servant.]   235

[To the king.]   Did Olaus bring these

   letters?

KING.   No, some spirit,

For he soon vanish'd. I have given my son

---

233. S.D. Enter King, Gotharus, with letters and servants]
after Exit. (l. 233) Q. A new scene, which would be required if the stage direction in Q. were allowed to stand,
should not be created here. Continuity in time and place is
indicated by Marpisa's sight of the king. Gifford creates a
new scene here without properly taking into account Marpisa's
exiting exclamation.

---

   232. something . . . us] the problem of what to do
with Turgesius.

To the most violent men under the planets,

These soldiers.

GOTHARUS.   And they'll cling to him like ivy,

Embrace him even to death.

KING.   Like breeze to cattle   240

In summer, they'll not let him feed.

GOTHARUS.   But make

Him fling, unquiet.--

KING.   Most repineful, spleeny.--

GOTHARUS.

Ready to break the twist of his allegiance.--

KING.

Which they fret every day.

GOTHARUS.

These put upon his young blood discontents.   245

---

238. most . . . planets] The most violent men in the
world. Also the bellicose nature of soldiers was explained
by the astrological influence of Mars upon them.

240. breeze] The breeze fly that inflicts stings upon
cattle.

242. fling] (1) in animals: "to be unruly and res-
tive," but (2) in humans: "to be angry and to complain"
(OED).

242. repineful] discontented.

242. spleeny] peevish.

243. twist] connection, used figuratively and derived
from the thread or cord formed by twisting or plaiting (OED).

244. fret] (1) fray, relating to the "twist", and (2)
irritate, chafe (OED).

KING.

    Dangerous--

GOTHARUS.   Extremely dangerous.

KING.   Swell him up

    With the alluring shapes of rule and empire--

GOTHARUS.

    And speak his strength with a proud emphasis;

    Yours, with a faint cold-hearted voice. Were ever

    Such peremptory lines writ to a father?   250

KING.

    Thy counsel, while the danger's yet aloof.

GOTHARUS.

    Aloof? Take heed; hills in a piece of landscape

    May seem to stand a hundred leagues, yet measure;

    There's but an inch in distance. Oh, ambition

    Is a most cunning, infinite dissembler,   255

    But quick i'th' execution.

KING.   Thy counsel.

GOTHARUS.

    He that aspires hath no religion;

    He knows no kindred.

KING.   I ask for thy advice.

GOTHARUS.

    Have you not seen a great oak cleft asunder

    With a small wedge cut from the very heart   260

249. Were] <u>Gifford</u>; was Q.

Of the same tree?

KING.   It frights me to apply it.

Oh, my misfortune; this is torment, not

A cure.

                    <u>Enter</u> Aquinus.

GOTHARUS.   Aquinus! [<u>To the king</u>.] Speak him gently,
    sir,

And leave me to encourage him in a service

Worth his attempt and needful to your safety.--   265

Noble Aquinus, our good king has sense

Of the affront you suffered from his uncle,

And as he is inform'd, for speaking but

The duty of a subject.

AQUINUS.   This is true, sir.

I wear his bloody favor still; I never   270

Took any blow so long on trust.

KING.

I know thy spirit's daring, and it shall become

My justice to reward thy suffering.

A storm now hovers o'er my kingdom;

When the air is clear and our sky fair again,   275

Expect, nay challenge, we shall recompence

---

266. <u>sense</u>] knowledge, probably with the implication
of sympathy.

270. <u>favor</u>] ironic, something to remember Olaus by.

276. <u>challenge</u>] claim as your right.

What thou hast suffer'd for us with a bounty

Worth all thy merits.   I'th' meantime, apply

Thyself to my Gotharus and be counsel'd.

Exit[, followed by servants].

AQUINUS.

My duty.

GOTHARUS.   Th'ast no alliance to my blood,   280

Yet, if thou think'st I do not flatter thee,

I feel a friendly touch of thy dishonor.

The blow, 'twas not well done of Duke Olaus.

AQUINUS.

You great men think you may do what you please,

And if y'ave a mind to pound us in a mortar,   285

We must obey.

GOTHARUS.   That law is none of nature's;

And this distinction of birth and royalty

Is not so firm a proof but there are men

Have swords to pierce it through and make the

    hearts

Of those that take this privilege from their

    blood   290

Repent they were injurious.

AQUINUS.

---

277. bounty] reward.

281-282. Yet . . . dishonor] i.e., if you do not believe I
am flattering you with what I am about to say, I take you as
a friend and, thereby, share in your dishonor.

My sword was quiet when he beat me.

GOTHARUS.

He did not, could not, beat thee?

AQUINUS.

'Twas worse; he cudgel'd me; I feel it yet,
Nor durst I strike again.

GOTHARUS.   It could not be   295
A tameness in thy spirit, but quick thought
That 'twas Olaus'. Not that in thy heart
There was no will to be reveng'd, for he
Is false to nature, loves his injury,
But that there was no safety to return   300
Thy anger on his person.

AQUINUS.   Y'are i'th' right;
That frighted me.

                    For he is not reveng'd
That kills his enemy and destroys himself
For doing his own justice. Therefore, men
That are not slaves, but free, these we receive   305
Born and bred gentlemen in fair employments
That have and dare bid high again for honor.
When they are wrong'd by men 'bove them in title,

---

295. <u>again</u>] back.

299. <u>loves</u>] who loves.

 300-301. <u>But</u> . . . <u>person</u>] i.e., there was no safe opportunity to return the blows. See 11. 302-304; and 313-317
for the conditions under which Gotharus believes it is safe
to avenge an injustice.

As they are thought worthy a personal wound,

In that are rais'd and level'd with the injurer.   310

And he that shall provoke me with his weapon

By making me his enemy, makes me equal,

And on those terms, I kill him. But there is

Another caution to wise men who ought

To cast and make themselves secure: that when   315

They have return'd full payment for their

    sufferings

In fame, they may be safe without a guard.

AQUINUS.

    That, sir, is the prudence.

GOTHARUS.   Yet I can direct thee

To be reveng'd with safety unto this.

What if I add therein, thou shalt do service   320

302-310. For . . . injurer] "This long-drawn perplexed tis-
sue of sophistry seems purposely calculated to bewilder the
honest soldier. It may be read twice without being fully com-
prehended" (Gifford, V, 131n.). The passage is a bit con-
fusing and certainly sophistic, but the essence of these and
the succeeding lines is generally clear: "A man who has
been injured by a high-born person has become, by that low
act, the equal of his injurer. He that is not a slave, but
a free individual who wishes to have his honor restored, may
take revenge; but by avenging himself, he must take care not
to destroy himself as well as his enemy. It must be remem-
bered by those who have been wronged and who wish to feel
secure in public that they must somehow avenge themselves
without endangering their future."

317. fame] public estimation.

318. prudence] practical wisdom.

That will oblige the commonwealth that groans

With fear of innovation and make

The king thy friend by one expense of courage?

And, having nam'd the king thus, it must make

Thy thoughts secure from future loss and in   325

The present act no danger.

AQUINUS.   Sir, be clear;

Make good what you have promis'd

And see if I be frighted. I have help'd

Many give up the ghost.

GOTHARUS.   Olaus us'd

Thee basely. How much would the kingdom suffer   330

If he were dead and laid into his tomb,

Perhaps a year sooner than nature meant

To make his bones fit?

AQUINUS.   I dare kill him, sir,

If I were sure the king would pardon me;

That, in my own revenge and any other   335

Whom he calls enemy without exception;

To this, I am bound in conscience. Sir, there

  needs

---

322. innovation] revolution.

323. expense] expenditure, i.e., act.

324. thus] as Aquinus' friend.

335. That] the murder of Olaus.

337. I . . . conscience] I am committed.

No conjuration for this, nor art,

To heighten me; let me but hear the king

Will have it, and secure me.

GOTHARUS.   Thou deserv'st him,   340

And may'st a statue for our great deliverer.

Yet, now I have thought better on't; we may

Save trouble in Olaus' tragedy

And kill him through another.

AQUINUS.   Whom?

GOTHARUS.   One that

Sits heavier on the king's heart and dwells in't   345

Such a disease as if no resolute hand

Cure him.--

---

338. conjuration] (1) persuasion by invoking sacred names, and (2) solemn oath (OED). Aquinus may very much wish to avoid a sworn bond with Gotharus in this plot.

339. heighten] excite.

341. may'st] may'st deserve.

342-344. Yet . . . another] It appears as if Gotharus' argument to follow runs like this: "If a certain other person [the prince] is killed, then Olaus will be powerless and in that sense 'killed'." No connection between the murder of the prince and the death of Olaus is made; in fact from this point until the actual "assassination" of the prince by Aquinus, no attention is given to Olaus' murder. Gotharus (and, or course, Shirley), with shellgame agility, has ingeniously and almost imperceptibly transformed the plot to kill Olaus into a plot to kill the prince. Of more importance, Shirley has cleverly constructed a scene in which a cunning Gotharus appears to have fooled and manipulated a malleable Aquinus but which actually makes completely credible Aquinus greater subtlety and cunning as events in the play   later prove.

347. Cure] could cure.

AQUINUS.   I'll be his chirurgeon.

GOTHARUS.   When I name him,

    One that has had no will to advance thee

    To thy deserts in wars for all thy former

    And thy late services, rewarded with   350

    A dull command of captain; but incens'd

    By Olaus now who rules his heart, less hope

    To be repair'd in fortune--

[AQUINUS].   Let him be the prince--

GOTHARUS.

    --'Tis he!

AQUINUS.   It honors my atttempt; and while

    His father holds him disobedient,   355

    I think him less than subject.

GOTHARUS.

    Disobedient?

            Shows [Aquinus] a letter.

                Look there!

AQUINUS.

    This is the prince's hand.

GOTHARUS.   But read his heart.

                [Aquinus reads.]

353.   S.P. Aquinus.] Huberman; Al. Q.

357.   S.D. Shows Aquinus a letter.] after there! Q.

358.   S.D. Aquinus reads.] Gifford.

_____

    347.   chirurgeon] surgeon.

AQUINUS.

>   Impious! Above the reach of common faith.
>
>   I am satisfied, he must not live. The way!   360
>
>   They would not trust me with his cup to poison it.
>
>   Show me the way.

>   Enter King and Marpisa
>
>   The king and queen.

GOTHARUS.   Let's study.

>   [Gotharus and Aquinus walk aside and talk.]

MARPISA.

>   You have a faithful servant in Gotharus.

KING.

>   Upon his wisdom we depend.

GOTHARUS [aside to Aquinus].   I have it,

>   He shall die like a soldier, thus--

>   Whispers.

MARPISA.   Their malice   365

>   Doth only aim at me, and if you please
>
>   To give me up a sacrifice to their fury,--

KING.

>   Not for a thousand sons; my life and honors
>
>   Must sit with thine, Marpisa.

362.   S.D. Enter King and Marpisa.] after study Q.

---

353.   repair'd] remedied, made up for.

361.   They] those around the prince.

365.   Their] Olaus and Turgesius.

QUINUS [to Gotharus].   Sir, 'tis done.

OTHARUS [to Aquinus].

    This act shall make thee great.--[To the king.]

        The king and queen   370

    Look cheerful, royal sir, and think of honor

    To crown the merit of this captain. Let

    No trouble shake a thought; he will deserve

    Your bosom, sir.

ING.   He shall possess it.

    --[Aside.]   How, my Gotharus?

OTHARUS [aside].   Pray, leave it to

        me;   375

    It is not ripe yet for your knowledge, sir.

ING.

    We'll trust thee.--Come, Marpisa.

OTHARUS.   Dearest

        madam.--

    Come, Aquinus.

QUINUS.   I attend your lordship.   Exeunt.

III. ii.]

nter Haraldus, Sueno [and] Helga, at a banquet.

UENO.

    My lord, you honor us.

---

369.   sit with] agree with (OED).

374.   bosom] figuratively, trust with confidence.

HELGA.   If we knew how

    to express our duties--

HARALDUS.   No more ceremony;

    Your loves engage me if some discontents

    Make me but seem unpleasant. Yet, I must

    Confess I was more prompted to th'acceptance   5

    In hope to cure a melancholy.

HELGA.   With your pardon,

    It does too much usurp on your sweet nature;

    But if your lordship please, there is a way

    To banish all those thoughts.

HARALDUS.   I would call him

      doctor

    That could assure me that.

SUENO.   I am of his   10

    Opinion, sir, and know the best receipt

    I'th' world for sadness.

HARALDUS.   Prithee, what?

SUENO.   Good wine.

HARALDUS.

    I have heard 'em talk so. If I thought

    There were that operation--

---

4. but] not Q. The line with <u>not</u> is nonsensical: "Your
loves win me over even if some discontents make me seem
pleasant.

---

   3.   <u>engage</u>] win over (<u>OED</u>).

 11.   <u>receipt</u>] recipe, prescription.

 14.   <u>operation</u>] result (<u>OED</u>).

HELGA.   Try sir.

SUENO [offering Haraldus wine].

    My humble duty. 'Tis excellent wine   15

HARALDUS drinks.

    Helga.

HELGA.   Your lordship's servant.

HARALDUS.   'Tis pleasant.

SUENO.

    It has spirit. Will you please another trial

    That prepares more sweetness? Health to the

      queen! [Drinks.]

HARALDUS.

    I thank you.

HELGA.   With your pardon, fill to me.--

    Your grace should have it last.

HARALDUS.   She is my mother.   20

SUENO.

    She is our royal mistress, heaven preserve her.

16.   S.D. drinks.] after pleasant Q.

18.   S.D. Drinks.] Gifford.

---

   18.   prepares] provides.

   19.   fill to me] fill my cup.

   20.   Your . . . last] Perhaps Haraldus, a novice at
drinking, is quaffing his wine, and Helga urges him to drink
more slowly. The next part of l. 20 (She is my mother.) may
be Haraldus' justification for his manner of drinking.

   21.   royal mistress Perhaps Sueno puns on the word
mistress.

Haraldus <u>drinks</u>.

Does not your lordship feel more inclination

To mirth? There is no spell 'gainst sorrow like

Two or three cups of wine.

HELGA.   Nothing, believe't,

Will make your soul so active. Take it liberally.   25

HARALDUS.

I dare not trust my brain.

SUENO.   You never tried.

HELGA.

You'll never know the pleasure then of drinking;

I have drunk myself into an emperor.

SUENO.

In thy own thoughts.

HELGA.   Why, is't not rare that wine,

Taken to the extent, should so delightfully   30

Possess the imagination? I have had my queens

And concubines--

HARALDUS.   Fine fancies.

HELGA.   The king's health

    [<u>Drinks</u>.]

21.1 S.D. Haraldus <u>drinks</u>.] <u>after</u> inclination (<u>1</u>. <u>22</u>) <u>Q</u>.

---

25. <u>your</u> . . . <u>active</u>] you spirited.

26. <u>You never tried</u>] You never gave drinking wine a
test.

Give me't in greater volume; these are acorns.

Sueno, to thee.   I'm sprightly but to look on't.

SUENO. [pouring wine].

What rare things will the flowing virtue raise   35

If but the sight exalt you?--[To Haraldus.]   To

   your grace. [Drinks.]

The king's health.   [Drinks.]

HARALDUS.   Let it come; I'll trespass

   once.   Drinks.

HELGA.

That smile became you, sir.

HARALDUS.   This cup doth warm me;

Methinks I could be merry.

SUENO.

Will your grace have any music?   40

HARALDUS.

Anything.

---

34.   on't] Gifford; out Q.

37.   S.D. (following health) Drinks.] Gifford.

37.   S.D. (following once) Drinks.] after me (1. 38) Q.

---

   33.   acorns] i.e., just the beginnings as an acorn is
merely the small start of a great oak.

   34.   I'm . . . on't] I became enlivened just to look at
the wine.

   35.   flowing virtue] wine.

   36.   exalt] stimulate, excite.

   37.   I'll trespass once] I'll transgress once; that is,
get drunk.

HELGA.   Strike lustily!   Music [within].

HARALDUS.

   I have begun no health yet, gentlemen.

SUENO.

   Now you must honor us.

HARALDUS.   Health to the prince.

HELGA.

   That is your title, sir, as you are son to a queen.

HARALDUS.

   My father was no king. Father? I'll drown   45

   The memory of that name.   Drinks.

HELGA.

   The Prince Turgesius' health. [Drinks.]

SUENO.   He's not far off

   By the court computation. Happiness now

   To Prince Haraldus' mistress.

HELGA.   With devotion.

        [They drink.]

HARALDUS.

   Alas, I am too young to have a mistress.   50

HELGA.

41. S.D. within] Gifford.

---

   42. begun no health] proposed no toast.

   48. court computation] court reckoning; that is, according to the talk in court.

Sir, you must crown it.

HARALDUS.   These are complements

At court where none must want a drinking mistress.

SUENO.

Methinks loud music should attend these healths.

HARALDUS.

So, shall we dance?   _Drinks_.

HELGA.   We want ladies.

HARALDUS.

I am as light--[_To_ Sueno.]-- Thou shalt go for a   55

lady.

SUENO.

Shall I?   [_They_] _dance_.

Is not this better than to sigh

Away our spirits now?

HARALDUS.   I'm hot.

HELGA.

A cup of wine is the most natural cooler.

HARALDUS.

You are my physicians, gentlemen.   _Drinks_.

SUENO.

Make it a health to my lord, Gotharus.   60

---

51. crown it] (1) achieve it; that is, get a mistress,
or (2) "fill it to overflowing or till the foam rises like
a crown above the brim," thus a reference to Sueno to fill
his cup fuller (Huberman, p. 242).

51. complements] accomplishments (OED).

53. healths] toasts.   54. want] lack.

I'll pledge it as heartily as he were my father.

HARALDUS.

  Whose father?

<u>Throws</u> <u>wine</u> <u>in</u> Sueno's <u>face</u>.

SUENO.   Mine, I said.

HARALDUS.   Cry mercy.

SUENO.

Nay, 'tis but so much wine lost; fill't again.

HARALDUS.

  I'll drink no more.

HELGA.   What think you of a song?

SUENO.

  A catch.--To't boys.

<u>Song</u>.

HARALDUS.   Shall we to bed, gentlemen?   65

I did not sleep last night.

HELGA.   If your grace

Desire to sleep, there's nothing to prepare it

Like t'other cup.

HARALDUS.   A health to both your mistresses.

  <u>Drinks</u>.

SUENO.

You do us grace.

65. S.D. <u>Song</u>.] <u>Gifford</u>; <u>after</u> song (<u>1</u>. <u>64</u>) Q.

---

62. <u>Cry</u> <u>mercy</u>] forgive me (<u>OED</u>).

65. <u>catch</u>] song.

HELGA [aside to Sueno]. There's hope of his conversion.

HARALDUS.

    I am not well; what wheels are in my brains?   70

    Philosophy affirms the earth moves not;

    'Tis here, methinks, confuted, gentlemen.

    You must be fain to lead me to some couch

    Where I may take a nap, and then I'll thank you.

    I'll come again tomorrow.

SUENO.   Everyday   75

    For a twelve-month.

HELGA.   That will make you a good

    fellow.

        Ex[eunt, Sueno and Helga helping Haraldus].

[III. iii.]

Enter [at one side,] Turgesius, Reginaldus [and] soldiers
marching; [at the other,] Olaus; they salute and whisper.

TURGESIUS.

    You tell me wonders.

[III. iii.]

0. S.D. Enter at one side, Turgesius, Reginaldus and soldiers marching; at the other, Olaus; they salute and whisper.] Gifford; Enter Prince Turgesius, Reginaldus, Souldiers
marching. Olaus meets, they salute and whisper. Q.

    71-72. Philosophy . . . gentlemen] The Ptolemaic theory,
which was used by poets long after the Copernican was generally accepted, proposed that the earth did not move.

    73. You . . . fain] You must be kind enough.

OLAUS.   'Tis all truth; we must

    Stand on our guard; 'tis well we are provided.

TURGESIUS.

    Is it not some device to make us fear

    That at our entertainment we may find

    Our joys more spacious.

OLAUS.   There is some device   5

      in't.

TURGESIUS.

    It is not possible a father should

    Be so unkind to his own blood and honor.

OLAUS.

    My life was threaten'd.

TURGESIUS.   Who durst threaten it?

OLAUS.

    The king, your father.

TURGESIUS.   Oh, say not so, good sir.

---

3.   device] harmless trick. Cf. device 1. 5 below.

4.   That] so that.

4.   entertainment] reception.

5.   device] evil trick. Cf. device 1. 3 above.

7.   unkind] (1) not kind, gentle, and (2) unnatural, in the sense of not acting as a father ought.

7.   honor] (1) Turgesius is the king's reputation, glory, and credit because of the young man's victories. (2) The king also would foul his own honor by plotting against his son.

OLAUS.

    And if you please him not with your behavior,   10

    Your head may be soon humbled to the ax

    And sent a token of his love to your stepdame,

    The queen; I trifle not.

TURGESIUS.   For what sins

    Hath angry heaven decreed to punish Norway

    And lay the scene of wrath in her own bowels?   15

    I did suspect when none came forth to meet

    Our victory to have heard of some misfortune,

    Some prodigies engend'ring. Down with all

    Our pride of war; the garlands we bring home

    Will but adorn us for the sacrifice,   20

    And while our hairs are deck'd with flowers

      and ribands,

    We shall but march more gloriously to death.

    Are all good women dead within the kingdom,

    There could be found none worth my father's love

    But one whose fame and honor are suspected?   25

18. engend'ring] engendring O (corrected); egendring Q
(uncorrected).

25. are] Gifford; is Q.

---

    15. bowels] (1) center of Norway, (2) "offspring or
children" (OED), (3) "seat of the tender and sympathetic emotions" (OED).

    18. prodigies engend'ring] monstrous or abnormal
things developing.

    19. pride of war] glory and magnificence of war, and,
in this case, the ornamentation and trappings of battle
(OED).

OLAUS.

Would they were but suspected.

TURGESIUS.   Marpisa!

OLAUS.

Her preferment was no doubt

Gotharus' act, for which 'tis whisper'd

She pays him fair conditions while they both

Case up the king's eyes or confine him to   30

Look through such cunning optics as they please.

TURGESIUS.

I'll have his heart.

OLAUS.   But how will you come by't?

He's safe in the king's bosom, who keeps warm

A serpent till he find a time to gnaw

Out his preserver.

26. Would] Gifford; Woulst Q.

---

29. She . . . conditions] She repays him well. Condition was a common legal term in contractual agreements.

30. case up] cover.

31. cunning optics] craftily or skillfully wrought
eye-glasses. The sense is that the sinister couple lead the
king to see things as they wish him to see them and not as
they are.

32. heart] his true feelings.

33-35. He's . . . preserver] Gotharus uses the king as
protection as long as it serves him to do so, but when the
time is ripe he will turn against his royal protector.
"These lines recall Aesop's fable . . . of the countryman
and the viper" (Huberman, p. 244). "To nourish a viper
(snake) in one's bosom." Tilley, pp, 698-699 (V68).

TURGESIUS.   Had we died with honor   35

    By the enemy's sword, something might have been

      read

    In such a fall as might have left no shame

    Upon our story, since 'tis chance of war,

    Not want of valor, gives the victory.

    This shipwrecks all and eats into the soul   40

    Of all our fame; it withers all the deeds

    Are owing to our name.

               Enter Cortes.

CORTES.

    Health to the prince.

OLAUS.   Cortes, welcome. What

      news?

CORTES.

    These letters will inform his highness.

OLAUS.

    Sent from the king, Cortes? Has he thought

      upon't   45

    Are we considerable at last, and shall

    The Lady Gew-gaw that is perch'd upon

35. Had we] We had Q.

42. are] is Q.

---

    46. Are we considerable] Are we to be considered?

    47. Gew-gaw] an insignificant plaything, a mere gaudy
ornament.

His throne be counsel'd not to take too much

Upon her? Will Gotharus give us leave

To be acquainted with the king again? Ha!   50

CORTES [gives letters to Turgesius].

These letters came, sir, from Aquinus.

OLAUS [aside].   How?

I hope he mentions not the broken pate

I gave him and complains on't to the prince;

I may be apt to make him an amends

With such another.

TURGESIUS [to Olaus].   Sir!

OLAUS.   What's the matter?   55

TURGESIUS [gives letters to Olaus].

Read, I am planet-struck! Cursed Gotharus!

What would the traitor have?

OLAUS.

'Tis here. I take it he would have you sent

Yonder and has took order with Aquinus

For your conveyance hence at both their charges.   60

48-49. to . . . her] (1) to presume authority, and (2)
the double-entendre concerning sexual activity. See Partridge, p. 200.

54-55. I . . . another] I may feel it necessary to give
him another.

56. planet-struck] bewildered, but more than simple
amazement. He is fearful, terrified as if he came under the
evil influence of a planet (OED).

59. Yonder] to another world.

59. has took order] is in league.

But now you know the plot, you wo'not trust

Your life as he directs.

TURGESIUS.   Not trust Aquinus?

OLAUS.

You are desperate. Hark you, I do suspect him,

And I ha' cause; I broke his head at court

For his impertinent counsel when I was   65

In passion with the king. You sha'not trust

  him.

This may be cunning to revenge himself;

I know he has a spirit. Come, you sha'not

Be cheated of your life while I have one

To counsel you.

TURGESIUS.   Uncle, I am unmov'd.   70

He is a soldier; to that name and honor

I'll trust a prince's life. He dares not be

A traitor.

OLAUS.   I have read that one prince was

So credulous, and 'scap'd. But Alexander,

Though he were great, was not so wise a gentleman   75

As heaven, in that occasion, might have made him.

The valiant confidence in his doctor might

Ha' gnawn his bowels up, and where had been

---

63. <u>desperate</u>] hopeless, perhaps, reckless (<u>OED</u>).

My gallant Macedonian?   Come, you shall

Consider on't.

TURGESIUS.   I am resolv'd already   80

March to the city; every thought doth more

Confirm me. Passion will not let you see,

Good uncle, with your pardon, the true worth

And inside of Aquinus; he is faithful.

Should I miscarry, 'tis my single life,   85

And 'tis obedience to give up our breath

When fathers shall conspire their children's

death.

                         Exeunt.

[IV.i]

Enter King [and] Gotharus.

GOTHARUS.

IV.i]

0.1. S.D. and] Gifford.

73-79. I . . . Macedonian] Olaus is referring to a story
of Alexander the Great. That famous conqueror, having been
informed that his friend and physician, Philip, was in the
pay of his enemy, Darius, to poison him, revealed his
trust in his friend and his own courage by presenting the
physician with the letter of charges as he received and drank
the medicine Philip brought him. See Plutarchus, The Lives
of the Noble Grecians and Romaines, Translated by Sir Thomas
North (London: Richard Field and Thomas Wight, 1603), p.
682. It is Olaus' point, of course, that Alexander was spared
death at this time not because he was trusting and courageous, but because heaven or fate decreed otherwise.

85. miscarry] perish (OED).

You may surrender up your crown; 'twill show

Brave on Turgesius' temples, whose ambition

Expects it.

KING.   Nay, Gotharus--

GOTHARUS.   Has my care

Cast to prevent your shame, how to preserve

The glories you possess by cutting off   5

A canker that would eat into your trunk

And hinder your fair growth; and do you make

A scruple to be cured?

KING.   I did but mention,

And nature may excuse, he is my son.

GOTHARUS.

The more your danger when he dares be impious,   10

The forfeit of his duty, in this bold

1.   'twill] Gifford; 'twell Q.

---

2.   Brave] handsomely, attractively.

3-4.   Has . . . shame] Have I made known to you my deep-
est worries to prevent your dishonor. . .

6.   canker] cancer.

7-8.   make a scruple] hesitate (OED).

9.   nature may excuse] nature may excuse me; i.e, it is
natural that I, his father, should mention that Turgesius is
my son.   The comment is in reference to something supposed
to have been said prior to the opening of this scene.

10.   impious] "wanting in natural reverence and duti-
fulness, esp. to parents. rare" (OED)

11.   forfeit] "breach or violation" (OED).

And hostile manner. To affright your subjects

And threaten you with articles, is already

The killing of your honor and a treason

Nature abhors, a guilt heaven trembles at;   15

And you are bound, in care of your own province,

To show your justice and not be partial

To your own blood. But let your kindgom suffer,

Her heart be torn by civil wars; 'tis none

Of mine. And let him, in the blood of many   20

Fathers, be made a king, your king; and you

That now command, be taught obedience.

Creep to your child, exchange your palace for

A prison, and be humbled till you think

Death a preferment. I have but a life--   25

KING.

Which I will cherish; be not passionate;

And I consent to all thou hast contained.

Thou art my friend.

GOTHARUS.

---

13. articles] "terms, conditions" (OED), in the sense
of demands.

14-15. and . . . at] i.e., the rebellion of a son against
a father.

16. province] (1) realm, and (2) duty.

27. contained] included, meaning all that Gotharus has
included in his charges and analyses. Gifford substitutes
the word "contrived" for contained, and Huberman (p. 247)
says: "This ingenious emendation [Gifford's] alters only
two letters." However ingenious the emendation, there is no
need for it.

I would be, sir, your honest chirurgeon,

And when you have a gangrene in your limb,   30

Not flatter you to death, but tell you plainly,

If you would live, the part so poison'd must be

Cut from your body.

KING.   And I wo'not shake

With horror of the wound, but meet my safety

And thank my best preserver. But art sure   35

Aquinus will be resolute?

GOTHARUS.

Suspect not; he is my creature.

                    Enter Hormenus.

HORMENUS.

The prince, your son--

KING.   Is a bold traitor,

And they are rebels join with him.

GOTHARUS.

What of the prince, Hormenus?   40

HORMENUS.

He is very near the city with his army.

KING.

Are the walls fortified?

HORMENUS.   They are.

---

29. chirurgeon] surgeon.

34. meet . . . safety] endure the surgery that would
assure my safety.

39. rebels join] rebels who join.

KING.

    We wo'not trust him,nor the ruffian,

    Olaus, that incendiary.

                Enter Marpisa.

GOTHARUS.   The queen!

MARPISA.

    0, sir!

KING.   There are more wounds in those sad accents   45

    Than their rebellion can give my kingdom.

MARPISA.

    My boy, my child, Haraldus,--

KING.   What of him?

MARPISA.

    Is sick, is dying, sir.

GOTHARUS.   Forbid it, heavens!

    He was in health--

MARPISA.   But if I mean to see him

    Alive, they say I must make haste.   50

    The comforts of my life expire with him.   Exit.

GOTHARUS.

    The devil's up in arms, and fates conspire

    Against us.

KING.   Mischiefs tumble like waves upon us.

44. S.D. Enter Marpisa.] after queen! Q.

---

   45. sad accents   sad sounds; i.e., sad voice (OED).

HORMENUS.

    Sir, it will be necessary

    You lend your person to direct what shall   55

    Be further done i'th'city. Aquinus hath

    Charge of the gate and walls that offer

    The first view to the enemy.

KING.   He is trusty

    And a daring soldier.--What, at stand, Gotharus?

GOTHARUS.

    I was thinking of the queen, sir, and Haraldus,   60

    And grieve for the sweet child.

KING.   Some fever.

    Would my

Son were in his state, but soon we shall

Conclude his destiny if Aquinus prosper.

But to the walls!

GOTHARUS.   I attend.--[Aside.] My very

    soul

Is in a sweat.--Hormenus.

HORMENUS.   I wait on you. Exeunt.   65

---

    59. at stand] frozen, not moving or acting (OED).

    62-63. we . . . destiny] we shall have him meet his fate,
or death.

    65. Is in a sweat] is in pains, trouble (OED).

[IV.ii]

Enter Turgesius, Olaus, Cortes, Reginaldus, [and]
    soldiers.

TURGESIUS.

    The gates are shut against us soldiers.

OLAUS.

    Let our engines tear 'em

    And batter down the walls.

TURGESIUS.   Good uncle,

    Your counsel I obey'd i'th' wars abroad.

    We did there fight for honor, and might use   5

    All the most horrid forms of death to fright

    Our enemies, and cut our way to victory;

    But give me leave to tell you, sir, at home

    Our conquest will be loss, and every wound

    We give our country is a crimson tear   10

    From our own heart. They are a viperous brood,

    Gnaw through the bowels of their parent; I

    Will rather die without a monument

    Than have it bear my name to have defaced

    One heap of stones.

IV.ii] Gifford.

0.1 S.D. and] Gifford.

    11-12. They . . . parent] see the note to III.iii.33-35.

    15. stones] stones of his city.

Enter [above,] on the walls, Gotharus, Hormenus

    [and] Aquinus.

CORTES.   Gotharus! On the walls!   15

OLAUS.

Hormenus and Aquinus! Now a speech

And 'twere at gallows, would become him better.

GOTHARUS.

Thus from my master to the Prince of Norway:

We did expect and had prepar'd to meet

Your victory with triumphs, and with garlands   20

Due to your fate and valors entertain'd you.

Nor has your army sacrific'd so many

Warm drops of blood as we have shot up prayers

That you might prosper and return the pledge

15. S.D. and] Gifford.

---

17. And 'twere] Though the meaning of the phrase is an 'twere or if 'twere, And 'twere is probably not a misprint, for that construction was quite proper in seventeenth-century English. See Abbott, p. 73.

20. triumphs] "a public festivity or joyful celebration" (OED).

21. fate] Possibly fate is a misprint for fame, but the former is retained as meaning "what the gods have done for you" while valors, two words later, refers to "what you have done for yourself." In short, Gotharus says that they would liked to have celebrated Turgesius' good fortune and bravery.

24. pledge] This word functions as a predicate nominative referring to Turgesius, not as a direct object, the result of Turgesius' action. Thus, pledge means security, and Gotharus' statement reads: "We prayed that you might prosper and return as the security for the nation's hope and glory." It is possible that pledge means "token" or "sign of favor" (OED). The statement, however, would still read essentially the same.

Of all our hope and glory. But when pride   25

Of your own fames and conquest in a war

Hath poison'd the obedience of a son,

And tempted you to advance your sword, new

  bath'd

In enemies' blood, 'gainst your country's bosom,

Thus, we receive you and declare your piety   30

And faith lost to your country and your father.

TURGESIUS.

My lord, all this concerns not me. We have

But done our duties and return to lay

The trophies at his feet whose justice did

Make us victorious more than our own valor;   35

And now, without all titles but his son,

I dare hell's accusation to blast

My humble thoughts.

GOTHARUS.   Sir, give us leave to fear,

Not your own nature, calm as the soft air

When no rude wind conspires a mutiny,--   40

OLAUS.

Leave rhetoric, and to'th'point. Why do not

The gates spread to receive us, and your joys

---

37. blast] discredit (OED)

38. give us leave] permit us.

38-40. Sir . . . mutiny] This is the first of several statements by Gotharus in which he implies that Olaus is responsible for inciting Turgesius to disloyal actions. Olaus is not insensitive to the implications.

Shoot up in acclamation? I would have

Thy house give good example to the city,

And make us the first-born fire.

GOTHARUS.   Good heaven knows 45

How willingly I would sacrifice myself

To do a grateful service to the prince,

And I could wish, my lord, you were less

   passionate,

And not inflame his highness' gentle spirit

To these attempts.

TURGESIUS.   I am ignorant, Gotharus,   50

Of what you mean. Where is the king, my father?

AQUINUS.

Where a sad father is, to know his son

Brings arms against his life.

TURGESIUS.   How now, Aquinus?

OLAUS.

Dare you be saucy?--Oh, that gentleman

Is angry; his head aches with the remembrance   55

---

53. Brings] Bring Q.

---

45. first-born fire] Gifford changes this to "first
bonfire" probably because bonfires were used in public cele-
brations, especially in connection with a victory. There is
little doubt that the fire to which Olaus refers is a bonfire in the sense just described, but there is no need to
amend the phrase; first-born is an appealing expression for
first-built, or first-created and is metrically more satisfactory than first-bonfire.

47. grateful] "pleasing" (Huberman, p. 248).

Of my truncheon.

AQUINUS.   'Twas a valiant act,

And did become the greatness of Olaus

Who, by the privilege of his birth, may do

A wrong and boast it.

OLAUS [to Turgesius].   Shall these grooms affront

us?

TURGESIUS [to Aquinus].

Have you commission to be thus insolent?--[To

Olaus.]   60

They do not know us.

GOTHARUS.   Yes, and in our hearts

Bleed that our fears of your unjust demands

Compel us to this separation.

TURGESIUS.

Demands? Is it injustice for a son

To ask his father's blessing? By thy duty,   65

Gotharus, I command thee, tell my father

His son desires access; let me but speak with him.

GOTHARUS.

I have not in your absence, sir, neglected,

What did become my service to your highness,

58.   Who] Q and O (corrected); Woh Q (uncorrected).

62.   demands] Gifford; demand Q.

---

56.   truncheon] a staff, cudgel.

59.   grooms] a contemptuous term, meaning literally "servants."

    To take his anger off.

TURGESIUS.   What riddle's this?   70
GOTHARUS.

    But let me with a pardon tell your grace,

    The letters you sent were not so dutiful;

    You were to blame to chide and article

    So with a king and father. Yet, I said,

    And pawn'd my conscience, 'twas no act of yours,   75

    I mean entire, but wrought and form'd by some

    Rash spirits to corrupt you with ambition,

    Feeding your youth with thought of hasty empire

    To serve their ends, whose counsel all this
        while

    Did starve that sweetness in you we all hop'd
        for.   80
OLAUS.

    Devices! More devices!

TURGESIUS.   I am amaz'd,

    And if the king will not vouchsafe me conference,

    I shall accuse thy cunning to have poison'd

    My father's good opinion.

                    Enter King [above].

_____

    70. To take his anger off] to reduce his anger.

    73. article] "bring charges against" (OED).

     75. pawn'd my conscience] risked telling my innermost
thoughts.

    81. Devices] tricks.

GOTHARUS.

    May thus be stain'd;--[To the king.] Pray, let

       your justice clear me.   85

KING.

    What would our son?

TURGESIUS.   Thus pay his filial duty.

KING.

    'Tis but counterfeit. If you bring no thought

    To force our blessing in this rude manner,

    How dare you approach? Dismiss your soldiers.

OLAUS.

    Not the meanest knapsack;   90

    That were a way to bring us to the mercy

    Of wolves indeed; Gotharus grinds his teeth

    Already at us.

KING [to Olaus]. We shall talk with you, sir,

    Hereafter.--[To Turgesius.] I command thee, by

      thy duty

    Thou ow'st a father and a king, dismiss   95

    Your troops.

TURGESIUS.   I will.

OLAUS.   You shall not; that were fine

---

    88. in . . . manner] with force of arms. Turgesius
has come to the city gates with his army, an act easily
understood by an objective person, for the prince and his
army are returning from battle. But to the king, whose
judgment has been impaired by Gotharus' treachery, Turgesius comes in armed revolt.

    90. meanest] least.

So we may run our heads into their noose.

You give away your safety.

TURGESIUS.   I will not

Dispute my power. Let my entreat prevail

For their dismission.

OLAUS.   You may dismiss   100

Your head and mine and be laugh'd at; these men

Are honest and dare fight for us.

TURGESIUS.   I know

Their love and will reward it, dear, dear uncle

[Speaks with the soldiers.]

GOTHARUS [aside to Aquinus].

How he prepares his tragedy, Aquinus.

Let not thy hand shake.

AQUINUS [aside to Gotharus]. I am resolute.   105

GOTHARUS.

And I, for thy reward. [Exeunt soldiers.]--'Tis

done, the soldiers

Disperse already.

OLAUS [to Turgesius]. If any mischief

103.   love] loves Q.

103.   reward] Gifford; rewa Q.

106.   S.D. Exeunt soldiers.] Gifford.

---

99.   entreat] request.

106.   And . . . reward] "There is a double meaning here.
Gotharus was planning to 'reward' Aquinus by killing him.
Cf. 1[1. 129-130 below]" (Huberman, p. 250).

Follow this, thank your credulity.

TURGESIUS [to the king].

May I now hope for access?

KING.

Descend, Gotharus and Aquinus,   110

To meet the prince; while he contains within

The piety of a son, we shall embrace him.

[Exeunt King, Gotharus, Hormenus, and Aquinus.]

TURGESIUS.

When I degenerate, let me be accurst

By heaven and you.

OLAUS [to Turgesius]. Are you not pale to think on't?

TURGESIUS [to Olaus].

It puzzles me to think my father guilty.   115

OLAUS.

I do not like things yet.

As the prince is going forth, a pistol is discharged

within; he falls.

TURGESIUS.

Oh, I am shot; I am murder'd!

[Enter Aquinus, below.]

117. S.D. Enter Aquinus, below.] Enter Aquinus, Gifford,
but after yet, l. 116.

---

113. degenerate] "fall away, revolt" (OED).

114. pale] fearful (OED).

115. It . . . me] I cannot believe.

OLAUS [to Aquinus].

    Inhuman traitor, villain!

                        Olaus wounds Aquinus.

    [Enter Gotharus, below.]

GOTHARUS [aside].

    So, so, his hand has saved my execution;

    'Tis not safe for me to stay. They are both sped

      rarely.   120

           Exit.

[Enter the king, below.]

OLAUS.

    Oh, my dear cousin; treason, treason.

KING.   Where?

OLAUS.

    In thy own bosom; thou hast kill'd thy son.

    --[To Reginaldus and Cortes.] Convey his body,

      guard it safe, and this

    Perfidious trunk, I'll have it punish'd

    Past death and scatter his torn flesh about   125

    The world to affright mankind.--[To the king.]

118. S.D. Enter Gotharus, below.] Gifford, but after yet,
1. 116.

126. S.D. To the king.] Gifford, but after art.

---

    119. execution] carrying out of the plot to kill
Aquinus.

    120. sped] killed (OED).

    121. cousin] nephew.

    124. trunk] Aquinus' body.

                                        Thou art

A murderer, no blood of mine.

    [Exeunt, <u>all</u> <u>save</u> <u>the</u> <u>king</u>, <u>bearing</u> <u>the</u> <u>bodies</u>.

       <u>Enter</u> Gotharus, <u>above</u>.]

GOTHARUS [<u>aside</u>].   'Tis done,

    And all the guilt dies with Aquinus, fall'n

    By Olaus' sword most happily, who but

    Prevented mine. This act concludes all fear.   130

KING.

    He was my son; I must needs drop a tear. <u>Exeunt</u>.

[IV.iii]

Haraldus, <u>discovered</u> <u>sick</u>, Marpisa, <u>physicians</u>[, <u>and</u>

    <u>officers</u>].

MARPISA.

    It is not possible he catch a fever

127. S.D. <u>Exeunt</u> . . . <u>bodies</u>.] <u>Exeunt</u>, <u>bearing</u> <u>the</u> <u>bodies</u>,
<u>Gifford</u>.

127. S.D. <u>Enter</u> Gotharus, <u>above</u>.] <u>Gifford</u>, <u>except</u> <u>Re-enter</u>.

[IV.iii]

0.1. S.D. <u>physicians</u>] <u>Gifford</u>; <u>Doctors</u> Q.

---

    130. <u>This</u> . . . <u>fear</u>] The killing of Aquinus, so Go-
tharus believes, ends <u>his</u> fear of being discovered as a plot
ter (1) to kill Turgesius, and (2) to gain the throne through
Haraldus.

[IV.iii]

    0.1. S.D. <u>discovered</u>] "The original [stage] direction
clearly calls for the use of the inner stage" (Huberman,
p. 251). See the note to 129 S.D. of this scene.

By excess of wine. He was all temperance.

[1 PHYSICIAN].

He had a soft and tender constitution,

Apt to be inflam'd. They that are most abstemious

Feel the disorder with more violence.   5

MARPISA.

Where? Who assisted him in this misfortune?

He had some company.

[2 PHYSICIAN].   He was invited,

He says, by Sueno and Helga to a banquet,

Where in their mirth they, careless of his health,

Suffered him drink too much.

MARPISA.   They poison'd him.   10

--[To officers.] Go apprehend the murders of

   my child.

                          [Exeunt officers.]

If he recover not, their deaths shall wait

Upon Haraldus.--But pray you, tell me gentlemen,

Is there no hope of life? Have you not art

Enough to cure a fever?

3. S.P. 1 Physician] Gifford; Do. Q.

7. S.P. 2 Physician] Gifford; Do. Q.

12. deaths] death Q.

12-13. wait / Upon] accompany, escort (OED).

[1 PHYSICIAN].   We find, madam   15

    His disease more malignant by some thought

    Or apprehensions of grief.

MARPISA.   What grief?

    Y'are all impostors and are ignorant

    But how to kill.

HARALDUS.   Is not my mother come?

MARPISA.

    Yes, my dear son, and here shall weep myself   20

    Till I turn Niobe unless thou givest me

    Some hope of thy own life.

HARALDUS.   I would say something

    Were you alone.

             --Leave us.   [Exeunt physicians.]

     Now my Haraldus,

    How is it with my child?

HARALDUS.   I know you love me,

    Yet, I must tell you truth, I cannot live.   25

    And let this comfort you: death will not come

    Unwelcome to your son; I do not die

15. S.P. 1 Physician] Gifford; Do. Q.

23. S.D. Exeunt Physicians] Gifford.

---

    17. apprehensions] feelings.   18. impostors quacks

  18-19. are . . . kill] Cf. I.i.264 and V.ii.244 and the
explanatory notes accompanying them.

  20-21. Yes . . . Niobe] Niobe, at the loss of her children, turned to stone with grief.

Against my will, and having my desires

You have less cause to mourn.

MARPISA.   What is't has made

The thought of life unpleasant, which does court   30

Thy dwelling here with all delights that nature

And art can study for thee, rich in all things

Thy wish can be ambitious of. Yet all

These treasures nothing to thy mother's love

Which to enjoy thee would defer a while   35

Her thought of going to heaven.

HARALDUS.

Oh, take heed, mother; heaven

Has a spacious ear and power to punish

Your too much love with my eternal absence.

I bet your prayers and blessing.

MARPISA.   Th'art dejected.   40

Have but a will and live.

HARALDUS.   'Tis in vain, Mother.

MARPISA.

Sink, with a fever, into earth? Look up;

Thou shalt not die.

HARALDUS.   I have a wound within

---

32. art] artifice.

32. study] devise (OED).

35. Which] who, referring to Marpisa rather than her
love. See Abbott, p. 181.

37-39. Oh . . . absence] another reference to the Niobe
myth.

You do not see, more killing than all fevers.

MARPISA.

A wound? Where? Who has murder'd thee?

HARALDUS.   Gotharus-- 45

MARPISA.

Ha! Furies persecute him.

HARALDUS.   Oh, pray for him!

'Tis my duty though he gave me death;

He is my father.

MARPISA.   How? Thy father?

HARALDUS.

He told me so, and with that breath destroy'd me;

I felt it strike upon my spirits. Mother,   50

Would I had ne'er been born!

MARPISA.   Believe him not.

HARALDUS.

Oh, do not add another sin to what

Is done already. Death is charitable

To quit me from the scorn of all the world.

MARPISA.

By all my hopes, Gotharus has abus'd thee;   55

Thou art the lawful burden of my womb;

---

50. spirits] (1) feelings and sensibilities (OED), and
(2) the vital spirits; i.e., "the operation of the vital
functions" (OED).

54. to quit] to release, deliver (OED).

55. abus'd] wronged, deceived (OED).

Thy father, Altomarus,--

HARALDUS.   Ha!

MARPISA.

--Before whose spirit long since taken up

To meet with saints and troops angelical,

I dare again repeat: thou art his son.   60

HARALDUS.

Ten thousand blessings now reward my mother.

Speak it again and I may live. A stream

Of pious joy runs through me; to my soul

Y'ave struck a harmony next that in heaven.

Can you, without a blush, call me your child   65

And son of Altomarus? All that's holy

Dwell in your blood forever; speak it once,

But once again.

MARPISA.   Here it my latest breath,

Thou art his and mine.

[HARALDUS.]   Enough, my tears do flow

To give you thanks for't. I would you could

    resolve me   70

---

69. S.P. Haraldus.] Lamb; no S.P. in Q.

---

63. pious] "Faithful to the duties naturally owed to
parents . . . characterized by loyal affections, esp. to
parents" (OED).

64. Y'ave . . . heaven] In the old cosmology, the per-
fection and order of the universe were reflected in the har-
monious music of the spheres. Possibly, Haraldus is also
referring to the proverbial singing of the choir of angels.

68. latest] last.

But one truth more: why did my lord, Gotharus,

Call me the issue of his blood?

MARPISA.

Alas, he thinks thou art--

HARALDUS.   What are those words?

I am undone again.

MARPISA.   Ha!

HARALDUS.   'Tis too late

To call 'em back; he thinks I am his son.   75

MARPISA [aside].

I have confess'd too much and tremble with

The imagination.--Forgive me, child,

And heaven, if there be a mercy to a crime

So black as I must now, to quit thy fears,

Say I have been guilty of. We have been sinful,   80

And I was not unwilling to oblige

His active brain for thy advancement by

Abusing his belief thou wert his own.

But thou hast no such stain; thy birth is

   innocent,

Or may I perish ever. 'Tis a strange   85

Confession to a child, but it may drop

76.   S.D. aside.] Gifford.

_____

77.   imagination] the picture he must imagine.

82.   active brain] plotting mind.

83.   abusing] deceiving.

A balsam to thy wound. Live, my Haraldus;

If not for this, to see my penitence

And with what tears I'll wash away my sin.

HARALDUS.

I am no bastard, then.

MARPISA.   Thou art not.   90

HARALDUS.

But I am not found while you are lost;

No time can restore you. My spirits faint.

MARPISA.

Will nothing comfort thee?

HARALDUS.

My duty to the king.

<u>Enter</u> King

MARPISA.   He's here.

KING.

How is't, Haraldus?--[<u>Aside</u> <u>to</u> Marpisa.] Death

    sits in's face.   95

HARALDUS.

Give me your blessing and within my heart

94.   S.D. <u>Enter</u> King.] <u>after</u> here Q.

96.   your] <u>Lamb</u>; you Q.

---

87.   <u>balsam</u>] a healing agent.

94.   <u>My</u> . . . <u>king</u>] This statement seems irrelevant to
the conversation and may have been introduced by Shirley to
contrast the loyalty of Haraldus, at this critical point,
with the disloyalty of his mother and Gotharus. It relates
to the entrance of the king and perhaps has no other function than to create a continuity in the action.

I'll pray you may have many. My soul flies

'Bove this vain world.--Good Mother, close mine

    eyes.

               [<u>Dies</u>.]

MARPISA.

    Never died so much sweetness in his years.

KING.

    Be comforted; I have lost my son, too;   100

    The prince is slain.

               <u>Enter</u> <u>officers</u> <u>with</u> Helga[, <u>drunk</u>].

                   --How now?

MARPISA.

    Justice upon the murderer of my son!

    This villain, Helga, and his companion,

    Sueno, have kill'd him.--Where's the other?

OFFICER.   Fled,

    Madam, but Helga does confess he made him drunk, 105

---

98. S.D. <u>Dies</u>.] <u>Gifford</u>.

---

    98. S.D. <u>Dies</u>] Haraldus' death is brought on by a fev-
er contracted through excessive drinking and complicated by
melancholy. This process of deterioration was easily accepted by Shirley's audience. According to Philip Barrough
in his seventeenth-century book on diseases and their cures,
melancholy by itself could cause a fever. Philip Barrough,
<u>The</u> <u>Method</u> <u>of</u> <u>Physick</u>, <u>Containing</u> <u>the</u> <u>Causes</u>, <u>Signes</u> <u>and</u>
<u>Cures</u> <u>of</u> <u>inward</u> <u>diseases</u> <u>in</u> <u>man's</u> <u>body</u>, <u>from</u> <u>the</u> <u>head</u> <u>to</u> <u>the</u>
<u>foote</u> (London: George Miller, 1634), p. 117.

    101. S.D. <u>drunk</u>] Only drunkenness would explain Helga's
imprudent statements in the following exchange. Helga is
no fool when it comes to saying the right thing to the king
and queen; thus, his ill-advised comments demand some explanation. Furthermore, he says in 1. 111 "I left no drink behind me."

HELGA.

But not dead drunk.--I do beseech you, madam,--

KING.

Look here what your base surfeit has destroy'd.

HELGA.

'Twas Sueno as well as I. My lord, Gotharus,

Gave us commission for what we did.

MARPISA [aside.]

Again, Gotharus; sure he plotted this.   110

KING.

Hang him up straight.

HELGA.   I left no drink behind me;

If I must die, let me have equal justice

And let one of your guard drink me to death, sir.

Of, if you please to let me live till

Sueno is taken, we will drink and reel   115

Out of the world together.

KING.   Hence, and hang him.

Exeunt [officers with

Helga].

Enter Hormenus.

HORMENUS.

Sir, you must make provision against

New danger; discontent is broke into

A wild rebellion and many of your subjects

116. S.D. officers with Helga.] Gifford.

Gather in tumults and give out they will   120

Revenge the prince's death.

KING.   This I did fear.

Where's Gotharus? Oh, my fright; my conscience

Has furies in't. Where's Gotharus?

HORMENUS.

Not in the court.

KING.   I tremble with confusions.

Ex[eunt King and Hormenus].

MARPISA.

I am resolv'd; my joys are all expir'd;   125

Nor can ambition more concern me now.

Gotharus has undone me in the death

Of my loved son; his fate is next. While I

Move resolute, I'll command his destiny. Exit.

124. S.D. Exeunt King and Helga.] Gifford; Exit. Q.

---

120. tumults] "a disorderly crowd, a mob" (OED).

122-123. Oh . . . in't] Oh, the terror; my mind is disturbed by fears.

125. am resolv'd] have decided.

128. fate] death.

128-129. While . . . destiny] As long as I remain resolute, I will be in control of his fate.

129. S.D. Exit] With Marpisa's exit the departure of
each character in this scene is accounted for, save one.
Haraldus' body remains on the stage, but because he has been
in the inner stage, the curtain to that stage could easily
be closed, obscuring his body.

[IV.iv]

<u>Enter</u> Gotharus.

[GOTHARUS].

How are we lost; the Prince Turgesius' death

Is of no use since 'tis unprofitable

To the great hope we stored up in Haraldus.

It was a cursed plot directed me

To raise his spirit by those giddy engines   5

That have undone him; their souls reel to hell

   for't.

How will Marpisa weep herself into

The obscure shades and leave me here to grow

A statue with the wonder of our fate.

                                        <u>Enter</u> Albina.

ALBINA.

   Sir.

GOTHARUS. Do not trouble me.

ALBINA.   Although   10

---

1. S.P. <u>Gotharus</u>] <u>Gifford</u>; <u>Ho.</u> Q.

1.   <u>How</u> . . . <u>lost</u>] an exclamation, not a question.

5.   <u>giddy engines</u>] foolish instruments; <u>i.e.</u>, Sueno and Helga.

7-9.   <u>How</u> . . . <u>fate</u>] An echo, with variations, of the Niobe myth. Cf. IV.iii.20-21 and 37-39.

8.   <u>obscure</u>] dark, gloomy (<u>OED</u>).

8.   <u>shades</u>] "the darkness of the nether world, the abode of the dead, Hades" (<u>OED</u>).

9.   <u>wonder</u>] "great distress of grief" (<u>OED</u>).

I am not partner of your joys or comfort,

Yet let your cruelty be so mindful of me,

I may divide your sorrows.

GOTHARUS.   Would thy sufferings

Could ease me of the weight, I would

Empty my heart of all that's ill to sink thee   15

And bury thee alive. Thy sight is hateful;

Ask me not why, but in obedience

Fly hence into some wilderness.

> Enter Marpisa.
>
> --The queen.
>
> Exit Albina.

GOTHARUS.

Great queen, did any sorrow lade my boson

But what does almost melt it for Haraldus,   20

Your presence would revive me. But it seems

Our hopes and joys in him grew up so mighty,

Heaven became jealous we should undervalue

The bliss of th'other world and build in him

A richer paradise.

18.   S.D. Enter Marpisa.] after queen Q.

18.   S.D. Exit Albina.] after Enter Marpisa. Q.

---

13.   divide] share.

19.   lade] laden.

21.   Your . . . me] For another reference by Gotharus
to Marpisa's life-giving powers, see I.i.310-314.

21-24. But . . . paradise] Perhaps another variation on
the Niobe myth. Cf. IV.iii.20-21 and 37-39, and IV.iv.7-9.

MARPISA.   I have mourn'd already   25

    A mother's part, and fearing thy excess

    Of grief, present myself to comfort thee.

    Tears will not call him back, and 'twill become

       us,

    Since we two are the world unto ourselves,

    Nothing without the circle of our arms,   30

    Precious and welcome, to take heed our grief

    Make us not oversoon like him that's dead

    And our blood useless.

GOTHARUS.   Were you present, madam,

    When your son died?

MARPISA.   I was.

GOTHARUS.   And did you weep

    And wish him live; and would not heaven, at   35

    Your wish, return your wandering ghost again?

    Your voice should make another out of atoms;

    I do adore the harmony, and from

    One pleasant look, draw in more blessings

32. that's] <u>Gifford</u>; that Q.

---

30. <u>without</u>] outside.

37. <u>atoms</u>] small particles of matter. The entire statement, <u>Your voice should make another out of atoms</u>, can be compared with Gotharus' earlier statement about the Promethean fire in Marpisa's eyes that has life-giving powers. See I.i.310-314.

38. <u>harmony</u>] the sound of her voice.

39. <u>look</u>] (1) a look from Marpisa, or (2) a look on Marpisa.

Than death knows how to kill.   40

MARPISA [aside].

He is recovered from his passion.

GOTHARUS.

What's this? Ha!

MARPISA.   Where?

GOTHARUS.   Here, like a sudden
winter

Struck on my heart. I am not well o'th sudden,
ha!

MARPISA.

My lord, make use of this; 'tis cordial.

Gives him a box of poison.

I am often subject to these passions   45
And dare not walk without this ivory box
To prevent danger. They are pleasant;
'Tis a most happy opportunity.

GOTHARUS.

Let me present my thanks to my preserver

41. S.D. aside.] Gifford.

---

41. passion] grief.

44. cordial] "A medicine . . . which invigorates the
heart and stimulates the circulation" (OED).

45. passions] attacks of illness.

48. 'Tis . . . opportunity] i.e., it is a very nice
coincidence that I happened to have the medicine with me.
The statement, of course, is heavily ironic.

Enter Albina.

And kiss your hand.

MARPISA.   Our lips will meet more

   lovingly.   50

ALBINA [aside].

   My heart will break.

MARPISA [to Gotharus]. Your lady; we are betray'd.

   She sees us kiss, and I shall hate her for't.

GOTHARUS [to Albina].

   Does this offend your virtue?

ALBINA.   Y'are merciless!

   You shall be a less tyrant, sir, to kill me.--

   Injurious queen!

MARPISA.   Shall I be here affronted?   55

   I shall not think Gotharus worth my love

   To let her breathe forth my dishonor which

   Her passion hath already dared to publish;

   Nor wanted she before an impudence

   To throw this poison in my face.

GOTHARUS.   I'll tame her.   60

    Exit.

52. sees] Huberman; see Q.

57. breathe] Gifford; breath Q.

---

   51. betray'd] exposed.

   58. passion] anger, hatred (OED)

   60. poison] accusations dishonoring Marpisa, a timely
metaphor.

ALBINA.

    I wo'not curse you, madam, but you are

    The cruel'st of all womankind. I am

    Prepared to meet your tyrannies.

       Enter Gotharus with a pistol; at the other door,

          a servant.

SERVANT.   My lord,

    We are undone; the common people are

    In arms and violently assault our house,   65

    Threat'ning your lordship with a thousand deaths

    For the good prince, whose murder they exclaim

    Contriv'd by you.

GOTHARUS.   The fiends of hell will show

    More mercy to me. Where shall I hide me?

MARPISA.

    Alas, they'll kill me too.   [Exit.]

SERVANT.   There's no staying;   70

    They have broke the wall of the first court.

    Down at some window, sir.

       [Gotharus drops] the pistol; Albina takes

        [it] up.

70. S.D. Exit.] Gifford.

72. S.D. Gotharus drops the pistol; Albina takes it up.]
Goth. drops the pistol, which Albina takes up. Gifford;
Albina takes up the Pistoll. Q.

---

    63. tyrannies] outrages, violences (OED)

    67. exclaim] exclaim was.

GOTHARUS.   Help me!

    Oh, help me; I'm lost. [_Exeunt_ Gotharus _and_

      servant.]

[REBELS] (_within_).   Down with the doors.

    This way, this way.

              Enter _rebels_.

ALBINA.   He that first moves this way

    Comes on his death; I can dispatch but one,   75

    And take your choice.

1 [REBEL].   Alas, good madam,

    We do not come to trouble you;

    You have sorrow enough. We would talk

    With my lord, your pagan husband.

2 [REBEL].

    Aye, Aye. Where is he?

3 [REBEL].   That traitor.   80

4 [REBEL].

    Murderer of our prince.

73. I'm] i'me Q _and_ O (_corrected_); i'me Q (_uncorrected_).

76. passim. S.P. 1 Rebel] Gifford; 1. Q. Whenever it is
omitted from Q, Gifford adds the word "Rebel" to the subsequent speech prefixes throughout the text.

80. Aye, Aye] Gifford; I, I Q.

---

    75. I . . . one] it is a one-shot pistol, the only
kind in the seventeenth-century.

    76. And] The word And is used emphatically here. See
Abbott, p. 71.

    79. pagan] heathenish, ungodly (OED).

ALBINA.   Y'are not well-informed;

Aquinus kill'd the prince.

2 [REBEL].

But by my lord's correction.

We know his heart and do mean to eat it;

Therefore, let him appear.--Knock down the lady   85

You with the long bill.

ALBINA.

How dare you run the hazard of your lives

And fortunes, thus, like outlaws, without

Authority to break into our houses.

When you have done, what fury leads you to't,   90

You will buy too dear repentance at the gallows.

2 [REBEL].

Hang the gallows and give us my lord, your

husband.

                    Enter servant.

SERVANT.

He's escap'd, madam; now they may search.

                    Enter more rebels.

ALBINA.

But where's the queen? She must not be betray'd.

---

83. correction] control, governance (OED).

84. We . . . heart] We know what he is really like.
Heart means "one's inmost being, character" (OED).

86. long bill] a halberd, a weapon in which an ax-
spear combination was attached to a long staff.

1 [REBEL].

    This way, this way; he got out of a window   95

    And leap'd a wall. Follow, follow.

                  [Exeunt rebels.]

[REBELS] (within).

    Follow, follow, follow.

ALBINA.   Oh, my poor Gotharus.

               [Enter Marpisa.]

    --Madam, you are secure. Though you pursued

    My death, I wish you safety.

MARPISA.   I have been

    Too cruel, but my fate compel'd me to't. Exit.   100

ALBINA.

    I am become the extremest of all

    Miseries. Oh, my unhappy lord. Ex[eunt Albina

       and servant].

[IV.v]

Enter Sueno, [disguised]

96. S.D. Exeunt rebels.] Gifford.

97. S.D. Enter Marpisa.] Gifford.

[IV.v]

0.1. S.D. disguised] Gifford. Huberman comments on Gifford's
emendation: "I can see no indication in the lines following,
however, that Sueno is not wearing his ordinary clothes."
Whatever clothes Sueno is wearing, it is clear that he has
on a false beard (1. 14.), and, therefore, is disguised.

---

    96. Follow, follow] "A hunting cry . . . . The pur-
suit of Gotharus by the rebels seems likened to a hunting
party, with hounds chasing their prey. 'Follow, follow' is
frequently repeated" (Huberman, p. 257).

SUENO.

Helga is hanged. What will become of me?

I think I best turn rebel; there's no hope

To walk without a guard, and that I shall not

Want to the gallows; heathen halbediers

Are used to have a care and do rejoice   5

To see men have good ends.

                Enter Gotharus.

GOTHARUS.   I am pursued.

SUENO [aside].

My lord, Gotharus? Worse and worse.

Oh, for a mist before his eyes.

GOTHARUS [attacking Sueno].

You sha'not betray me, sir.

SUENO.

Hold, my lord; I am your servant, honest Sueno.   10

GOTHARUS.

Sueno! Off with that case; it may secure me.

---

3.   that] a guard.   4.   Want] lack.

4.   halbediers] soldiers armed with halberds. In this case, those who accompany a condemned person to the gallows and who may also perform the execution.

5.   Are . . . care] take care in their work.

8.   Oh . . . eves] To cast a mist before one's eyes is proverbial, meaning to deceive one, to blind him from reality. Tilley, p. 466 (M1017). Sueno does not want the politician to recognize him, a wish he shortly repents when he discovers that he is in more danger unrecognized.

11.   case] clothes.

Quickly, or--

SUENO.   Oh, my lord, you shall command my

skin.

Alas, poor gentleman, I'm glad I have it

To do your lordship service.

GOTHARUS.   Nay, your beard,

too!

SUENO.

Yes, yes, anything. [They exchange clothes.] Alas,

my good lord   15

How comes this?

GOTHARUS.   Leave your untimely prating, help.

You'll not betray me?

SUENO.   I'll first be hanged.

[REBELS] (within).

Follow, follow.

GOTHARUS.

Hell stop their throats. So, so.--Now thy reward.

SUENO.

It was my duty; troth, sir, I will have nothing.   20

GOTHARUS.

Yes.

Wounds him.

Take that,

[Wounds him again.]

21. S.D. Wounds him.] after Haraldus Q.

and that for killing Haraldus.

Now I'm sure you will not prate.

SUENO.   Oh, murder!

[REBELS] (within).

Follow, follow.

GOTHARUS.

I cannot 'scape. Oh, help invention.

He bloodies himself with Sueno's blood, and falls down
as dead.

Enter rebels.

1 REBEL .

This way they say he went. [Discovering Gotharus
    disguised.]

What's he?   25

2 [REBEL].

One of our company, I think.

3 [REBEL].

Who kill'd him?

4 [REBEL].   I know not.

2 [REBEL].   Let's away.

If we can find that traitor, he shall pay for all.

4 [REBEL].

Oh, that I had him here, I'd teach him--

2 [REBEL].

---

24. invention] inventiveness, or a scheme, a plan (OED).

25. What's he] who's he? See Abbott, pp. 173-174 on
the use of what for who in the seventeenth-century.

        This way, this way.

SUENO.   Oh--

3 [REBEL].   Stay, there's one groans.   30

SUENO.

      Oh--

2 [REBEL]. Nay, 'twas here abouts. Another dead?

4 [REBEL].

      He has good clothes. Gotharus! The very cur!

3 [REBEL].

      'Tis Gotharus! I have seen the dog.

2 [REBEL].

      'Tis he, 'tis he.

SUENO.   Oh--   Exit Gotharus.

2 [REBEL].   Now, 'tis not he.--

      If thou canst speak, my friend,--

SUENO.   Gotharus murdered

          me   35

      And shifted clothes. He cannot be far off. Oh--

                                          [Dies.]

1 [REBEL].

      That's he that lies dead yonder.

      Oh, that he were alive again that we

      Might kill him one after another.

3 [REBEL].

      He's gone.

      _____

      30. one groans] one who groans.

2 [REBEL].   The devil he is. Follow, follow.   40

3 [REBEL].

    This way, he cannot 'scape us.--[To Sueno.]

      Farewell, friend.

    I'll do thee a courtesy.--Follow, follow.

                  Ex[eunt rebels].

[IV.vi]

Enter Olaus, Turgesius, [disguised,] Aquinus[, and

    Cortes].

OLAUS [to Turgesius].

42. S.D. Exeunt rebels] Gifford; Exit. Q.

[IV.vi]

0.1. S.D. and Cortes] Gifford.

    41-42. Farewell . . . follow] It is not perfectly
clear as to what actually occurs here. It is apparent that
Sueno has received a mortal wound from Gotharus and as the
toady does not appear in the play again, it is obvious that
he dies. In order to make this fact clear to the audience,
it is likely that he dies in this scene; thus, the stage
direction emendation at l. 36. Just what the third rebel
does to Sueno (and it is difficult to account for another
"friend"; see the second rebel's reference to Sueno as
"friend" in l. 35.) is unclear. Perhaps, the last courtesy
is to carry off Sueno's body (the body needs to be removed)
or perhaps he respectfully covers the dead courtier's face.
Huberman apparently believes the rebel's statement refers
to avenging Sueno's murder: "The thoughtless rebel seems to
forget that Sueno will probably be dead before this promise
can be fulfilled" (p. 259).

So, so, in this disguise you may to'th 'army

Who, though they seem to scatter, are to meet

By my directions.--Honest Aquinus,

You wait on the prince.--[To Turgesius.] But sir--

    Whispers.

CORTES [to Aquinus].

Were you not wounded?

AQUINUS.   I prepared a   5

Privy coat, for that I knew Gotharus

Would have been too busy with my flesh else.

But he thinks I'm slain by the duke and hugs

His fortune in't.

TURGESIUS [to Olaus]. You'll follow.

OLAUS.

And bring you news. Perhaps the rabble are   10

In hot pursuit after the politician.

He cannot 'scape them; they'll tear him like so

Many hungry mastiffs.

TURGESIUS.   I could wish they had him.

OLAUS.

Lose no time.

3. Aquinus] Gifford; Aquinus you Q.

---

    1. you] To whom you refers is not completely clear.
Very probably Olaus is referring to the prince, for their
plans would be disturbed if the populace were to discover
the prince alive (see ll. 23-24 below). There is evidence
that Turgesius is disguised in a later scene (see V.i.33-38).
Thus, the emendation to 0.1 is made.

    6. Privy coat] "a coat of mail worn under the ordinary
dress" (OED).

Ex[eunt Turgesius and Aquinus].

--Cortes, stay you with me.

Not that I think my house will want your guard.   15

CORTES.

Command me, sir.

OLAUS.   Was ever such a practise.

By a father to take away his son's life?

[CORTES.]

I would hope he may not be so guilty,

Yet I know not how his false terrors,

Multiplied by the art of this Gotharus,   20

May prevail upon him and win consent.

OLAUS.

Aquinus has been faithful

And deceived all their treasons, but the prince

Is still thought dead. This empty coffin shall

Confirm the people in his funeral,   25

To keep their thoughts revengeful.

[REBELS] (within).   Follow, follow.

Till we are posses'd of him that plotted all.

CORTES.

14. S.D. Exeunt Turgesius and Aquinus] Gifford; Exit. Q.

18. S.P. Cortes] Gifford; Pr. Q.

---

15. want] lack.

23. deceived] frustrated, disappointed (OED).

25. Confirm . . . funeral] convince the people of his
death.

The cry draws this way; they are excellent

   bloodhounds.

                        Enter Gotharus.

GOTHARUS.

   As you are men, defend me from the rage

   Of the devouring multitude; I have   30

   Deserv'd your anger and a death, but let not

   My limbs inhumanly be torn by them.

   Oh, save me!

[REBELS] (within).   Follow, follow.

OLAUS.   Blest occasion.

GOTHARUS.

   I am forced to take your house, and now implore

   Your mercy but to rescue me from them   35

   And be your own revenger.   Yet my life

   Is worth your preservation for a time;

   Do it, and I'll reward you with a story

   You'll not repent to know.

OLAUS.   You cannot be

   Safe here.   Their rage is high, and every door   40

   Must be left open to their violence,

32.   inhumanly] Gifford; inhumanely Q.

33.   Follow, follow] Gifford; Follow, foll-- Q.

---

   34.   to take] to take to

   40-41.   and . . . violence] The rebels must be allowed access to wherever they wish, else they will force their way.

Unless you will obscure you in this coffin,

Prepared for the sweet prince that's murder'd,

And but expects his body which is now

Embalming.

GOTHARUS.   That? Oh, y'are charitable.   45

[REBELS] (within).

Follow, follow.

GOTHARUS.

Their noise is thunder to my soul.

He goes into the coffin.

So, so.

Enter rebels.

OLAUS.

How now, gentlemen; what means this tumult?

Do you know that I possess this dwelling?

[1] REBEL.

Yes, my lord, but we were told my Lord   50

Gotharus enter'd, and we beseech you

Give him to our justice; he is the common

Enemy, and we know he killed the prince.

OLAUS.

You may search, if you please;

He can presume of small protection here.   55

46.   Follow, follow] Gifford; Follow, fol--Q.

---

42.   obscure you] hide yourself (OED).

55.   presume of] lay claim to, expect (OED).

But I much thank you for your loyalties

And service to the prince whose bloodless ruins

Are there and do but wait when it will please

His father to reverse a cruel sentence

That keeps him from a burial with his ancestors.   60

We are forbid to do him rights of funeral.

1 [REBEL].

How? Not bury him?

2 [REBEL].   Forbid to bury

Our good prince? We'll bury him

And see what priest dare not assist us.

3 [REBEL].

Not bury him? We'll do't and carry   65

His body in triumph through the city

And see him laid i'th' great tombs.

1 [REBEL].

Not bury our prince? That were a jest, indeed.

CORTES [to Olaus].

'Tis their love and duty.

2 [REBEL].   We'll pull the church

down,

But we'll have our will.

3 [REBEL].   Dear prince, how sweet he

smells.   70

1 [REBEL].

Come, countrymen, march, and see

Who dares take his body from us.

CORTES [aside to Olaus].

> You cannot help.

OLAUS [aside to Cortes].   They'll bury him alive.

CORTES.

> He's in a fright.

OLAUS.   So may all traitors thrive.

> Exeunt [rebels with the coffin, followed by Cortes
> and Olaus].

[V.i]

Enter King and Marpisa.

KING.

> Oh, I am lost and my soul bleeds to think
>
> By my own dotage upon thee.

MARPISA.   I was curst

> When I first saw thee, poor wind-shaken king.
>
> I have lost my son.

KING.   Thy honor, impious woman,

> Of more price than a son or thy own life.   5
>
> I had a son too whom my rashness sent
>
> To another world; my poor Turgesius.
>
> What sorcery of thy tongue and eyes betray'd me?

74.1 S.D. rebels with coffin, followed by Cortes and Olaus]
Gifford.

[V.i]

> 2. By] "as a consequence of." Abbott, p. 99.

MARPISA.

    I would I had been a basilisk, to have shot

    A death to thy dissembling heart when I   10

    Gave myself up thy queen. I was secure

    Till thou with the temptation of greatness

    And flattery didst poison my sweet peace.

    And shall thy base fears leave me now a prey

    To rebels?

KING.   I had been happy to have left   15

    Thee sooner, but begone! Get to some wilderness

    Peopled with serpents and engender with

    Some dragon like thyself.

MARPISA.   Ha, Ha.

KING.

    Dost laugh thou prodigy? Thou shame of woman.

MARPISA.

    Yes, and despise thee dotard. Vex till thy soul   20

    Break from thy rotten flesh; I will be merry

    At thy last groan.

---

    9. basilisk] "a fabulous reptile . . . alleged to be
hatched by a serpent from a cock's egg . . . its breath, and
even its look was fatal" (OED). For a complete contemporary
description of this legendary beast see Edward Topsell's
Historie of Serpents, 1608 in Byrne, pp. 127-132. A basilisk was also called a cockatrice (see V.ii.123).

    16-18. Get . . . thyself] The dragon echoes the basilisk
(1. 9 above) and the entire charge reminds one of Gotharus'
similar dismissal of Albina IV.iv.17-18.

    19. prodigy] monster (OED).

    20. vex] grieve.

KING.

> Oh, my poor boy, my son.
>
> His wound is printed here, that false Gotharus,
>
> Your wanton goat I fear, practis'd with thee
>
> His death.

MARPISA.   'Twas thy own act and timerous heart   25

> In hope to be secure. I glory in
>
> The mention thou murderer of thy son.

> Enter Hormenus.

HORMENUS.

> O sir, if ever, stand upon your guard.
>
> The army which you thought scattered and broke
>
> Is grown into a great and threat'ning body   30
>
> Lead by the Duke Olaus, your lov'd uncle,
>
> Is marching hither; all your subjects fly to
>
> him. Exit.

MARPISA.

> Ha, Ha!

KING.   Curse on thy spleen!

> Is this a time for laughter, when horror
>
> Should afflict thy guilty soul? Hence, mischief!   35

---

24. wanton goat] Goats were associated with lechery.
See Partridge, p. 122.

24. practis'd] worked.

33. spleen] In this case spleen means feelings of laugh-
ter and mirth as opposed to those of melancholy and peevish-
ness (OED).

35. mischief] a direct reference to Marpisa meaning
trouble, wickedness or the devil (OED).

MARPISA.

    Not to obey thee, shadow of a king,

    Am I content to leave thee, and but I wo'not

    Prevent thy greater sorrow and vexation.

    Now I would kill thee, coward!

KING.   Treason! Treason!

MARPISA.

    Aye, Aye. Who comes to your rescue?

KING.   Are all fled? 40

MARPISA.

    Slaves do it naturally.

KING.   Canst thou hope to 'scape?

MARPISA.

    I am mistress of my fate and do not fear

    Their inundation. Their army coming,

    It does prepare my triumph. They shall give

    Me liberty and punish thee to live.   45

KING.

    Undone, forsaken, miserable king.   Exeunt

    severally.

40. Aye, Aye] Gifford; I, I Q.

---

36. shadow . . . king] Cf. II.i.42.

[V.ii]

__Enter__ Turgesius, Olaus, Cortes, Aquinus, [__and__]
    __soldiers__.

TURGESIUS.

    Worthy Aquinus, I must honor thee.

    Thou has preserv'd us all; thy service will

    Deserve a greater monument than thanks.

AQUINUS.

    Thank the duke for breaking o'my pate.

OLAUS.

    I know 'twas well-bestowed, but we have now   5

    Proof of thy honest heart.

AQUINUS.   But what, with your

    Highness' favor, do you mean to do

    With your father?

TURGESIUS.   Pay my duty to him.

    He may be sensible to his cruelty

    And not repent to see me live.   10

OLAUS.

    But, with your favor, something else must be

    Considered. There's a thing he calls his queen,

0.1. S.D. __and__] __Gifford__.

---

    7. __favor__] permission.

    9. __sensible to__] aware of.

    10. __repent__] regret, be sorry.

A limb of Lucifer; she must be roasted

For the army's satisfaction.

AQUINUS.

They'll ne'er digest her;   15

The king's hounds may be kept hungry

Enough, perhaps, and make a feast upon her.

TURGESIUS.

I wonder how the rabble will bestow

The coffin.

OLAUS.   Why, they'll bury him alive,

I hope.

TURGESIUS.   Did they suppose my body there?   20

OLAUS.

I'm sorry; he will fare so much the better.

I would the queen was there to comfort him;

Oh, they would smell and sweat together rarely.

AQUINUS.

He dare as soon be damn'd as make a noise,

Or stir, or cough.

OLAUS.   If he should sneeze--   25

CORTES.

---

18. bestow] dispose of.

22. comfort] double-entendre, "To soothe and solace
with love's caresses and with yet intimacy." Partrige, p.
90.

23. Oh . . . rarely] literal reference to both persons
being buried alive, but also a double-entendre referring to
Gotharus' and Marpisa's scandalous liaison. See Partridge,
pp. 198-199.

'Tis his best course to go into the ground

With silence.

TURGESIUS.   March on!--[A trumpet sounds

within.]

Stay, what trumpet's

that?

Enter rebels with a trumpet before the coffin,

marching.

OLAUS.

They are no enemies; I know the coffin.

AQUINUS.

What rusty regiment ha' we here?

OLAUS.

They are going to bury him; he's not yet discover'd. 30

Oh, do not hinder 'em; 'tis a work of charity.

Yet, now I do consider better on't.--[To

Turgesius.]

You may do well to show yourself; that may

Be a means to waken the good gentleman

And make some sport before the rascal smell.   35

---

27. S.D. A trumpet sounds within] Trumpet sounded within.
after that? Gifford.

---

26. course] a pun on the word "corpse," pronounced
"corse" as well as "corpse" in the seventeenth century.   See
a discussion of the pronunciation in OED citation of
corpse.

29. rusty] rough, rude (OED).

    And yet he's in my nostril; he has perfum'd

    His box already.   [Turgesius reveals himself.]

OMNES REBELS.

    'Tis he, 'tis he! The prince alive! Hey!

They see the prince, throw down the coffin, and run to

kneel and embrace him.

AQUINUS.

    What would he give but for a knife to cut

    His own throat now?

OMNES REBELS.   Our noble prince alive?   40

TURGESIUS.

    That owes himself to all your loves.

AQUINUS.   What?

    What trinkets ha' you there?

[1] REBEL.   The Duke Olaus

    Told us 'twas the prince's body which we

    Resolv'd to bury with magnificence.

AQUINUS.

    So it appears.

OLAUS.   'Tis better as it is.   45

2 REBEL.

    There's something in't; my shoulder is

---

37. S.D. Turgesius reveals himself.] Turgesius discovers
himself Gifford.

---

    45. 'Tis . . . is] a comment declaring reality (the
prince alive and Gotharus caught) is better than appearance
(see Aquinus' statement So it appears, l. 44). Olaus' comment is appropriate to his blunt, plain and direct character.

Still sensible. Let's search, stand off.

OLAUS.

Now, do you scent him, gentlemen?--He w'od

   forgive

The hangman to dispatch him out o'th' way.

Now, will these masties use him like a cat;   50

Most dreadful rogues at an execution.

Now, now--   [They open the coffin.]

1 REBEL.   'Tis a man. Ha, Gotharus,

The thing we whet our teeth for.

OMNES REBELS.   Out with the

   traitor.

And with the murderer. Hey, drag him!

OLAUS.   I told you.

1 REBEL.

Hold, you know your duty fellow renegades.--   55

We do beseech thee, high and mighty prince,

Let us dispose of what we brought, this traitor.

He was given us by the duke; fortune has

Thrown him into our teeth.

OLAUS.   And they'll devour

   him.

48.   scent] Gifford;   sent Q.

52.   S.D. They open the coffin.] Gifford.

46-47. is . . . sensible] still feels the weight of the
coffin.

50.   masties] mastiffs.

OMNES [REBELS].

 We beseech your highness.

OLAUS [<u>to</u> Turgesius].   I do acknowledge it. 60

 Good sir, grant their boon and try the cannibals.

2 [REBEL].

 I'll have an arm.

3 [REBEL].   I'll have a leg; I am

 A shoemaker; his shinbone may be useful.

4 [REBEL].

 I want a sign; give me his head.

TURGESIUS.

 Stay, let's first see him. Is he not stifled? 65

3 [REBEL].

 I had rather my wife were speechless.

OLAUS.

 The coffin, sir, was never close.

TURGESIUS.

 He does not stir.

1 [REBEL].   We'll make him stir. Hang him;

 He's but asleep.

2 [REBEL].   He's dead, hum.

 62-63. <u>I'll</u> . . . <u>useful</u>] The shoemaker probably wants the shinbone to use as a form with which to shape and make boots.

 64. <u>I</u> . . . <u>head</u>] A rather macabre joke; this rebel wants Gotharus' head to hang outside his shop as a sign.

 67. <u>close</u>] closed.

OLAUS.   Dead?   Then the

Devil is not so wise as I took him.   70
TURGESIUS.

He's dead and has prevented all their fury.
AQUINUS.

He was not smother'd; the coffin had air enough.
OLAUS.

He might ha' liv'd to give these gentlemen

Some content.
1 REBEL.   Oh, let us tear his limbs.
TURGESIUS.

Let none use any violence to his body.   75

I fear he has met reward above your

Punishment.
2 [REBEL].   Let me have but his clothes--
3 [REBEL].

He is a tailor.
2 [REBEL].   --Only to cut out

A suit for a traitor by 'em,

Or any man my conscience would wish hang'd.   80
4 [REBEL].

Let me have a button for a relic--
TURGESIUS.

No more!

---

76.   reward] punishment (OED).

OLAUS.   There is some mystery in his death.

Enter King.

    The king! Obscure a little, nephew. [Turgesius

      retires.]

KING.

    To whom now must I kneel? Where is the king?

    For I am nothing and deserve to be so.--   85

    Unto you, uncle, must I bow and give

    My crown. Pray, take it; with it give me leave

    To tell you what it brings the hapless wearer

    Beside the outside glory, for I am

    Read in the miserable fate of kings.   90

    You think it glorious to command, but are

    More subject than the poorest pays you duty;

    And must obey your fears, your want of sleep,

    Rebellion from your vassals, wounds even from

    Their very tongues whose quietness you sweat for,   95

    For whose dear health you waste and fright your

      strength

    To paleness and your blood into a frost.

    You are not certain of a friend or servant

83. S.D. Turgesius <u>retires</u>.] <u>Gifford</u>.

---

    83. <u>obscure</u>] hide yourself.

    90. <u>Read</u>] experienced, instructed.

    92. <u>poorest pays</u>] poorest who pays.

    95. <u>sweat</u>] (1) labor, and (2) suffer (<u>OED</u>).

> To build your faith upon. Your life is but
> Your subjects murmur and your death their sacrifice. 10
> When looking past yourself to make them blest
> In your succession, which a wife must bring you,
> You may give up your liberty for a smile
> As I ha' done, and in your bosom cherish
> More danger than a war or famine brings.   105
> Or if you have a son,--my spirits fail me
> At naming of a son.

TURGESIUS [coming forward]. Oh, my dear father.
KING.

> Ha! Do not fright me in my tears, which should
> Be rather blood for yielding to thy death.
> I have let fall my penitence though I was   110
> Counsel'd by him whose truth I now suspect
> In the amaze and puzzle of my state.

TURGESIUS.

> Dear sir, let not one thought afflict you more;
> I am preserv'd to be your humble son still.
> Although Gotharus had contriv'd my ruin,   115
> 'Twas counterplotted by this honest captain.

KING.

> I know not what to credit. Art Turgesius?

TURGESIUS.

107. S.D. coming forward.] Gifford.

---

108. Ha . . . tears] The king believes Turgesius to be
his son's ghost.

And do account your blessing and forgiveness,

If I have err'd, above the whole world's empire.

The army, sir, is yours.

OLAUS.   Upon conditions--   120

TURGESIUS [to Olaus]. Good sir!--[To the king.] And

    all safety meant your person.

OLAUS.

Right. But for your gypsy-queen, that cockatrice--

KING.

She's lost.

OLAUS.   The devil find her.

KING.   She's false.

OLAUS.

That gentleman jack-in-a-box, if he could speak,

Would clear that point.

KING [to Turgesius].   Forgive me, gentle boy.   125

TURGESIUS.

Dear sir, no more.

AQUINUS.   Best dismiss these gentlemen.

---

122. gypsy-queen] According to OED gypsy is: "a contemptuous term for a woman, as being cunning, deceitful,
fickle, or the like; a 'baggage', 'hussy', etc."

122. cockatrice] same as basilisk (see V.i.10 and the
accompanying note). Huberman says that cockatrice is "here
used as a cant term of reproach, equivalent to prostitute or
whore" (p. 266).

124. jack-in-a-box] a common word for a particular
kind of thief or con-man as well as an obvious macabre joke
on Gotharus' present condition.

OLAUS.

> The prince's bounty. [Gives them money.] Now
>> you may go home.
>
> And d'ye hear? Be drunk tonight; the cause
> Requires it.

1 REBEL.   We'll show ourselves good subjects.

OMNES [REBELS].

> Heaven bless the king and prince and the good duke. 130
>
>> Exeunt [rebels].

KING.

> My comforts are too mighty; let me pour
> More blessings on my boy.

TURGESIUS.   Sir, I am blest

> If I stand fair in your opinion.

KING.

> And welcome, good Olaus.

OLAUS.   Y'are deceiv'd;

> I am a ruffian, and my head must off   135
> To please the monkey-madam that bewitch'd you,
> For being too honest to you.

KING.   We are friends.

OLAUS.

> Upon condition that you will--

127. S.D. Gives them money.] Gifford.

---

129. good subjects] (1) loyal and non-rebellious, and
(2) good drinkers (see l. 128).

136. monkey-madam] Monkeys are associated with lechery.
See Partridge, p. 155.

KING.   What?

OLAUS.

    Now have I forgot what I would have.

    Oh, that my lady Circe that transform'd you   140

    May be sent--whither? I ha' forgot again--

    To the devil; any whither, far enough.

    A curse upon her; she troubles me both when

    I think on her and when I forget her.

             Enter Albina.

KING.

    Gotharus' wife, the sorrowful Albina.   145

ALBINA.

    If pity dwell within your royal bosom,

    Let me be heard. I come to find a husband.

    I'll not believe what the hard-hearted rebels

    Told me, that he is dead; they lov'd him not

    And wish it so; for you would not permit   150

    His murder here. You gave me, sir, to him

    In holy marriage; I'll not say what sorrow

    My poor heart since hath been acquainted with,

    But give him now to me and I'll account

    No blessing like that bounty. Where, oh where   155

    Is my poor lord? None tell me? Are you all

---

    140. Circe] the sorceress who transformed Odysseus'
men into swine.

    142. any whither] anywhere.

Silent or deaf as rocks? Yet they sometimes

Do with their hollow murmurs answer men.

This does increase my fears; none speak to me?--

I ask my lord from you, sir; you once lov'd him.   160

He had your bosom. Who hath torn him thence?

Why do you shake your head and turn away?

Can you resolve me, sir?--The prince alive,

Whose death they would revenge upon Gotharus?--

Oh, let me kiss your hand. A joy to see   165

You safe doth interrupt my grief; I may

Hope now my lord is safe too. I like not

That melancholy gesture. Why do you make

So dark your face and hide your eyes as they

Would show an interest in sorrow with me?   170

Where is my lord?--Can you or any tell me

Where I may find the comfort of mine eyes,

My husband. Or but tell me that he lives,

And I will pray for you. Then he is dead;

Indeed I fear.

TURGESIUS.   Poor lady.

AQUINUS.   Madam, be comforted.   175

---

157. Silent . . . rocks] Two proverbs are here com-
bined: (1) "As still as a stone," Tilley, p. 633 (S877),
and (2) "As deaf as a stone," Tilley, p. 633 (S879).

159. This] the silence.

163. resolve] answer, satisfy (OED).

170. an . . . sorrow] sympathy.

ALBINA.

 Why, that's well said; I thank you, gentle sir.

 You bid me be comforted; blessing on you.

 Show me now reason for it; tell me something

 I may believe.

AQUINUS.   Madam, your husband's dead.

ALBINA.

 And did you bid me, sir, be comforted   180

 For that? Oh, you were cruel. Dead? Who

  murdered him?

 For though he lov'd not me in life, I must

 Revenge his death.

TURGESIUS.   Alas, you cannot.

ALBINA.   No?

 Will not heaven hear me think you? For I'll pray

 That horror may pursue the guilty head   185

 Of his black murderer; you do not know

 How fierce and fatal is a widow's curse.

 Who kill'd him? Say!

AQUINUS.   We know not.

ALBINA.   Y'are unjust.

TURGESIUS.

 Pursue not sorrow with such inquisition

 Lady.

190. Lady] Ladie Q (corrected); Lodie Q and O (uncorrected).

---

188. unjust] dishonest (OED).

ALBINA.   Not I?   Who hath more interest?   190

KING.

> The knowledge of what circumstance depriv'd him
>
> Of life will not avail to his return;
>
> Or, if it would, none here know more than that
>
> He was brought hither, dead, in that enclosure.

ALBINA.

> Where?

AQUINUS.   In that coffin, lady.

ALBINA.   Was it charity   195

> Made this provision for him?--[Going to the
>
>   coffin] Oh, my lord,
>
> Now may I kiss thy wither'd lip, discharge
>
> Upon thy bosom a poor widow's tears.
>
> There's something tempts my heart to show more
>
>   duty
>
> And wait on thee to death, in whose pale dress   200
>
> Thou dost invite me to be reconcil'd.

KING.

> Remove that coffin.

ALBINA.   Y'are uncharitable!

> Is't not enough that he is robb'd of life
>
> Among you, but you'll rob me of his body,
>
> Poor remnant of my lord?   I have not had,   205

  199-201. There's . . . reconcil'd] The temptation of suicide.

  Indeed, so many kisses a great while;

  Pray do not envy me, for sure I sha'not

  Die of this surfeit. He thought not I was

  So near to attend him in his last and long

  Progress that build this funeral tenement   210

  Without a room for me. The sad Albina

  Must sleep by her dead lord; I feel Death coming

  And, as it did suspect I durst not look

  On his grim visage, he has drawn a curtain

  Of mist before my eyes. [Swoons.]

ING.   Look to the lady!   215

URGESIUS.

  Look to Albina!--Our physicians!

  There is not so much virtue more i'th' kingdom.

  If she survives this passion, she is worth

  A prince, and I will court her as my blessing.

      [Enter physicians.]

  Say, is there hope?

1] PHYSICIAN.   There is.   220

215. S.D. Swoons.] Gifford.

219. S.D. Enter physicians.] Gifford, but after Our phyi-
cians!

---

  210. progress] journey, in this case, death.

  210. funeral tenement] coffin.

 214-215. he . . . eyes] Cf. IV.v.8.

  218. passion] attack of illness, here arising from
great strain on the emotions which makes the word doubly
appropriate.

TURGESIUS.

Above your lives preserve her.

[2] PHYSICIAN.   With our best

art and care.   Ex[eunt] with Albina.

OLAUS.

She has almost made me woman too.   But

Come, to other business.

Enter Marpisa.

AQUINUS.   Is not this the queen?

OLAUS.

The queen of hell; give her no hearing, but

Shoot, shoot her presently without more repentance! 225

There is a lecherous devil in her;

Give him more fire; his hell's not hot enough.

Now shoot!

TURGESIUS.   Be temperate, good sir.

MARPISA.

Nay, let his choleric highness be obey'd.

AQUINUS.

221. S.D. Exeunt] Gifford; Exit. Q.

---

222. She . . . too] She has almost made me weep.

225. repentance] regret, in the sense of without
worrying about doing wrong.

226-227. There . . . enough] Send her and the devil, who
resides in her, to hell. Compare this reference to Marpisa's eyes with all of the previous comments in praise of
them, especially Gotharus' about their life-giving powers.

She is shot-free.

MARPISA.   The prince alive? Where is   230

Gotharus?

OLAUS.   Your friend that was?

MARPISA.   It is confess'd.

OLAUS.

Your stallion.

MARPISA.   He has more titles, sure.

OLAUS.

Let but some strangle her in her own hair.

MARPISA.

The office will become a noble hangman.

OLAUS.

Whore--

MARPISA.   I'll not spend my breath upon thee;   235

I have more use on't. Does Gotharus live?

AQUINUS.

You may conjecture, Madam, if you turn

---

230. shot-free] shot-proof. She has more practical
reasons for not fearing the shot of a pistol. See 11. 251-
253 below.

231. friend] paramour.

232. stallion] a crude reference to Gotharus' role in
his and Marpisa's relationship.

236. on't] for it.

237. conjecture] infer, in the sense of reading signs
or omens (OED). In this case Aquinus is telling Marpisa
that she can interpret the meaning of the sign (the coffin)
for herself.

Your eyes upon that object.

MARPISA.   It has wrought then.

KING.

What has wrought?

MARPISA.   His physic, sir, for the state

megrim.

A wholesome poison which, in his poor fears   240

And fainting when the rebels first pursu'd him,

It was my happiness to minister

In my poor boy's revenge, kill'd by his practise.

TURGESIUS.

Poison'd!

OLAUS.   She is turn'd doctor.

MARPISA.   He becomes

Death's pale complexion, and now I'm prepar'd.   245

TURGESIUS.

For what?

MARPISA.   To die.

OLAUS.   Prepar'd to be damned.

---

239.   physic] medicinal cure, purge.

240.   wholesome] curative (OED).

240-241.   A . . . him] Either Marpisa or Shirley has forgotten when and why the poison, as medicine, was given to
Gotharus. It was before he even knew of the rebels, and
the distraught state for which he took the cordial was
brought on by excessive grief over Haraldus' death. See
IV.iv.34-69.

244.   She . . . doctor] See IV.iii.18-19 and the accompanying note.

244-245.   He . . . complexion] Death fits Gotharus well.

A seven-years' killing will be too little.

MARPISA.

I pity your poor rage; I sha'not stay so long,

Nor shall you have the honor, sir, to kill me.

OLAUS.

No, let me try.

MARPISA.   Ha, ha.

OLAUS.   Dost thou laugh, hellcat?   250

MARPISA.

Yes, and scorn all your furies. I was not

So improvident to give Gotharus all

My cordial; you may trust the operation.

Here's some to spare if any have a mind

To taste and be assur'd.--[To Olaus.] Will you,

    my lord?   255

'Twill purge your choler rarely.

OLAUS.

I'll not be your patient, I thank you.

MARPISA.

This box was every my companion,

Since I grew wicked with that politician,

To prevent shameful death. Nor am I coy   260

To pleasure a friend in't.

---

252.   improvident] unmindful of the future.

260.   coy] reluctant.

261.   pleasure] please.

OLAUS.   Devil's charity.

MARPISA.

   It works with method and doth kill discreetly

   Without a noise; your memory is a rude

   And troublesome destroyer to this medicine.--

   I feel it gently seize upon my vitals;   265

   'Tis now the time to steal into my heart.

KING.

   Hast thou no thought of heaven?

MARPISA.   Yes, I do think

   Sometimes, but have not heart enough to pray.

   Some vapor now rises 'twixt me and heaven;

   I cannot see't; lust and ambition ruin'd me.   270

   If greatness were a privilege i'th'other

   World, it were a happiness to die a queen.

   I find my conscience too late; 'tis bloody

---

270. cannot] Q (corrected); annot O (uncorrected).

---

   262. method] Medically, a method means: "The regular, systematic treatment proper for the cure of a specific disease" (OED).

   263. mercury] "This refers probably to mercuric chloride, commonly known as corrosive sublimate, or to some other mercury compound. Liquid mercury taken internally is not ordinarily painful or poisonous" (Huberman, p. 269). But Howard W. Haggard, in his history of medicine and medical practise, says that mercury, first used as a medicine to cure syphilis in the sixteenth-century, could be poisonous. Howard W. Haggard, Devil's Drugs, and Doctors: The Story of the Science of Healing (London: William Heineman, Ltd., 1929), p. 349. OED includes references to several poisonous plants under the citation of mercury.

   273. conscience] sense of right and wrong.

And full of stains. Oh, I have been so wicked;

'Twere almost impudence to ask a pardon;   275

Yet for your own sakes, pity me. Survive

All happy, and if you can, forgive, forgive.

Moritur.

KING.

Those accents yet may be repentance.

TURGESIUS.   She's dead.

KING.

Some take their bodies hence.

TURGESIUS.   Let them have

burial.

[Exeunt several soldiers with the bodies of Gotharus

and Marpisa.]

KING.

'Tis in thee, Turgesius,   280

To dispose all, to whom I give my crown.--

Salute him, king, by my example!

TURGESIUS.   Stay,

Upon your duty, stay! Will you be traitors?

---

279. S.D. Exeunt several soldiers with the bodies of Gotharus and Marpisa.] Gifford, omitting several.

---

278. accents] comments.

280-294. 'Tis . . . duty] During these two speeches, the
king attempts to place the crown on Turgesius' head, and the
prince refuses it and returns that symbolic item to the king.
The pronoun it used by Turgesius in his reply to the king always refers to the crown.

Consent your lawful king should be depos'd?--

Sir, do not wound your son and lay so great   285

A stain upon his hopeful, his green honor.

I now enjoy good men's opinions;

This change will make 'em think I did conspire

And force your resignation. Wear it still

By justice and yourself; it shall not touch   290

My brow till death translate you to a kingdom

More glorious, and you leave me to succeed,

Better'd by your example in the practise

Of a king's power and duty.

KING.   This obedience

Will with excess of comfort kill thy father   295

And hasten that command thou wouldst decline.

TURGESIUS [presents Aquinus].

Receive this captain and reward his faith

To you and me.

KING.   Be captain of our guard.--

289. Wear] Gifford; were Q.

297. S.D. presents Aquinus] Gifford, but after me (1. 298).

---

286. green] not fully developed or matured (OED).

288. This change] the king's abdication and the prince's assumption of the throne.

291. translate] transform, transport.

296. command] position.

And, my good uncle, to your care I leave

The soldiers. Let the largess speak our bounty   300

And your love.

OLAUS.   Aye, this sounds well, fellow

    soldiers.

Trust me, beside your pay, for the king's bounty.

SOLDIERS.

Heaven preserve the king and prince!

OLAUS.

Not a short prayer for me?

OMNES SOLDIERS.

Heaven bless the duke! Heaven bless the duke!   305

OLAUS.

Why so. Money will do much.

KING.

A bright day shines upon us. Come, my son,

Too long a stranger to the court. It now

Shall bid thee welcome. I do feel my years

Slide off and joy drown sorrow in my tears.   310

Exeunt omnes.

FINIS.

299. care] Gifford; eare Q.   301. Aye Gifford; I Q.

303. S.P. Soldiers] Gifford; Within soldiers Q.

---

300. largess] in this case, a generous gift of money
by the king to the soldiers.

300. bounty] gratitude.

310. joy . . . tears] His tears of joy dispatch sorrow.

APPENDIX I

ADDITIONAL BIBLIOGRAPHICAL AND TEXTUAL NOTES

(A)

The following symbols designate the copies of The Politician, 1655, that were collated for this present study. Each is a single volume unless otherwise noted.

QUARTO

T4   John H. Wrenn Collection in the University of Texas Library, Wh/Sh66/655p, Austin. This copy was used as the copy-text for the present edition.

BN4   Bibliothèque Nationale, Catalogue Général Auteurs 172, Yk 397, Paris.

BM4   British Museum, 644.c.65., London.

BM4a   British Museum, C.12.f.18.(5.), London. (Bound with The Gentleman of Venice, Love's Cruelty, The Constant Maid, The Coronation, Cupid and Death, and Andromana.)

A4   Ashley Library, Ashley 1725, in the British Museum, London.

V4   Dyce Collection, Dyce Collection Catalogue, II, 302, no. 9141, D25.C.90., in the Victoria and Albert Museum, London.

F4   Folger Shakespeare Library, S3482, Washington, D.C.

OCTAVO

T8   John H. Wrenn Collection in the University of Texas Library, Wh/Sh66/655pa, Austin.

BM8   British Museum, 641.b.1.(2.), London. (Bound with The Gentleman of Venice.)

A8   Ashley Library, Ashley 1726, in the British Museum, London.

V8   Dyce Collection, <u>Dyce</u> <u>Collection</u> <u>Catalogue</u>, II, 302, no. 9141 (incorrectly cited as a quarto), D25.E.39., in the Victoria and Albert Museum, London. (Bound with <u>The</u> <u>Gentleman</u> <u>of</u> <u>Venice</u>.)

V8a   Dyce Collection, <u>Dyce</u> <u>Collection</u> <u>Catalogue</u>, II, 302, no. 9141 (incorrectly cited as a quarto), D25.E.38., in the Victoria and Albert Museum, London. (Bound with <u>The</u> <u>Gentleman</u> <u>of</u> <u>Venice</u> and with <u>Six</u> <u>New</u> <u>Playes</u>.)

LC8   Library of Congress, PR3144/.P6/1655/Office, Washington, D.C.

(B)

Collations of the above copies of <u>The</u> <u>Politician</u>, 1655.

ALL QUARTOS: 84 pp. (i-vi, 1-74, with numbers 39-42 repeated). A-K in fours, L1-L2. [A1^r] Title-page, [A1^v] blank, A2 "The Epistle Dedicatory," A3 "The names and small Characters of the Persons." The text begins on A4.

ALL OCTAVOS (except A8 and T8): 84 pp. (i-vi, 1-74, with numbers 39-42 repeated). A-D in eights, E1-E2. [A1^r] Title page, [A1^v] blank, A2 "The Epistle Dedicatory," A3 "The names and small Characters of the Persons." The text begins on A4.

A8: same collation as regular octavo with quarto cancels A4, A8, B4, B8, C2 (reads E2), C4, C7-C8, D-4, D-8, E-4, E7-E8.

T8: same collation as regular octavo with quarto cancels A2, A3, C3 (reads E3), C5-C6 (reads F1-F2), D2-D3 (reads G2-G3), D6 (reads H2).

(C)

The variants appearing in the 1655 edition that are referred to in the textual notes merely as occurring in <u>O</u> or <u>Q</u> are here identified with specific copies of the first edition.

I.i.247
    Visit 't 'the (<u>uncorrected</u>) V8, V8a.
    Visit the (<u>corrected</u>) the other eleven copies.

III.iii.18
    engendring (<u>corrected</u>) all octavo copies.
    egendring (<u>uncorrected</u>) all quarto copies.

IV.ii.58
    Woh (uncorrected) V4.
    Who (corrected) the other twelve copies.

IV.iv.73
      i'me [single quote mark or comma directly above the
        i] (uncorrected) the Duke University Library
        quarto. The entire quarto has not been collated
        for the present text; only the page containing
        this word has been examined.
      i'me (corrected) the thirteen copies collated for the
        present text.

V.ii.190
    Ladie (corrected) V4.
    Lodie (uncorrected) the twelve copies

V.ii.270
    cannot (corrected) all quarto copies.
    annot (uncorrected) all octavo copies.

(D)

    The lines of the play have been regularized in accord-
ance with dramatic blank verse tradition; generally, the
copy-text posed no special problems in this regard. The following lines, however, were found to be unusually irregular
in quarto.

I.i	IV.iii
46-49	73-75
138-141	90-95
	102-105
II.i	
1-38	IV.iv
75-90	61-102
193-194	
228-237	IV.v
284-285	7-42
III.i	IV.vi
95-126	1-74
374-378	
	V.i
III.ii	25-27
1-76	33-41
IV.i	V.ii
52-65	6-8
	41-82
IV.ii	278-282
1-3	
106-109	

APPENDIX II

A BRIEF BIOGRAPHY OF SIR WALTER MOYLE (1627-1701)

The "very much honored WALTER MOYLE, Esq." to whom
Shirley dedicated The Politician in 1655 is a shadowy figure in English history. He is found in the Dictionary of
National Biography only through the entry on his father,
John Moyle (1592?-1661), as one of "numerous sons"[1] and the
entry on his more famous namesake, his son and the writer,
Walter Moyle (1672-1721).[2] Thumbnail biographies of Walter
Moyle of Shirley's dedication are found in Alumni Oxonienses
by Joseph Foster[3] and in J. L. Vivian's edition of The Visitations of Cornwall,[4] in which are given approximate dates
of Moyle's birth and death, and a few citations of honors
bestowed upon him.

A member of a Cornish family of longstanding, Moyle of
Bake in St. Germans, Walter Moyle was born probably in the

---

[1]Sir Leslie Stephen and Sir Sidney Lee, eds., DNB (Oxford: University Press, 1917), XIII, 1141.

[2]DNB, XIII, 1143.

[3]Joseph Foster, Alumni Oxonienses . . . 1500-1714 (Oxford: Parker and Co., 1891), III, 1044.

[4]J. L. Vivian, ed., The Visitations of Cornwall (Exeter:
William Pollard & Co., 1887), p. 335.

186

first week of March, 1627/1628, for according to the parish register of St. Germans, he was baptized on 9 March 1627.[5] On 12 November 1650, Moyle matriculated at Exeter College, Oxford[6] at the age of twenty-two years, rather late for a seventeenth-century student. Three years later, in November, 1653, Moyle was admitted to the Inner Temple.[7] Shortly after his admission to the Inn, he was elected to Parliament representing Cornwall. This parliament, called the First Protectorate Parliament, sat in September, 1654, and Moyle's election was only the first of several that he was to win.[8] Moyle is included in a group of members of this house of 1654 that has been described as "strong parliamentarians."[9] Also in 1654, Moyle's name appears in the will of Richard Moyle who had died that same year and who appointed Walter Moyle and John Vivian to be "overseers of the will."[10] In 1655 James Shirley dedicated his play, The Politician, to "the very much honored, WALTER MOYLE, Esq."

---

[5] Vivian, p. 335, and Foster, III, 1044.

[6] Foster, III, 1044.

[7] [W. H. Cooke, ed.,] Students Admitted to the Inner Temple (London: William Clowes and Sons, [1877]), p. 351.

[8] Mary Coate, Cornwall in the Great Civil War and Interregnum: 1642-1660 (Oxford: Clarendon Press, 1933), p. 379.

[9] William Prideaux Courtney, The Parliamentary Representation of Cornwall to 1832 (London: Thomas Pettit & Co., 1889), p. 398.

[10] J. L. Vivian and Henry H. Drake, eds., The Visitation of the County of Cornwall in the Year 1620 (London: Mitchell and Hughes, 1874), p 149.

Two years after his first election to Parliament, Moyle
was again chosen to represent Cornwall in Commons. In a
letter dated 7 September 1656, written to Sir Edward Nicholas
Secretary of State to both Charles I and Charles II, Edward
Hyde, the historian and Royalist statesman, said of this
Second Protectorate Parliament: "All letters agree that
Cromwell is in great perplexity, and that in all places people choose persons for Parliament of very different affections to his purpose."[11] Another Royalist, John Fisher,
wrote on 22 September 1656 concerning this same parliament
that there were "precautions [taken] against Cavaliers."[12]
And on 24 October of the same year, a John Jennings wrote
Hyde that "One hundred and forty members were excluded from
the house by Cromwell, and since then eighty have left of
their own accord."[13] The excluded members published a
remonstrance for having been deprived of their duly elected
seats, and protested that Cromwell had assumed powers which
were not rightly his. Walter Moyle's name is among this
excluded and protesting group.[14]

Though the statement that the Protector was taking
"precautions against Cavaliers" cannot be ignored in trying

[11]O. Ogle, et al., eds., Calendar of the Clarendon
State Papers (Oxford: Clarendon Press, 1876), III, 168.

[12]Ogle, III, 179.   [13]Ogle, III, 189.

[14]Bulstrode Whitelock, Memorials of the English Affairs
(Oxford: the University Press, 1853), IV, 280. See also
Coate, p. 295, and Courtney, p. 422.

to determine the nature of the excluded members in general and of Walter Moyle in particular, one must be careful in identifying Moyle as a strong Royalist. In his letter to Hyde, Jennings says of the excluded members: "Cromwell's information of persons was, as many think, but bad, for he excluded many who, if not his friends, would not have ventured to be his enemies."[15] Moyle is among a group of members of the 1656 Parliament referred to as "moderate" and "Presbyterian" by another historian.[16] Furthermore, according to Jennings, Cromwell's speech was hardly designed to warm the hearts of "moderates" and "strong parliamentarians": "His speech to the Parliament was insolent beyond all show of prudence, . . . he derided government by a commonwealth, and cried up monarchy, which he said, he was never against in his judgment, but was violenced by a giddy generation."[17] This report agrees with the protest of the excluded members who said that the Protector had assumed powers that were not rightly his.

From this slight information, one could rather easily arrive at two contradictory conclusions about Moyle: he could have been a dedicated republican who decried Cromwell's movement toward greater dictatorship, or he could

---

[15]Ogle, III, 189.

[16]Coat, pp. 294-295. See also pp. 311 and 314.

[17]Ogle, III, 189.

have been a dedicated Royalist who opposed Cromwell completely. Perhaps he was simply mistakenly placed by Cromwell in a group the Protector believed hostile to him. It seems more likely, however, that Moyle was a moderate with leanings toward the monarchy, for though he was a member of the Cromwellian parliaments, he nevertheless was from an old, established and prominent family in Cornwall, and his later years under Charles II indicate that he was considered favorably by that royal government which succeeded the Protectorate.

After Oliver Cromwell's death, Moyle was returned in January, 1659, to the so-called Parliament of Richard Cromwell.[18] This time he represented Lostwithiel in Cornwall and won his seat in a close contest, receiving nineteen votes to his two opponents' eighteen and nine votes.[19] One chronicler of Cornish history describes Moyle at this time as a man "of influence and position . . . who belonged to a Cornish family with ample estates and influential connexions among the chief families of the Duchy."[20] Richard Cromwell dissolved this parliament after four months,[21] and Moyle was one of thirty-seven Cornishmen who petitioned the Council of State in December, 1659, for a "Free Parliament."[22] A few months later Moyle was returned from Lostwithiel as its

---

[18]Coate, p. 380.

[20]Courtney, p. 212.

[22]Coate, p. 307.

[19]Coate, p. 300.

[21]Coate, p. 301.

representative to the Convention Parliament of 1660,[23] a

parliament called in April to prepare for the return of

Charles II in May.

Shortly after the Restoration, Moyle's career, such as

it had been, began to climb. On 26 May 1661 in Parliament,

he was called to the bar at Inner Temple.[24] At Whitehall,

on 4 February 1663/4, he was made Knight Bachelor.[25] Just

when Moyle married is not known, but in Joseph Polsue's

history of Cornwall, Sir Walter is shown to have married

Thomasine Morice, the daughter of Sir William Morice, Secre-

tary of State to Charles II.[26] The union certainly occurred

before 1672, for it was in that year that Moyle's son, Wal-

ter, was born.

The association with the crown grew; in 1671 Sir Walter

was appointed by the king to the office of Sheriff of Corn-

wall.[27] Nothing is known of Moyle's activities after this

appointment until 1689 when he was chosen to represent his

---

[23]Coate, p. 382.

[24]F. A. Inderwick, ed., A Calendar of the Inner Temple Records (London: Stevens and Son, 1901), III, 3.

[25]William A. Shaw, comp., The Knights of England (London: Sherratt and Hughes, 1906), II, 239, and George W. Marshall, Le Neve's Pedigrees (London: Mitchell and Hughes, 1873), p. 180.

[26][Joseph Polsue, ed.,] A Complete Parochial History of the County of Cornwall (London: John Camden Hotten, 1868), II, 63. Sir William's name is also among those who were excluded from the Second Protectorate Parliament in 1656. See DNB, XIII, 944.

[27]Polsue (1872), IV, 129.

parish of St. Germans in the Convention Parliament of 1689 which was called to prepare the way for William of Orange to assume the throne. Courtney writes of this election of Moyle: "Sir Walter Moyle, a Cornish knight and a prominent personage in the parish of St. Germans, obtained the second seat in the Convention of 1689, . . . but his connection with the borough lasted . . . for one parliament only."[28]

There exists today one item written by Moyle; it is a holograph letter written to William Blaythwayt, Secretary of War to both James II and William III. The letter is dated 31 March 1694, is written from Plymouth, and apparently is a business letter in which Moyle, the barrister, discusses Blaythwayt's responsibilities as guardian to the latter's fatherless nephew and widowed sister.[29]

The exact date of Moyle's death is not known; in fact, there is some confusion as to the exact date of his burial. Foster says that he was buried in St. Germans on 11 September 1701;[30] Vivian says the burial took place on 17 September according to the parish register;[31] and the monumental inscription in the church at St. Germans reads: "Depositum

---

[28]Courtney, p. 287.

[29]Sir Walter Moyle, Letter to William Blaythwayt, 31 March 1694, Folger Shakespeare Library, X.d./436/(55). The red sealing wax carries the Moyle family insignia: a side view of a mule with a raised forefoot.

[30]Foster, III, 1044.

[31]Vivian, p. 335.

Walter Moyle, _Equitis_, _obiit_ 19 _die_ Septembris, Anno Domini
1701; _Vitae_ _sue_ 75,"[32]

It is impossible from this information to say when Shirley met Moyle, what their relationship was, and specifically
why in 1655 the playwright dedicated The Politician to this
young Cornish gentleman. But in a search for a general
explanation for the dedication, two things should be noted:
(1) by 1655 Moyle had been admitted to the Inner Temple and
judging from his activities from 1656 onward, we can assume
that those who knew him at the time of publication of The
Politician, late 1655, knew him to be a Royalist-moderate;
and (2) Shirley, certainly a Royalist, also reveals a long
association with the Inns of Court.

In February, 1633/34, the playwright's extraordinarily
lavish masque, The Triumph of Peace was presented by the members of the four Inns of Court at Whitehall at the enormous
cost of twenty thousand pounds. The masque, which expressed the devotion and loyalty of the Inns to the crown,
was dedicated by Shirley to the four legal societies.[33] At
the time of this masque's presentation, Shirley was living
at Gray's Inn where he had resided since early 1624/25.[34]

---

[32]Polsue II, 41.

[33]Alexander Dyce, The Dramatic Works and Poems of James
Shirley, eds. William Gifford and Alexander Dyce (London:
John Murray, 1833), I, xxiii-xviii, and Inderwick (1898),
II, xlvii-xlviii.

[34]Arthur H. Nason, James Shirley: Dramatist (New York:
Arthur H. Nason, 1915), p. 36.

During the Interregnum, he lived in Whitefriars, adjacent to the Temple.[35] In 1663 and in 1664 respectively, The Brothers and Changes, or Love in a Maze, both by Shirley, were performed at the Inner Temple.[36] In 1666, the year of his death, he was living in a "house close to Inner Temple Gateway."[37] And in the dramatist's will, money and a ring are left to his "worthy friend Mr. John Warter of the Inner Temple" and to Warter's wife and son.[38]

Aside from his place of residence, nothing is known to connect Shirley with Inner Temple in particular or with the Inns of Court in general during the 1650's; but, then, hardly anything is known about Shirley during the late 1640's and throughout the 1650's. But it is highly unlikely that one who was associated so closely with the Inns in the 1630's and 1660's and who lived near the Temple during the Interregnum, would be estranged from the Inns and their members in the 1640's and 1650's. Thus, it is quite natural that the Royalist dramatist and a friend and associate of the Inns of Court and their members from at least 1633 until his death in 1666 should, in 1655, dedicate a play to a man who is a member of the Inner Temple and a Royalist-moderate member of Parliament.

---

[35]Anthony à Wood, Athenae Oxonienses, quoted in Nason, p. 138. His will, dated July, 1666, begins: "I, James Shirley of White Fryers, London . . ." Nason, p. 158.

[36]Hugh H. L. Bellot, The Inner and Middle Temple (London: Methuen & Co., 1902), p. 197.

[37]Bellot, p. 270.   [38]Nason, p. 159.

BIBLIOGRAPHY

A. BOOKS

Abbott, E. A. A Shakespearian Grammar: An Attempt to Illustrate Some of the Differences Between Elizabethan and Modern English. New Edition. London: MacMillan and Company, 1886.

Adams, Joseph Quincy, ed. The Dramatic Records of Sir Henry Herbert, Master of Revels, 1623-1673. New Haven: Yale University Press, 1917.

Apollodorus. The Library. Trans. Sir James G. Frazer. 2 vols. London: William Heinemann, 1921-1946.

Arber, Edward, ed. A Transcript of the Registers of the Company of Stationers of London; 1554-1640 A.D. 5 vols. London: n.p., 1875-1894.

Babb, Lawrence. The Elizabethan Malady: A Study of Melancholia in English Literature from 1580 to 1642. East Lansing: Michigan State College Press, 1951.

[Baker, David Erskine.] The Companion to the Playhouse: or an Historical Account of all the Dramatic Writers (and their Works) that have appeared in Great Britain and Ireland. 2 vols. London: T. Beckert, P. A. Dehondt, C. Henderson, and T. Davies, 1764.

Baker, D. E., Isaac Reed and Stephen Jones. Biographia Dramatica. 3 vols. London: Longman, Hurst, Rees, Orme, and Brown, 1812.

B[aron]., R[obert]. Mirza. A Tragedie. London: Humphrey Moseley and T. Dring, 1655.

Barrough, Philip. The Method of Physick, Containing the Causes, Signes, and Cures of inward diseases in man's body, from the head to the foote. London: George Miller, 1634.

Baugh, Albert C., ed. A Literary History of England. New York: Appleton-Century-Crofts, Inc., 1948.

195

196

[Chetwood, William Rufus.] Theatrical Records: or, An Account of English Dramatic Authors and Their Works. London: R. and J. Dodsley, 1756.

Clark, William Smith. The Early Irish Stage: The Beginnings to 1720. Oxford: The Clarendon Press, 1955.

Coate, Mary. Cornwall in the Great Civil War and Interregnum: 1642-1660. Oxford: The Clarendon Press, 1933.

[Cooke, W. Y., ed.] Students Admitted to the Inner Temple. London: William Clowes and Sons [, 1877].

Cooper, Thomas. Thesavrvs Lingvae Romana & Britannica . . . Accessit Dictionarivm Historicvm & poeticum. London: [Henry Bynneman,] 1584.

Courtney, William Prideaux. The Parliamentary Representation of Cornwall to 1832. London: [Thomas Pettit and Company,] 1889.

Dibdin, Charles, the elder. A Complete History of the English Stage. 5 vols. London: [published by the author, 1800.]

[Dryden, John.] Mac Flecknoe, or a Satyr upon the True-Blew-Protestant Poet, T. S. London: D. Green, 1682.

Dunham, S. A. Lives of the Most Eminent Literary and Scientific Men of Great Britain. 3 vols. London: Longman, Orme, Brown, Green and Longmans, 1838.

Eckhardt, Edward. Das Englische Drama Der Spätrenaissance (Shakespeares Nachfolger). Berlin und Leipzig: Walter De Gruyter and Company, 1929.

[Egerton, John and Thomas, comps.] Egerton's Theatrical Remembrancer. London: T. and J. Egerton, 1788.

Eglinton, John. Anglo-Irish Essays. New York: John Lane Company, 1918.

Eyre, G. E. Briscoe, ed. A Transcript of the Registers of the Worshipful Company of Stationers: From 1640-1708 A. D. 3 vols. London: n.p., 1913-1918.

Fleay, F. G. A Biographical Chronicle of the English Drama, 1559-1642. 2 vols. London: Reeves and Turner, 1891.

Forsythe, Robert Stanley. The Relations of Shirley's Plays to the Elizabethan Drama. New York: Columbia University Press, 1914.

Beaumont, Francis and John Fletcher. The Works of Francis
Beaumont and John Fletcher. Variorum Edition. Ed. A. H.
Bullen. 4 vols. London: George Bell and Sons and
A. H. Bullen, 1904-1912.

Bellot, Hugh H. L. The Inner and Middle Temple. London:
Methuen and Company, 1902.

Bentley, Gerald Eades. The Jacobean and Caroline Stage. 5
vols. Oxford: The Clarendon Press, 1941-1956.

Boase, George Clement and William Prideaux Courtney. Biblio-
theca Cornubiensis. 3 vols. London: Longmans, Green,
Reader, and Dyer, 1874-1882.

Bowers, Fredson T. Elizabethan Revenge Tragedy, 1587-1642.
Gloucester, Mass.: Peter Smith, 1959.

Briggs, K. M. Pale Hecate's Team: An Examination of the
Beliefs on Witchcraft and Magic among Shakespeare's
Contemporaries and His Immediate Successors. London:
Routledge and Kegan Paul, 1962.

Brome, Richard. Five New Playes. London: Humphrey Moseley, Richard Marriot, and Thomas Dring, 1653.

B[urnell]., H[enry]. Landgartha: A Tragi-Comedy. Dublin:
n.p., 1641.

[Burton, Robert.] The Anatomy of Melancholy. Fifth Edition.
Oxford: Henry Cripps, 1638.

Byrne, M. St. Clare, ed. The Elizabethan Zoo: Selected
from Philemon Holland's Translation of Pliny 1601 and
Edward Topsell's "Historie of Foure-Footed Beasts" 1607,
and his "Historie of Serpents" 1608. London: Frederich Etchells and Hugh MacDonald, 1926.

Camp, Charles W. The Artisan in Elizabethan Literature.
New York: Columbia University Press, 1924.

Campbell, Thomas. Specimens of the British Poets: with
Biographical and Critical Notices and An Essay on
English Poetry. 7 vols. London: John Murray, 1819.

Carlell, Lodowick. The Passionate Lovers, a Tragi-Comedy.
London: Humphrey Moseley, 1655.

Chalmers, G. An Apology for the Believers in the Shakespeare Papers. London: Thomas Egerton, 1797.

198

Foster, Joseph. Alumni Oxonienses: The Members of the University of Oxford, 1500-1714. 4 vols. Oxford: Parker and Company, 1891.

Foxon, D. F. Thomas J. Wise and the Pre-Restoration Drama: A Study in Theft and Sophistication. London: The Bibliographical Society, 1959.

Gagen, Jean E. The New Woman: Her Emergence in English Drama, 1600-1730. New York: Twayne Publishers, 1954.

Genest, John. Some Account of the English Stage from the Restoration in 1660 to 1830. 10 vols. Bath: H. E. Carrington, 1832.

Gerber, Richard. James Shirley: Dramatiker der Dekadenz. Bern: Friedrich Gegenbauers, 1952.

Godfrey, Elizabeth. Home Life Under the Stuarts. New York: E. P. Dutton and Company, 1903.

G[offe]., T[homas]. The Careless Shepherdes, A Tragicomedy . . . with an Alphabeticall Catalogue of all such Plays that ever were Printed. London: Richard Rogers and William Ley, 1656.

Greg, W. W. A Bibliography of the English Printed Drama to the Restoration. 4 vols. London: The Bibliographical Society, 1939-1959.

Haggard, Howard W. Devils, Drugs, and Doctors: The Story of the Science of Healing from Medicine-Man to Doctor. London: William Heinemann, Ltd., 1929.

Halliwell, J. O. A Dictionary of Old English Plays. London: John Russell Smith, 1860.

Harbage, Alfred. Annals of English Drama, 975-1700. Philadelphia: University of Pennsylvania Press, 1940.

_____. Cavalier Drama: An Historical and Critical Supplement to the Study of the Elizabethan and Restoration Stage. London: Oxford University Press, 1936.

_____. Thomas Killigrew: Cavalier Dramatist, 1612-83. Philadelphia: University of Pennsylvania Press, 1930.

_____, and Samuel Schoenbaum. Annals of English Drama, 975-1700. London: Methuen and Company, Ltd., 1964.

Hazlitt, W. C. Collections and Notes, 1867-1876. London: Reeves and Turner, 1876.

Heywoode, Thom[as]. Γunaikeion: or, Nine Bookes of Various History Concerninge Women; Inscribed by ye names of ye Nine Muses. London: Adam Islip, 1624.

Hole, Christina. A Mirror of Witchcraft. London: Chatto and Windus, 1957.

Holinshed, Raphaell. The Chronicles of England, Scotland, and Irelande. 2 vols. London: Lucas Harrison and George Bishop, 1577.

Hotson, Leslie. The Commonwealth and Restoration Stages. Cambridge, Mass.: Harvard University Press, 1928.

Hoy, Cyrus. The Hyacinth Room: An Investigation into the Nature of Comedy, Tragedy and Tragicomedy. New York: Alfred A. Knopf, 1964.

Inderwick, F. A., ed. A Calendar of the Inner Temple Records. 3 vols. London: Stevens and Son, 1896-1901.

Ingelo, Nathaniel. Bentivolio and Urania in Six Books. Second Edition. London: T. Dring, J. Starkey and T. Basset, 1669.

J[acob]., G[iles]. The Poetical Register: or, the Lives and Characters of the English Dramatick poets with an account of their Writings. London: E. Curll, 1719.

Kavanagh, Peter. The Irish Theatre: Being a History of the Drama in Ireland from the Earliest Period to the Present Day. Tralee: The Kerryman Limited, 1946.

Killigrew, Thomas. The Pilgrim, a Tragedy. London: Henry Herringman, 1663.

[Kirkman, Francis.] A True, perfect, and exact Catalogue of all the Comedies, Tragedies, Tragi-Comedies, Pastorals, Masques and Interludes, that were ever yet printed and published till this present year 1661. [London: Francis Kirkman,] 1661.

_____. A True, perfect, and exact Catalogue of all the Comedies, Tragedies, Tragi-Comedies, Pastorals, Masques and Interludes, that were ever yet Printed and Published till this present year 1671. London: Francis Kirkman, 1671.

[Kramer, Heinrich and James Sprenger.] Malleus Maleficarum. Trans. Montague Summers. London: The Pushkin Press, 1948.

Lamb, Charles. Specimens of English Dramatic Poets, who lived about the time of Shakespeare. London: Longman, Hurst, Rees, and Orme, 1808.

Langbaine, Gerard. An Account of the English Dramatick Poets. Oxford: George West and Henry Clements, 1691.

_____. Momus Triumphans: or The plagaries of the English Stage. London: Nicholas Cox, 1688.

_____ [, and Charles Gildon]. The lives and characters of the English Dramatick poets. London: Nicholas Cox and William Turner, 1699.

[_____, and Nicholas Cox.] An Exact Catalogue of all the Comedies, Tragedies, Tragi-Comedies, Operas, Masks, Pastorals and Interludes that were ever yet Printed and Published, till this present year 1680. Oxford: Nicholas Cox, 1680.

[London, William.] A Catalogue of the Most Vendible Books in England. London: [William London,] 1658.

MacCarthy, B. G. Women Writers: Their Contribution to the English Novel, 1621-1744. Third Impression. Dublin: Cork University Press, 1946.

McKerrow, Ronald B. An Introduction to Bibliography for Literary Students. Oxford: The Clarendon Press, 1928.

Magnus, Olaus. A Compendious History of the Goths, Swedes, & Vandals, and other Northern Nations. London: J. Streater, 1658.

Malone, Emdond. An Historical Account of the Rise and Progress of the English stage and of the Economy and Usages of Our Ancient Theatres. London: Henry Baldwin, 1790.

_____. The Plays and Poems of William Shakespeare with Corrections and Illustrations of Various Commentators: Comprehending a Life of the Poet and an Enlarged History of the Stage. London: C. Baldwin, 1821.

Marshall, George W., ed. Le Neve's Pedigrees of the Knights Made by King Charles II, King James II, King William III and Queen Mary, King William alone, and Queen Anne. London: Mitchell and Hughes, 1873.

Mascal, Leonard. The Gouernment of Cattell. London: Thomas Harper and John Harrison, 1633.

Massinger, Philip. Three New Playes. London: Humphrey Moseley, 1655.

_____, Thomas Middleton and William Rowley. The Excellent Comedy, called The Old Law: or A new way to please you . . . . Together with an exact and perfect catalogue

of all the Playes, with the authors Names, and what are
Comedies, Tragedies, Histories, Pastoralls, Masks,
Interludes, more exactly Printed then ever before.
London: Edward Archer, 1656.

Murray, James A. H. et al., eds. The Oxford English Dictionary. 10 vols. Oxford: The Clarendon Press, 1888-
1928.

Nabbes, Thomas. The Vnfortunate Mother: A Tragedie. London: Daniell Frere, 1640.

Nason, Arthur H. James Shirley: Dramatist: A Biographical
and Critical Study. New York: Arthur H. Nason, 1915.

Nicoll, Allardyce. A History of Restoration Drama, 1660-
1700. Second Edition. Cambridge: The University
Press, 1928.

Nissen, P. James Shirley: Ein Beitrag zur englischen Litteraturgeschichte. Hamburg: Lütcke and Wülff, 1901.

North, Sir Thomas, trans. The Lives of Epaminondas, of
Philip of Macedon, of Dionysius the Elder, and of Octa-
vius Caesar Augustus: Collected out of good authors.
London: Richard Field, 1603.

O'Brien, George, ed. Advertisements for Ireland: Being a
description of the State of Ireland in the reign of
James I. Dublin: The Royal Society of Antiquities of
Ireland, 1923.

Olge, O., et al., eds. Calendar of the Clarendon State
Papers. 4 vols. Oxford: The Clarendon Press, 1869-
1932.

Ornstein, Robert. The Moral Vision of Jacobean Tragedy.
Madison: University of Wisconsin Press, 1960.

Oulton, Walley Chamberlain, ed. Barker's Complete List of
Plays. London: Barker and Son[, 1804].

_____. Barker's Continuation of Egerton's Theatrical
Remembrancer. London: Barker and Son, 1801.

[_____.] The Drama Recorded; or, Barker's List of Plays.
London: J. Barker, 1814.

Partridge, Eric. Shakespeare's Bawdy: A Literary and
Psychological Essay and a Comprehensive Glossary. London: Routledge and Kegan Paul, 1955.

Pausanias. Description of Greece. Trans. W. H. S. Jones. 5 vols. London: William Heinemann, Ltd., 1918-1935.

Peers, Edgar Allison. Elizabethan Drama and Its Mad Folk. Cambridge, Mass.: W. Heffer and Sons, Ltd., 1914.

The Playhouse pocket-companion, or Theatrical Vade-mecum. London: Richardson and Urquhart, 1779.

Plomer, Henry R. A Dictionary of the Booksellers and Printers who were at Work in England, Scotland and Ireland from 1641 to 1667. London: Blades, East and Blades, 1907.

Plutarchus. The Lives of the Noble Grecians and Romaines . . . . Translated out of the Greek into French by by James Amiot . . . and out of French into English, By Sir Thomas North, Knight. London: Richard Field, 1603.

[Polsue, Joseph, ed.] A Complete Parochial History of the County of Cornwall. 4 vols. London: John Camden Hotten, 1867-1872.

Praz, Mario. Machiavelli and the Elizabethans. London: Humphrey Milford Amen House, 1928.

S., J. Andromana: or the Merchant's Wife: A Tragedy. London: John Bellinger, 1660.

[Saxo Grammaticus.] The First Nine Books of the Danish History of Saxo Grammaticus. Trans. Oliver Elton. With some considerations on Saxo's sources, Historical methods and Folk-Lore by Frederich York Powell. London: David Nutt, 1894.

Schelling, Felix E. Elizabethan Drama. 2 vols. Boston: Houghton Mifflin, 1908.

Scherrer, Gebhard Josef. James Shirleys Nachruhm. Zurich: Juris-Verlag, 1951.

Schipper, J. James Shirley: Sein Leben und Seine Werke. Wien und Leipzig: Wilhelm Braumüller, 1911.

Schoenbaum, Samuel. Middleton's Tragedies: A Critical Study. New York: Columbia University Press, 1955.

Seaton, Ethel. Literary Relations of England and Scandinavia in the Seventeenth Century. Oxford: The Clarendon Press, 1935.

Shakespeare, William. Cymbeline. Ed. J. M. Nosworthy, London: Methuen and Company, Ltd., 1955.

_____. Macbeth. Ed. Kenneth Muir. New York: Random House, Inc., 1964.

Shaw, William A., comp. The Knights of England. 2 vols. London: Sherratt and Hughes, 1906.

Shirley, James. The Dramatic Works and Poems of James Shirley. Eds. William Gifford and Alexander Dyce. 6 vols. London: John Murray, 1833.

_____. The Gentleman of Venice: A Tragi-Comedie. London: Humphrey Moseley, 1655.

_____. James Shirley. Ed. Edmund Gosse. London: Vizetelly and Company, 1888.

_____. A Pastoral Called the Arcadia. London: John Williams, 1640.

_____. The Polititian: A Tragedy. London: Humphrey Moseley, 1655.

_____. The Royal Master. London: T. Cotes and John Crooke, 1638.

_____. Six New Playes. London: Humphrey Robinson and Humphrey Moseley, 1653.

Sidney, Sir Philip. The Countess of Pembroke's Arcadia: The Original Quarto Edition (1590) in Photographic Facsimile with a Bibliographical Introduction. Ed. H. Oskar Sommer. London: Kegan Paul, Trench, Trübner and Company, Ltd., 1891.

Stephen, Sir Leslie and Sir Sidney Lee, eds. The Dictionary of National Biography. 22 vols. Oxford: The University Press, 1917.

Stockwell, La Tourette. Dublin Theatres and Theatre Customs, 1637-1820. Kingsport, Tenn.: Kingsport Press, 1938.

Sturgis, Russell, et al. A Dictionary of Architecture and Building, Biographical, Historical, and Descriptive. 3 vols. New York: The Macmillan Company, 1901-1902.

Sugden, E. H. A Topographical Dictionary to the Works of Shakespeare and His Fellow Dramatists. Manchester: University of Manchester Press, 1925.

Tannenbaum, Samuel A. and Dorothy R. James Shirley (A Concise Bibliography). New York: n.p., 1946.

Thorndike, Ashley H. Tragedy. London: Constable and Company, Ltd., [1908].

Tilley, Morris Palmer. A Dictionary of the Proverbs in England in the Sixteenth and Seventeenth Centuries. Ann Arbor: University of Michigan Press, 1950.

Van Lennep, William, ed. The London Stage, 1660-1800: A Calendar of Plays, Entertainments and Afterpieces. Part 1: 1660-1700. Carbondale: Southern Illinois University Press, 1965.

Vivian, J. L., ed. The Visitations of Cornwall, Comprising the Heralds' Visitations of 1530, 1573, and 1620. Exeter: William Pollard and Company, 1887.

_____. and Henry H. Drake, eds. The Visitation of the County of Cornwall in the Year 1620. London: Mitchell and Hughes, 1874.

Ward, Adolphus William. A History of English Dramatic Literature to the Death of Queene Anne. New and Revised Edition. 3 vols. London: MacMillan and Company, Ltd., 1899.

_____, and A. R. Waller, eds. The Cambridge History of English Literature. 15 vols. Cambridge: The University Press, 1907-1917.

Warner, William. Albions England. London: R. Moore, 1612.

Whitelocke, Bulstrode. Memorials of the English Affairs from the Beginning of the Reign of King Charles the First to the Happy Restoration of King Charles the Second. 4 vols. Oxford: The University Press, 1853.

Winstanley, William. The Lives of the Most Famous English Poets. London: H. Clarke, 1687.

Wise, Thomas J., ed. A Catalogue of the Library of the late John Henry Wrenn. Comp. Harold B. Wrenn. 5 vols. Austin: University of Texas Press, 1920.

_____. The Ashley Library: A Catalogue of Printed Books, Manuscripts and Autograph Letters. 11 vols. London: Dunedin Press, Ltd., 1924.

Wroath [Wroth], Lady Mary. The Countesse of Mountgomeries Urania. London: John Marriott and John Grismand, 1621.

[Yonge, Charlotte Mary.] History of Christian Names. 2 vols. London: Parker, Son and Bourn, 1863.

B. PERIODICALS

The American Quarterly Review, 16 (1834), 103-166.

Fleay, F. G. "Annals of the Careers of James and Henry Shirley," Anglia, 8 (1885), 405-414.

Greg, W. W. "The Printing of Mayne's Plays," Oxford Bibliographical Society: Proceedings and Papers, I (1922-1926), 255-262.

Harbage, Alfred. "The Authorship of the Dramatic Arcadia," Modern Philology, 35 (1938), 233-237.

Harrison, T. P., Jr. "A Source of Sidney's Arcadia," Studies in English, 6 (1926), 54-71.

Hoy, Cyrus. "Renaissance and Restoration Dramatic Plotting," Renaissance Drama, 9 (1966), 247-264.

Huberman, Edward. "Bibliographical Note on James Shirley's The Polititian," The Library, 18 (1937), 104-108.

K. Q. X. "On the Character and Writings of James Shirley," The London Magazine, 1 (May, 1820), 525-530 and II (July, 1820), 36-41.

McGrath, Juliet. "James Shirley's Uses of Language," Studies in English Literature, 6 (1966), 323-339.

Morillo, Marvin. "Shirley's 'Preferment' and the Court of Charles I," Studies in English Literature, 1 (1961), 101-117.

O'Connor, John J. "James Hay and 'The Countess of Montgomerie's Urania'," Notes and Queries, 200 (1955), 150-152.

Quarterly Review, 49 (1833), 1-29.

Reed, John Curtis. "Humphrey Moseley, Publisher." Oxford Bibliographical Society Proceedings and Papers, 2 (1927-1930), 57-142.

Reed, Robert R., Jr. "James Shirley, and the Sentimental Comedy," Anglia, 73 (1955), 149-170.

Smith, G. Barnett. "Shirley," The Gentleman's Magazine, 246 (1880), 584-610.

Stevenson, Allan H. "James Shirley and the Actors at the First Irish Theater," Modern Philology, 40 (1942), 147-160.

_____. "Shirley's Dedications and the Date of His Return to England." Modern Language Notes, 61 (1946), 79-83.

_____. "Shirley's Publishers: The Partnership of Crooke and Cooke," The Library, 25 (1945), 140-161.

_____. "Shirley's Years in Ireland," Review of English Studies, 20 (1944), 19-28.

Stoye, J. W. "The Whereabouts of Thomas Killigrew 1639-1641," Review of English Studies, 25 (1949), 245-248.

Swinburne, A. C. "James Shirley," Fortnightly Review, 53 (1890), 461-478.

Wright, Louis B. "The Reading of Plays during the Puritan Revolution," The Huntington Library Bulletin, 6 (November, 1934), 73-108.

C.   UNPUBLISHED MATERIALS.

Huberman, Edward. "James Shirley's 'The Polititian.'" Diss. Duke University 1934.

Moyle, Sir Walter. Letter to William Blathwayt. 31 March 1694. Folger Shakespeare Library, Washington, D. C.